Kieler Studien · Kiel Studies 313
Horst Siebert (Editor)
Kiel Institute of World Economics

Christian Pierdzioch

Noise Trading, Central Bank Interventions, and the Informational Content of Foreign Currency Options

 Springer

332.45
P61n

Professor Horst Siebert
President
Kiel Institute of World Economics
D-24100 Kiel
http://www.uni-kiel.de/ifw/

Dr. Christian Pierdzioch
Financial Markets Research Division
Kiel Institute of World Economics
D-24100 Kiel
c.pierdzioch@ifw.uni-kiel.de
JK

Die Deutsche Bibliothek – CIP-Einheitsaufnahme

Pierdzioch, Christian:
Noise trading, central bank interventions, and the informational content of foreign currency
options / Christian Pierdzioch. – Berlin ; Heidelberg ; New York ; Barcelona ; Hongkong ;
London ; Milan ; Paris ; Tokyo : Springer, 2001
  (Kieler Studien ; Bd. 313)
  ISBN 3–540–42745–7

© Springer-Verlag Berlin · Heidelberg 2001

Printed in Germany

ISSN 0340-6989

Preface

Since the breakdown of the Bretton Woods system in 1973, issues related to the hedging of the risk caused by the volatility of floating foreign exchange rates have become a particularly important facet in the risk management of agents acting in international financial markets. As a result, the markets for foreign exchange related derivative products have developed rapidly over the past two decades.

Flexible instruments to insure against adverse exchange rate movements are options on foreign currency. In real-world markets, a relatively simple baseline foreign currency option pricing model is often used to address pricing and hedging issues. As the volatility of the exchange rate process is the only unobservable input variable in this theoretical valuation model, it has become common practice to discuss the empirical fit of the baseline foreign currency option pricing model in terms of volatility quotes implicit in actual option prices. Because of the specification of the exchange rate process utilized to price options on foreign currency, the baseline foreign currency option pricing model predicts that the implied volatility of spot rate returns is constant over time and assumes a fixed numerical value regardless of the moneyness of the option contract. The results of many empirical studies, however, document that this invariance property of volatilities implicit in option prices does not hold in actual foreign currency option markets.

In this study, I investigate whether a noise trader approach can help to explain the empirically observed mispricing of the baseline option pricing model. To this end, I construct a noise trader foreign currency option pricing model and discuss how the presence of noise traders affects foreign currency option prices. In a first step, I show that the model allows empirical regularities in real-world foreign currency option markets to be explained. In a second step, I implement volatility-based empirical tests to assess whether the assumptions of the theoretical model are valid from an empirical point of view. In line with the predictions of the theoretical model, the results of the tests show that the dynamics of the conditional volatility of exchange rate returns contain a significant state-contingent component. Further, I conduct alternative econometric tests which confirm this result.

While the noise trader literature helps to explain the observed mispricing of the baseline option pricing model, a related literature has examined how policymakers can exploit the pricing errors of these frameworks. This study also contributes to this literature. I examine how option pricing theory can be applied to assess the effectiveness of central bank interventions in foreign exchange markets. To carry out this analysis, I use a model of exchange rate determination to set up a foreign currency option pricing model featuring infrequent central bank interventions. Based on the predictions of this model, I analyze the effectiveness of the intervention policy of the Deutsche Bundesbank during the Louvre period using a multifactor success criterion. This success criterion allows the impact of interventions on the level and on the volatility of the exchange rate to be modeled within a unified framework. Using this success criterion, I estimate an ordered probit model. The results suggest that central banks should be somewhat cautious when the question arises whether interventions are an appropriate instrument to support the domestic currency.

In preparing this study, I greatly benefited from the discussions with Professor Horst Siebert and Professor Thomas Lux. I would like to thank the former for keeping the Kiel Institute of World Economics such a hospitable and stimulating research environment. My thanks go to Claudia M. Buch and Ralph P. Heinrich, my colleagues of the Institute's Research Area Financial Markets, for encouraging discussions and for many insightful comments. I also owe a lot of thanks to Professor Joachim Scheide and my other colleagues of the Institute's Business Cycle Department. Jörg Döpke was a constant source of inspiration and a challenging discussant whose ideas and patience helped tremendously to improve the econometric work presented in this study. I am also indebted to Georg Stadtmann, my coauthor of a number of related papers, for carefully reading the manuscript and ferreting out mistakes. The Deutsche Forschungsgemeinschaft provided financial support, which I gratefully acknowledge.

Karin Kristahl and Hannelore Owe patiently handled various earlier versions of the manuscript. Kerstin Stark efficiently handled the final version of the manuscript and brought it into a professional form. Dietmar Gebert, Paul J. Kramer, and Itta-M. Schulte carefully edited the study.

I dedicate this study to my parents who encouraged me in all respects.

Kiel, August 2001   Christian Pierdzioch

Contents

1 The Setting   **1**

**2 The Valuation of Foreign Currency Options and Exchange Rate
Dynamics**   **7**

  2.1 The First-Generation FX Option Pricing Model   8

    2.1.1 The Basic Model for European Options on Foreign
Currency   8

    2.1.2 Option Sensitivities   11

    2.1.3 Extension to American Options   14

  2.2 Risk-Neutral Valuation   19

  2.3 Models with a Variable Diffusion Term   23

    2.3.1 Constant Elasticity of Variance Models   24

    2.3.2 Stochastic Volatility Models   27

  2.4 Models Featuring Discontinuous Exchange Rate Paths   38

  2.5 Summary   43

3 Noise Trader Trigger Rates, FX Options, and Smiles   **46**

  3.1 Implicit Price Barriers, Exchange Rate Dynamics, and Smiles 50

    3.1.1 Implicit Price Barriers and Exchange Rate Dynamics   57

    3.1.2 The Foreign Currency Option Valuation Model   67

    3.1.3 Implicit Trading Regimes and the Volatility Strike
Structure   72

  3.2 Implicit Trading Triggers and Exchange Rate Volatility: The
Traditional View   81

    3.2.1 Identification of Potential Trading Triggers in FX
Markets   83

    3.2.2 Modeling the Link between Trading Triggers and
Exchange Rate Volatility   85

    3.2.3 Exchange Rate Data   89

    3.2.4 Conditional Exchange Rate Volatility and the Barriers
Hypothesis   91

3.3   Technical FX Trading and the Barrier-Smile Hypothesis:
      A Rival Empirical Model   98
      3.3.1   Mechanical Trading and Implicit Trading Regimes in
              FX Markets   101
      3.3.2   Implicit Trading Regimes and the Dynamics of Con-
              ditional Exchange Rate Volatility   104
      3.3.3   Robustness of the Results   114
3.4   Noise Trader in a Heston-Style Model: A Primer   124
      3.4.1   The Structure of the Economy   125
      3.4.2   Noise Trader and Foreign Currency Options   132
3.5   Summary   136
      3.5.1   Policy Implications   141

4   Exchange Rate Policy and FX Options   **144**
4.1   Central Bank Interventions and FX Option Pricing   145
      4.1.1   The FX Option Pricing Model   149
      4.1.2   The Impact of Infrequent Central Bank Interventions on
              FX Option Prices   152
4.2   Implied Volatilities and the Effectiveness of Central Bank
      Interventions   159
      4.2.1   Results Reported in the Literature   161
      4.2.2   Discussion of the Research Strategy   167
      4.2.3   The Data   171
      4.2.4   The Effectiveness of Bundesbank Foreign Exchange
              Market Interventions   178
4.3   Summary   183

5   Conclusion   **186**

References   **190**

Index   **206**

List of Tables

Table 2.1: Sensitivities of the Garman–Kohlhagen Currency Option Pricing Formula   13

Table 3.1: Descriptive Statistics for the Levels of the Currency Pairs under Investigation   90

Table 3.2: Diagnostic Statistics for the Returns of the Exchange Rates under Investigation   90

Table 3.3: Implicit Price Barriers and Exchange Rate Volatility   92

Table 3.4: Diagnostic Statistics for the Models of Implicit Price Barriers and Exchange Rate Volatility (Model I)   95

Table 3.5: Alternative Moving Average Specifications and the Number of Realizations in the Trading Regimes under Different Threshold Assumptions   104

Table 3.6: Implicit Trading Triggers and Exchange Rate Volatility (MA_{150} representation)   106

Table 3.7: Implicit Trading Triggers and Exchange Rate Volatility (MA_{50} representation)   108

Table 3.8: Implicit Trading Triggers and Exchange Rate Volatility (MA_{100} representation)   110

Table 3.9: Diagnostic Statistics for the Models of Implicit Trading Regimes and Exchange Rate Volatility (Model II, MA_{100} -target value)   113

Table 3.10: A Nonparametric Test for the Link between Conditional Exchange Rate Volatility Options and Implicit Trading Regimes   116

Table 4.1: Modeling Conditional Stock Market Volatility   175

Table 4.2: Reaction Function Derived by Estimating a Tobit Model   177

Table 4.3: Ordered Probit Model for Individual Effects of Explanatory Variables   179

Table 4.4: Estimates of Joint Effects in the Ordered Probit Model   180

Table 4.5: Estimates of Joint Effects in the Ordered Probit Model
Including a Dummy for Reported Interventions   181

Table 4.6: Probabilities, Marginal Effects, and Elasticities in the Ordered
Probit Model   182

List of Figures

Figure 2.1: Implications of the Absolute Diffusion Model for the Pricing
of FX Options   26

Figure 2.2: The Time-Varying Nature of Annualized Volatilities Implicit
in At-the-Money Forward US/DM and Yen/DM Options (time to expiry:
one month)   28

Figure 2.3: Stochastic Volatility and the Premia of a European Call on
Foreign Currency   33

Figure 2.4: The Vega of the Garman and Kohlhagen Option Premia 33

Figure 2.5: Implications of Exchange Rate Jumps for Currency Option
Prices and Hedge Ratios   41

Figure 3.1: State-Contingent Market Entry and Exit of Technical Traders
and Exchange Rate Dynamics   65

Figure 3.2: Noise Trading and a U-Shaped Implied Volatility Strike
Structure   73

Figure 3.3: Distant Technical Trading Thresholds and the Convexity of
the Volatility Smile   75

Figure 3.4: The Aggressiveness of Noise Traders and the Shape of the
Volatility Strike Structure   77

Figure 3.5: Asymmetrically Spaced Trading Thresholds and Skewness in the Smile   78

Figure 3.6: Actual versus Fitted Cumulative Distribution Function for the Standardized Residuals of the CAN/US Returns   97

Figure 3.7: Estimated State-Contingent Empirical Conditional Volatility Densities   119

Figure 3.8: Selected Impulse Response Functions for the Estimated Bivariate Systems   123

Figure 3.9: Noise Trading and Exchange Rate Volatility   129

Figure 4.1: The Impact of the Intervention Probability on At-the-Money FX Options in the Managed Float: Part I   155

Figure 4.2: The Impact of the Intervention Probability on At-the-Money FX Options in the Managed Float: Part II   157

Figure 4.3: The Impact of a Variation in the Intervention Probability on In-the-Money Options in the Managed Float: Part III   158

Figure 4.4: Time Series Used in the Empirical Analyses   172

List of Abbreviations

CAPM	capital asset pricing model
CEV	constant elasticity of variance
ECB	European Central Bank
EMS	European Monetary System
FX	foreign exchange
GARCH	generalized autoregressive conditional heteroskedasticity
GED	generalized error distribution
GK	Garman and Kohlhagen
HW	Hull and White
KS	Kolmogorov–Smirnov test
MA	moving average
PHLX	Philadelphia Stock Exchange
TARCH	threshold GARCH
VAR	vector autoregression

List of Symbols

Chapter 2

Roman variables and indices

C valuation function for a European call option

C^A valuation function for an American call option

Cov   conditional covariance operator

c consumption flow

cf characteristic function of risk-neutral probability that an option expires in-the-money in stochastic volatility models

d   differential operator

$\mathrm{d}p$ differential of a Poisson counting process

$\mathrm{d}Z$ adjustment factor used to transform a semimartingale into a martingale

E exchange rate (domestic currency units in terms of a foreign currency unit)

E^* optimal exercise price of an American option

$\mathbb{E}$ expectations operator

e natural logarithm of the exchange rate

exp   exponential function

F forward price of a currency

FX   foreign exchange

g objective probability measure

$\tilde{g}$ equivalent martingale measure

H Heaviside function

h^V conditional distribution of volatility

$\hbar$ relative risk-aversion parameter

IM   imaginary number

J jump size of Poisson counting process

ℓ parameter used to compute jump intensity of a Poisson counting process

ln   natural logarithm of a variable

n	number of jumps in a Poisson counting process
P	valuation function for a European put option
Q	risk-neutral probability that an option expires in-the-money in stochastic volatility models
r	domestic risk-free interest rate
$r*$	foreign risk-free interest rate
T	time of expiry of a contingent claim
t	time
$U(c)$	utility as a function of consumption flow
V	stochastic volatility of exchange rate process
$\overline{V}$	expected average volatility over the time-to-expiry of a contingent claim
W	Wiener process
X	strike price of a contingent claim

Greek variables and indices

γ	risk premium
δ^D	Dirac delta function
∂	operator denoting partial differentiation
ε	standard normally distributed error term
Θ	early exercise premium of an American option
θ	mean reversion level of a stochastic process
ι	mean jump size of a Poisson counting process
κ	mean reversion coefficient of a stochastic process
λ	constant used to compute volatility risk premium
$\tilde{\lambda}$	general form of volatility risk premium
μ	drift component of a stochastic process
μ_C	expected rate of return of holding a call option
ν	elasticity parameter in CEV models
ξ	diffusion coefficient of a stochastic process
ρ	coefficient of correlation
σ	diffusion coefficient of a stochastic process
σ_C	expected standard deviation of holding a call option
σ_J	standard deviation of jump size of a Poisson counting process

τ	time-to-maturity of a contingent claim
Φ	standard normal distribution function
ω	integration argument of characteristic function
$\tilde{\Omega}$	hedge portfolio

Chapter 3

Roman variables and indices

A_j	constant of integration ($j = 1,2$)
B_j	constant of integration ($j = 1,2$)
$\hat{C}$	call value estimated by running a Monte Carlo simulation
D_j	constant of integration ($j = 1,2$)
$D(\cdot)$	density function of the disturbance term of a GARCH model
d	differential operator
$\tilde{d}$	day-of-week dummy
d_a	logarithm of the relative demand for domestic currency denominated assets
$\mathbb{E}$	expectations operator
e	natural logarithm of the exchange rate
e_0	medium-term target exchange rate of technical traders
$\bar{e}$	upper trading trigger of technical traders
$\underline{e}$	lower trading trigger of technical traders
f	natural logarithm of economic fundamentals
$\tilde{f}$	augmented fundamentals
$\bar{f}$	realization of economic fundamentals at which $e(t) = \bar{e}$
$\underline{f}$	realization of economic fundamentals at which $e(t) = \underline{e}$
G_{RF}	relative frequency of conditional volatilities
$\tilde{G}$	Radon–Nikodym derivative
$\tilde{g}$	equivalent martingale measure
g_{e_0}	parameter associated with the stochastic growth component of e_0
g_K	kernel density
g_s	parameter associated with the stochastic growth component of s

h_t	conditional volatility at time t
$\mathbf{I}$	(2 x 2) identity matrix
$\mathfrak{I}$	indicator function denoting whether technical traders participate in spot trading
K_w	kernel function based on band width of w
k	parameter used to allocate the international interest rate differential between domestic and foreign interest rates
L	lag operator
LL	log-likelihood function
M	parameter used to identify the position of the exchange rate relative to implicit trading triggers in the traditional test for implicit price barriers in FX markets
$MA_{t,i}$	moving average of length i observed in period t
M1	test for a mean of zero
M2	test for a variance of unity
M3	test for a skewness of zero
N	number of observations
$\mathbf{P}$	elements of a correlation matrix of a Wiener processor
P^l	price of a discount bond ($l = D, F$, where the index D (F) denotes a domestic (foreign) variable)
$q(t)$	stochastic state variable affecting e_0
R_j	a (2×2) matrix in a VAR
$r - r^*$	international interest rate differential
r_D	level of the domestic locally risk-free interest rates
r_F	level of the foreign locally risk-free interest rates
$\bar{r}$	base level of interest rates
s_a	logarithm of the relative supply of domestic currency denominated assets
U_i	a (2×2) matrix in a VAR
u_t	stochastic disturbance term in a GARCH model
$\mathbf{W}$	(1 x 2) vector of a Wiener processor
W	Wiener process
Y_t	vector of variables in a vector autoregression
$y(t)$	stochastic state variable affecting the relative supply of domestic assets

Greek variables and indices

α	market share of rational investors
$\alpha_{j,l}$	parameters of the equation defining domestic and foreign locally risk-free interest rates (with $j = 1,2,3$ and $l = D, F$, where the index D (F) denotes a domestic (foreign) variable)
α_p	parameter of the variance equation of a GARCH model
β	coefficient in day-of-week regressions
β_q	parameter of the variance equation of a GARCH model
Γ	gamma function
γ_j	parameters summarizing the trading behavior of technical spot traders ($j = 1,2$)
Δ	difference operator
δ	noise trading coefficient in the variance equation of a GARCH model
η_t	independently identically distributed error term
θ_q	mean reversion level of the process $q(t)$
θ_y	mean reversion level of the process $y(t)$
ϑ	scaling factor used to define the neighborhood of moving average
κ_q	speed of mean reversion of the process $q(t)$
κ_y	speed of mean reversion of the process $y(t)$
$\overline{\kappa}$	tail parameter of the GED density
λ	roots of the characteristic equation of a differential equation
μ_s	drift of the process specified for domestic assets
$\overline{\mu}$	drift of E in the second noise trader model discussed in Chapter 3
ξ_q	diffusion coefficient of the process $q(t)$
ξ_y	diffusion coefficient of the process $y(t)$
σ_{e_0}	volatility of the process specified for e_0
σ_s	volatility of the process specified for domestic assets
ς	weighting function used in kernel density estimation
ς_c	elasticity of chartists' demand for foreign-currency-denominated assets
ς_f	elasticity of fundamentalists' demand for foreign-currency-denominated assets
υ	interest-semielasticity of money demand
Φ	standard normal distribution function
ϕ	trading elasticity of technical traders

φ_c	trend-chasing parameter of chartists
φ_f	mean reversion parameter of fundamentalists
ψ	market share of fundamentalists
Ω_t	information set in period t
ω	parameter of the variance equation of a GARCH model
1	indicator function

Chapter 4

Roman variables and indices

b	coefficient vector in an ordered probit model
dev_t	absolute deviation of the spot rate from the target value $\overline{E}$ in period t
E	exchange rate
$\overline{E}$	implicit central parity of the exchange rate
e	logarithm of the exchange rate
f	intervention-augmented fundamentals
f^*	economic fundamentals net of changes in the monetary base due to central bank FX market interventions
G	call option as a function of economic fundamentals
I_t	central bank intervention in period t
I^*	central banks' propensity to intervene
k	weighting factor used to decompose the international interest rate differential
L	lag operator
LL	log-likelihood function
LR	likelihood ratio
$\overline{r}$	central interest rate
$r - r^*$	international interest rate differential
r_D	level of the domestic locally risk-free interest rates
r_F	level of the foreign locally risk-free interest rates
S	function indicating the state in which the latent variable of an ordered probit model has settled
S_j	threshold levels in an ordered probit model ($j = 1,2$)

S^*	latent state variable of an ordered probit model
W	Wiener process
x	vector of explanatory variables in an ordered probit model

Greek variables and indices

ε^*	disturbance term in a Tobit model
μ	drift of economic fundamentals
μ_b	mean of the instrument computed for central bank interventions
$\tilde{\pi}$	probability of a central bank intervention
σ	constant diffusion coefficient
σ_b	standard deviation of the instrument computed for central bank interventions
σ^*	standard deviation of the disturbance term in a Tobit model
σ_ε	standard deviation of the disturbance term in an ordered Probit model
v	interest elasticity of money demand

1 The Setting

During the past two decades, international financial markets have grown rapidly. Technological progress has lowered information and communication costs considerably. The majority of legal restrictions on cross-border capital movements has been abolished. A battery of new financial instruments tailor-made to control risks arising when positions in globally diversified portfolios are taken has been designed. As a consequence, a large and steadily expanding risk management and asset allocation industry has developed which is concerned with the administration of rapidly increasing global capital flows. In particular, issues related to the hedging of the risk caused by the volatility of floating foreign exchange (FX) rates have become an important facet of the risk management of agents acting in international financial markets since the breakdown of the Bretton Woods system in 1973.[1] Particularly flexible instruments used by agents to insure against risks caused by the volatility of floating FX rates are options on foreign currency. To value FX options and to compose hedge portfolios, most dealers and risk managers around the world use the continuous-time currency option pricing model which traces back to Garman and Kohlhagen (1983). These authors adopted the preference- and arbitrage-free valuation principle originated by Black and Scholes (1973) and Merton (1973) to show how to adjust FX option prices for the forward premium/discount caused by the differential in international rates of interest.[2] As in the case of the classical Black–Scholes–Merton setup, the first-generation currency option pricing model is based on the assumption that financial market prices are driven by an exogenously given stochastic process with a constant instantaneous volatility parameter.

---

[1]   The Bank for International Settlements (1996) estimated that at the end of March 1995 the outstanding global notional amount and gross market value in global over-the-counter foreign currency options markets net of local and cross-border inter-dealer double counting amounted to US$ 2,379 and US$ 71 billion, respectively. The corresponding estimates for the notional amount and gross market values of all over-the-counter foreign exchange derivatives contracts (including not only FX options but also, e.g., forward contracts and foreign exchange swaps) outstanding at the end of March 1995 were US$ 13,095 and US$ 1,048 billion.

[2]   Similar valuation models can be found in Giddy (1983), Grabbe (1983), and Biger and Hull (1983).

Empirical Pricing Errors and the Discussion in the Literature

The widespread adoption of the basic foreign currency option valuation model to address pricing and hedging issues contrasts with its relatively poor empirical performance. As the volatility of the exchange rate process is the only un-observable input variable in this theoretical valuation model, it has become common practice to discuss the empirical fit of the baseline FX option pricing model in terms of volatility quotes implicit in actual option prices. Because of the specification of the exchange rate process utilized to price options on foreign currency, the Garman and Kohlhagen (henceforth abbreviated as GK) (1983) model predicts that the implied volatility of spot rate returns is constant over time and assumes a fixed numerical value regardless of the moneyness of the option contract. The results of many empirical studies, however, document that this invariance property of volatilities implicit in option prices does not hold in actual FX option markets.[3] The most obvious feature of volatilities implicit in options on foreign currency (and on other assets as well) is that they are not constant over time. In addition, many empirical studies report that the magnitude of volatilities inferred from option prices changes as the maturity of the contract is varied. This implies that the term structure of volatilities implicit in foreign currency options does not show the zero slope predicted by the GK model.[4] Moreover, many empirical studies obtain convex curves resembling smiles or skewed smirks rather than straight horizontal rays when plotting volatilities implicit in actual FX option quotes as a function of the strike price/forward rate ratio (see, e.g., Shastri and Wethyavivorn 1987). This implies that at-the-money options usually tend to have lower implicit volatilities than options with strike prices above or below the prevailing forward rate. The consequence of skewness in the smile curve is that the implied volatility of an out-of-the-money call differs from the volatility implicit in a corresponding out-of-the-money put.

The disappointing empirical performance of the first-generation FX option valuation models has been attributed to the fact that the distributional assumptions underlying these models do not accurately describe the statistical properties of actual exchange rate data. As a consequence, several attempts have been undertaken in the option pricing literature to relax the restrictive assumption of the basic FX option pricing setup that exchange rates follow a simple geometric Brownian diffusion process. Various extensions of the baseline Garman and Kohlhagen (1983) model have been suggested. For example, Melino and

---

[3]   See, for example, Goodman et al. (1985), Shastri and Tandon (1986) or Bodurtha and Courtadon (1987b).

[4]   See Campa and Chang (1995) for a recent example; see also Xu and Taylor (1994).

Turnbull (1991) have examined whether a model belonging to the class of constant elasticity of variance (CEV) models introduced by Cox and Ross (1976) fits real-world foreign currency option prices better than the first-generation valuation models. Other authors including Hull and White (1987a) and Heston (1993) have developed stochastic volatility models to account for the empirically observed pricing errors of the first-generation FX option pricing models.[5] Yet another strand of the literature resorts to pure jump or jump-diffusion models to capture some of the characteristics of actual exchange rate data.[6] Finally, Amin and Jarrow (1991) and others have elaborated on a pricing model featuring stochastic domestic and foreign instantaneous interest rates.

Alternative Economic Theories of the Smile

These extensions of the first-generation option valuation model championed by Garman and Kohlhagen (1983) help to generate theoretical option prices which are more in line with the patterns detected in real-world FX option premia than those predicted by the baseline valuation model. From an economic point of view, however, these contingent claim valuation approaches have drawbacks, one of which is that the models of exchange rate dynamics utilized to replace the specification employed by Garman and Kohlhagen are given by exogenously prespecified stochastic differential equations. A consequence of this modeling strategy is that the smile and smirk effects shown by the real-world FX options implied volatility strike structures are also treated as exogenously given phenomena. Hence, the extensions of the basic GK model discussed in many contributions to the literature offer a technical rather than an economic rationale for the volatility smile.

An important avenue of research which has been followed in the option pricing literature to cope with this problem elaborates on the consequences of the trading behavior of economic agents to explain the shape of the volatility smile. In this literature, particular attention has been paid to the role of noise trading and technical market analysis in financial markets for option premia and the corresponding implied volatilities. For example, Grossman and Zhou (1996) have shown that the dynamic spot market interplay between technical portfolio insurers adhering to a convex risk management technique and noninsurers can result in a skewed volatility strike structure implicit in the corresponding options

---

[5] See also the work of Koch (1992), Bakshi and Chen (1997), Bakshi et al. (1997), and Scott (1997), and the references cited therein.

[6] Examples of this approach include the contributions of Borensztein and Dooley (1987), Jorion (1988), and Malz (1996).

contracts. A related approach has been developed by Platen and Schweizer (1998), who have analyzed the volatility smile in a continuous-time microeconomic equilibrium model with heterogeneous agents. In their model, the trading behavior of program traders gives rise to an endogenously determined stochastic asset price which renders it possible to generate endogenous convex volatility strike structures. Yet another approach has been introduced into the literature by Cherian and Jarrow (1998). These authors have discussed the properties of the volatility smile within a partial equilibrium call option market economy with heterogeneous trader groups. Their model generates smile effects in the volatility strike structure which can then be discussed in terms of structural parameters which summarize the trading behavior and the relative strengths of the various trader groups.

Because it is a well-documented stylized fact that the volatility of exchange rates exceeds the volatility of macroeconomic fundamentals at shorter- and medium-term horizons, a noise trading perspective on contingent claim valuation problems might also help to explain theoretically volatility smiles inferred from the options on foreign currencies.[7] Given this situation, one purpose of this study is to contribute to the noise trading literature on the volatility smile. On the theoretical side, this study utilizes a noise trader foreign currency option valuation model to analyze the shape of the volatility strike structure. To set up a framework of analysis, a heterogeneous agents monetary model of exchange rate determination tracing back to Krugman and Miller (1993) is modified to incorporate chartists and fundamentalists who implement state-contingent investment strategies. The exchange rate dynamics generated by this exchange rate model are then used to construct a continuous-time noise trader foreign currency option valuation model. Numerical simulations of the model show that smile effects can arise when spot traders implement a trend-extrapolative technical trading rule. The shape of the smile depends upon the width of the interval of inaction of technical traders, the position of the spot rate relative to noise traders investment thresholds, and the aggressiveness characterizing the trading behavior of technical investors. Based on the insights of this model, empirically testable hypotheses are derived and volatility-based quantitative tests are performed to present new evidence which allows the empirical relevance of the noise trading hypothesis of the volatility strike structure implicit in foreign currency options to be assessed.

---

[7]   Empirical evidence on the link between exchange rate volatility and the variability of economic fundamentals is documented, inter alia, in Flood and Rose (1995). For many more references on noise trading, the reader is referred to the introductory section of Chapter 3.

How Policymakers Can Use the Informational Content Embedded in FX Options

While the noise trader option pricing literature helps to *explain* the observed mispricing of the first-generation option pricing models, a significant and rapidly growing related strand of research has developed techniques allowing the pricing errors of the first-generation option pricing models to be exploited. Researchers working in this field of economics have, for example, applied techniques allowing the information embedded in option prices to be extracted in order to study problems arising in the context of corporate risk management. In recent years, however, it has been recognized that the pricing biases of the first-generation option pricing models might also constitute an important source of information for policymakers and monetary authorities alike.[8] In particular, it has been acknowledged that foreign currency option prices give central banks the opportunity to extract otherwise unobservable higher-order moments of the expected (risk-neutral) exchange rate distribution employed by option traders when pricing contingent claims. This is in sharp contrast to the informational content of, e.g., more conventional forward contracts which give central banks only an impression of the market sentiment regarding the expected rate of change of the external value of a currency and, thus, of the first moment of this distribution.

Motivated by this insight, a substantial body of research has explored the informational content of foreign currency options to address issues related to exchange rate policy. In particular, foreign currency option prices have been used to assess the effectiveness of central bank foreign exchange market interventions.[9] The contributions to this literature include the work of Bonser-Neal and Tanner (1996) and of Dominguez (1998), who have used at-the-money volatilities implicit in foreign currency options in regression-based analyses to shed light on the success or failure of the FX market operations of major central banks. Galati and Melick (1999) have discussed the effectiveness of perceived central bank interventions in spot markets for foreign currency by exploring the informational content implicit in the cross-section of foreign currency option premia. They have examined whether actual option prices suggest that the implied risk-neutral probability densities inferred from these contracts have become more skewed in the direction suggested by the central bank intervention.

---

[8]   Söderlind and Svensson (1997) provide an overview of these techniques and present applications demonstrating how central banks can use these new quantitative tools.

[9]   Some authors have also discussed whether derivative securities can be used by monetary authorities to conduct interventions in foreign exchange markets (see, e.g., Garber and Spencer (1996) and Breuer (1999)).

This study also contributes to this strand of research. A theoretical FX option pricing model featuring infrequent central bank interventions is used to derive empirically testable hypotheses regarding the impact of central bank foreign exchange market interventions on the level of the spot rate and on its volatility as anticipated by option traders. Exploiting the predictions of the theoretical model, the effectiveness of central bank foreign exchange market interventions is analyzed using a multifactor success criterion. The success criterion is utilized as the dependent variable in an ordered qualitative response model. It allows the impact of central banks' FX market interventions on the level and on the expected volatility of the spot rate to be studied within a unified framework. Moreover, framing the analysis in terms of this success criterion offers empirical researchers an additional degree of flexibility because central bank foreign exchange market interventions can be rated as effective, partially effective, or ineffective. More traditional success criteria, in contrast, typically allow one to differentiate only between completely effective or completely ineffective FX market interventions of monetary authorities.

Organization of the Study

This study is organized as follows. To set the stage for the analyses, Chapter 2 reviews the existing option pricing literature. In Chapter 3, a noise trader foreign currency option valuation model is constructed and the implications of technical spot trading for the shape of the volatility strike structure are discussed. Volatility-based testing techniques are utilized to analyze whether a link between technical trading, spot rate dynamics, and exchange rate volatility can be established empirically. The quantitative analyses are used to shed light on the empirical relevance of the noise trader hypothesis of the volatility smile. In Chapter 4, option pricing theory is applied to set up a framework which allows the effectiveness of central bank foreign exchange market interventions to be discussed. A quantitative model is applied to assess the effectiveness of the FX market interventions of the German central bank conducted after the Louvre Summit held in Paris in 1987. Chapter 5 concludes and summarizes the main lessons that can be drawn from the analyses.

2 The Valuation of Foreign Currency Options and Exchange Rate Dynamics

The purpose of this chapter is to introduce the basic Garman and Kohlhagen (1983) model and to provide a comprehensive review of the various extensions and refinements of the first-generation foreign exchange (FX) option pricing model discussed in the literature. The fundamental partial differential equation describing the premium of exchange rate contingent claims derived by Garman and Kohlhagen (GK) is analyzed and the characteristics of its particular solution that applies in the case of European currency options are discussed. Moreover, the complications arising in the context of the pricing of American options are studied. The chapter also includes a discussion of the risk-neutral option valuation model introduced by Cox and Ross (1976).

The analysis then proceeds by reviewing FX option valuation models designed to capture some of the pricing errors associated with the first-generation currency option pricing models. I first elaborate on approaches featuring a diffusion term for the volatility of the returns of the underlying asset price, which either is modeled as a deterministic function of the level of the exchange rate or is assumed to be itself driven by stochastic shocks potentially correlated with exchange rate innovations. At this stage of the analysis, the constant elasticity of variance (CEV) model tracing back to Cox and Ross (1976), as well as stochastic volatility models, are introduced. Special emphasis is put on the analysis of the stochastic volatility model introduced by Heston (1993). The interest in this model is fostered by the fact that it was the first stochastic volatility model for which a closed-form solution has been derived. The review of the extensions of the baseline GK model also contains a discussion of the so-called jump-diffusion approach originated by Merton (1976) as an example for the class of models emphasizing the implications of discontinuous exchange rate paths for the pricing of options on foreign currency.

The final section of the chapter offers a brief summary of the main results of the various approaches suggested in the literature to reconcile option valuation theory with empirically observed pricing patterns. It also provides further motivation for the analyses outlined in later chapters of this study.

2.1   The First-Generation FX Option Pricing Model

2.1.1   The Basic Model for European Options on Foreign Currency

The currency option pricing model developed by Garman and Kohlhagen (1983) is applicable to European options on foreign currency. A European foreign currency call (put) option gives its holder the right to buy (to sell) the underlying currency at the maturity of the option at an exchange rate (strike price) fixed when the contract is struck. The model is built on the presumptions that international financial markets are frictionless, that the risk-free domestic r and the risk-free foreign $r*$ interest rates are constant, and that the only source of risk is fostered by the stochastically evolving value of foreign currency. It is further assumed that the essential characteristics of exchange rate fluctuations can adequately be described by a standard geometric Gauss–Wiener process. The exchange rate E defined as the foreign currency price of domestic currency is thus assumed to evolve according to the following stochastic differential equation:

$$(2.1) \quad dE = \mu E dt + \sigma E dW.$$

The parameter μ reflects a constant drift term, σ is a time-invariant positive diffusion coefficient, and $\{W_t, t \geq 0\}$ is a standard Brownian motion with differential

$$(2.2) \quad dW = \varepsilon(t)\sqrt{dt},$$

where $\varepsilon(t)$ denotes a standard normally distributed random variable. Together, equations (2.1) and (2.2) imply that future realizations of the exchange rate are lognormally distributed.

Given this continuous-time setting, consider now an investor who can either hold a European call option on foreign currency or the underlying currency itself. Also let γ denote the market price of exchange rate risk. The expected excess returns from holding one unit of foreign currency arising in an arbitrage-free international asset pricing framework can then be expressed as:

$$(2.3) \quad \gamma\sigma = (\mu + r*) - r \quad \Leftrightarrow \quad \gamma = \frac{(\mu + r*) - r}{\sigma}.$$

The constant risk premium γ can, thus, be divided into four components. The numerator of equation (2.3) summarizes the expected excess return from holding foreign currency. It is obtained by subtracting the interest on the domestic risk-free asset from the sum of the expected appreciation of the foreign currency and the yield on the riskless foreign interest-bearing asset. The market price γ per unit of risk is then computed by dividing these excess returns with the standard deviation of the return on holding foreign currency.

In perfect analogy, the premium on holding a European call option on the foreign currency can be expressed as $\gamma = (\mu_C - r)/\sigma_C$, where μ_C and σ_C represent the expected rate of return and standard deviation of holding this financial security, respectively. Let the premium of such an FX option with time to expiry $\tau \equiv T - t$, $T \geq t$ be denoted by the function $C(E,\tau)$. Assuming that $C(E,\tau)$ is twice differentiable in E and once differentiable with respect to time, τ, and applying Ito's lemma (see, e.g., Elliott and Kopp 1998: Section 6.4) yields (Garman and Kohlhagen 1983: 233)

$$(2.4) \quad dC = C_E \mu E dt + C_E E \sigma dW - C_\tau dt + 0.5 C_{EE} \sigma^2 E^2 dt,$$

where subscripts denote the respective partial derivatives. From equation (2.4) one obtains

$$\mu_C C = C_E \mu E - C_\tau + 0.5 C_{EE} \sigma^2 E^2 \quad \text{and} \quad \sigma_C C = C_E E \sigma.$$

Utilizing this set of equations to reexpress γ and ruling out arbitrage opportunities by setting the resulting expression equal to equation (2.3) yields the following contingent claim valuation equation:

$$(2.5) \quad 0.5 C_{EE} \sigma^2 E^2 + (r - r^*) E C_E - rC = C_\tau.$$

Compared with the baseline pricing model for European options on a non-dividend paying stock developed by Black and Scholes (1973) and Merton (1973), this valuation equation features one prominent additional term of the format $r^* E C_E$. This term enters into the valuation equation of the GK model because the interest accrued by holding foreign assets takes a similar part in the valuation of contingent claims on foreign currency as the continuous leakage of value from holding the underlying in valuation models for European options on stocks yielding a dividend rate proportional to the level of the stock price (Merton 1973). As can be seen from equation (2.5), the presence of this "dividend" correction term in the valuation equation implies that the differential in domestic and foreign instantaneous riskless rates of interest plays a prominent role in the pricing of derivatives on foreign currency.

The risk premium γ is the same for *any* arbitrary financial security i. It follows that equation (2.5) not only describes the value of FX options but also the price of any financial security i which can be described by a sufficiently smooth function $C_i(E, \tau_i)$. In order to pin down a particular solution to equation (2.5) that applies only in the case of currency options, it is necessary to close the valuation model by specifying an appropriate set of boundary conditions. The boundary conditions utilized to distinguish the price $C(E,\tau)$ of a European call option from the value function describing other contingent claims can be formalized as follows:[10]

$$(2.6) \qquad C(E,0) = [E_T - X]^+, \quad \lim_{E \to 0} C(0,\tau) = 0, \quad C(E,\tau) \le E.$$

The first boundary condition in equation (2.6) states that the payoff realized at expiry of the contract determines the terminal value of the option, i.e., one has $C(E,0) = E_T - X$ for $E_T > X$ and $C(E,0) = 0$ otherwise. The second side condition reflects that zero is an absorbing barrier of the geometric Wiener process specified in equation (2.1), i.e., if $E(t') = 0$ for some $t' \ge t_0$, then $E(t') = 0$ for all $t \ge t'$, and the probability that the option will expire in-the-money is zero. The third boundary condition provided in equation (2.6) reflects that in an arbitrage-free setting the price of the European call option can never exceed the price of the underlying financial asset.

Given the set of boundary conditions specified in equation (2.6), the restrictive assumptions underlying the GK valuation model render it possible to obtain a pricing formula applicable to European-style options on foreign currency in closed form. The traditional approach used to tackle the boundary value problem (2.5)–(2.6) is to apply a change of variables technique as suggested by Black and Scholes (1973) and to transform equation (2.5) into the heat diffusion equation of mathematical physics. This equation is well known and solution strategies can be found in many books on partial differential equations (see, e.g., Humi and Miller (1992) or Wilmott et al. (1995: 97–101)). Alternatively, one can resort to the risk-neutral pricing approach (Cox and Ross 1976) to express the option premium as the present discounted value of the expected terminal payoff of the contract computed under a so-called risk-neutral or equivalent martingale measure.[11] This latter solution strategy will be discussed in detail in Section 2.2. Both approaches lead to the following option pricing formula (Garman and Kohlhagen 1983: 233)

$$(2.7) \qquad C(E,\tau) = \exp(-r^*\tau)E\Phi(d_1) - \exp(-r\tau)X\Phi(d_2),$$

---

[10]   See, e.g., Ingersoll (1987: 312). Note that the partial differential equation (2.5) is of order two in the E-direction and of order one in the t-direction. Hence, three boundary conditions are needed to determine a particular solution to this equation.

[11]   A martingale is an adapted stochastic process defined relative to a filtration and a probability measure with finite unconditional forecasts and with conditional forecasts equal to the current realization of the process, that is, future realizations of a martingale are completely unpredictable (Neftci 1996: 103).

where $\Phi(\cdot)$ represents the standard normal distribution function and d_1 and d_2 are given by

$$d_1 = \frac{\ln\left(\dfrac{E}{X}\right) + \left(r - r^* + 0.5\sigma^2\right)\tau}{\sigma\sqrt{\tau}} \quad \text{and} \quad d_2 = d_1 - \sigma\sqrt{\tau}.$$

The value $P(E,\tau)$ of a corresponding European put option can now be determined from the no-arbitrage condition known as put-call-parity:[12]

(2.8) $P(E,\tau) = C(E,\tau) + X\exp(-r\tau) - E\exp(-r^*\tau).$

An important implication of the GK option pricing formula outlined in equation (2.7) is that the exchange rate risk premium γ is irrelevant for the arbitrage-free "fair" price of currency options. The reason for this interesting result is that γ cancels out in the derivation of the valuation equation (2.7), so that the formula derived for $C(E,\tau)$ does not depend on this risk premium. It follows that the "fair" price of the option can be computed without recurring to the preferences of economic agents with respect to exchange rate risk. This, in turn, implies that the currency option price $C(E,\tau)$ is not only arbitrage-free but also preference-free. Because the risk tolerance of option traders does not enter into equation (2.7), it is perfectly valid to price options *as if* economic agents were risk-neutral. This fact will be exploited in Section 2.2 where a risk-neutral option valuation approach will be discussed.

2.1.2   Option Sensitivities

The GK option pricing formula provided in equation (2.7) highlights that the value of a position involving currency options depends on the level of the exchange rate, the strike price, the time-to-maturity of the contract, the domestic and foreign risk-free interest rates, and the volatility parameter of the exchange rate process. The sensitivities of options with respect to these parameters play a central role in the management of the risk associated with the taking of positions in derivative securities. They can be expressed formally as the partial derivatives of the option pricing formula with respect to the argument under investigation.

---

[12]   This strict form of put-call-parity does only applies in the case of European options on assets with nonstochastic dividends. In the case of American options, an observed price of a call option can only be utilized to deduce bounds on the premium of the corresponding put option (see, e.g., Hull 1993: 193–167).

Table 2.1 provides a summary of the sensitivities of a European call option on foreign currency used by practitioners to evaluate the exposure of their portfolios with respect to movements in several variables. The corresponding sensitivities obtaining in the case of a European put option can be derived using put-call-parity.

The option sensitivities provided in Table 2.1 can be used to gauge and to manage the risk of positions consisting of individual options or of portfolios of derivatives.[13] Conversely, if a financial institution or a firm intends to insure an open position in foreign currency against adverse exchange rate fluctuations it can resort to these option sensitivities to reduce the exchange rate exposure of this position. For example, if exchange rate fluctuations are the only source of risk, a portfolio, $\tilde{\Omega}$, composed of one European call on foreign currency and $-C_E E$ units of the underlying becomes insensitive to an *infinitesimal* variation of the level of the exchange rate. As the delta C_E of the option is utilized to construct such a portfolio, the position is said to be delta-neutral. However, as can be seen by checking the formula provided in Table 2.1, the delta of an option is itself a function of the level of the exchange rate. This implies that though a delta-neutral position is essentially riskless in the context of the GK valuation model with respect to small exchange rate movements, a substantial change in the level of the underlying alters the delta of the option and necessitates an adjustment of the fractions of wealth invested in the underlying and in the option. As gamma measures the sensitivity of the delta of a position to a change in the spot rate, the investment is said to be gamma-sensitive. The impact of a change in delta on the value of a portfolio can only be controlled by using a second FX option tailored to make the investment gamma-neutral (Hull and White 1987b) or by implementing a dynamic delta hedging strategy requiring a continuous reshuffling of financial wealth allocated in the long (short) position in the option and the corresponding opposite short (long) position in the underlying.

The power of dynamic hedging schemes based on the GK option sensitivities to efficiently manage the risk caused by the acquisition of a multicurrency portfolio or an investment involving currency options depends upon the empirical

---

[13]   In the derivation of the formulas presented in Table 2.1, the fact was used that the various partial derivatives which must be computed to obtain the option sensitivities can be simplified significantly by using the relation

$$\Phi'(d_1)/\Phi'(d_2) = \exp[(d_2^2 - d_1^2)/2] = X/F ,$$

where $\Phi'(d_i) \equiv \partial \Phi / \partial d_i$, $i = 1,2$ denotes the standard normal density function and $F = E\exp[(r - r^*)\tau]$ represents the forward price (for a discussion, see, e.g., Zhang 1996: 74).

Table 2.1: Sensitivities of the Garman–Kohlhagen Currency Option Pricing Formula

	Economic interpretation	Mathematical interpretation	Formula
Delta	Sensitivity of the option price to changes in the underlying	C_E	$\exp(-r^*\tau)\Phi(d_1)$
Gamma	Sensitivity of an option's delta to changes in the underlying	C_{EE}	$\dfrac{\exp(-r^*\tau)\Phi'(d_1)}{E\sigma\sqrt{\tau}}$
Vega	Sensitivity of the option price to changes in the volatility	C_σ	$\exp(-r^*\tau)E\sqrt{\tau}\Phi'(d_1)$
Rho	Sensitivity of the option price to changes in the interest rate r	C_r	$X\tau\exp(-r\tau)\Phi(d_1)$
Theta	Sensitivity of the option price to changes in the time to maturity	C_τ	$\dfrac{E\Phi'(d_1)\sigma\exp(-r^*\tau)}{2\sqrt{\tau}}$ $-r^*\exp(-r^*\tau)E\Phi(d_1)$ $+r\exp(-r\tau)X\Phi(d_2)$

Source: Kolb (1997: 224).

question of whether the assumptions made to derive the GK formula are satisfied in real-world foreign exchange markets. The poor empirical performance of the GK model mentioned in the introductory chapter of this study indicates that this tends not to be the case. For example, the time-varying nature of volatilities implicit in option prices and the existence of smile and smirk effects in the volatility strike structure impressively demonstrate that this first-generation FX option pricing model can safely be expected to be misspecified. Given the mentioned stylized facts, several attempts have been discussed in the literature to construct models which allow the empirical pricing errors observed when implementing the GK valuation model to be minimized and more accurate option sensitivities to be computed. Before discussing these approaches in later sections of the present chapter, I first complete the analysis of the first-generation FX option pricing framework by offering some remarks on problems arising in the context of American options and by examining the risk-neutral valuation model tracing back to Cox and Ross (1976).

2.1.3   Extension to American Options

European options can only be exercised at expiry of the contract. American options, in contrast, can be exercised at any time during the remaining time to maturity of the option. The actual exercise time of the security is, therefore, uncertain when the option contract is struck. The additional right to optimally choose the exercise time makes an American option potentially more valuable for its owner than its European counterpart. This argument directly implies that the following inequality must hold at every instant of time and for every realization of the exchange rate process

$$(2.9) \quad C^A(E,\tau) \geq C(E,\tau),$$

where the superscript A is utilized to express that an option is of the American style. A corresponding inequality can be formulated for American put options. The central problem in the pricing of American options is transforming this inequality into an equality by determining the value of the early exercise premium of an American option. Thus, denoting the market price of this additional flexibility by Θ, it is possible to write

$$(2.10) \quad C^A(E,\tau) = C(E,\tau) + \Theta, \quad \text{with} \quad \Theta \geq 0.$$

The first point to note in tackling this problem is to recognize that the fundamental FX contingent claim valuation equation provided in equation (2.5) and derived for an economy with only one source of risk (stochastic exchange rate fluctuations) has been built by resorting to a preference-free no-arbitrage argument. Therefore, the valuation equation itself can be employed to characterize any derivative security with a premium depending only on the level of the exchange rate and on the remaining time-to-maturity of the contract. From this argument it follows directly that equation (2.5) also applies in the case of American FX options. Only the boundary conditions imposed to specify completely the valuation problem distinguish American options on foreign currency from their European counterparts and other derivative securities. These boundary conditions must be derived from economic considerations. As in the case of a European foreign currency call option, no-free-lunch arguments can be utilized to obtain the appropriate set of boundary conditions for an American FX call. To derive these boundary conditions, I follow the presentation outlined in Kim (1990).

Ruling out arbitrage at the absorbing barrier of the exchange rate process, a first boundary condition must be $\lim_{E \to 0} C^A(0,\tau) = 0$. The second side condition can be posited by recognizing that in an arbitrage-free economy any option must have a nonnegative value. From the condition of put-call parity, it then follows that a lower boundary for a European FX call option is given by $P(E,\tau) \geq 0$ or $C(E,\tau) \geq E \exp(-r^*\tau) - X \exp(-r\tau)$. For nonnegative interest rates and $\tau > 0$, this can result in $E \exp(-r^*\tau) - X \exp(-r\tau) < E - X$ for large E.[14] This inequality reveals that the value of a European FX option might lie below the payoff realized at expiry of the option. But this cannot be the case for an American option, as arbitrageurs could implement the following round trip transaction: go long on the call, exercise it immediately, and realize a positive riskless profit of $E - X - C(E,\tau) > 0$ (see, e.g., Wilmott et al. 1995: 54). Therefore, the lower boundary of an American FX call is given by

(2.11) $\quad C^A(E,\tau) \geq [E(t) - X]^+$ for all $\quad \tau \geq 0$.

The no-arbitrage argument just mentioned above implies that this inequality changes into an equality if it is optimal to exercise the American option immediately. Consequently, equation (2.11) reduces to a strict inequality if the investor should optimally hold the option during the next infinitesimal period of time. Assuming that it is optimal to exercise the option if $E(t) \geq E^*$, this can be formalized by stating that $C^A(E,t) = E(t) - X$ for $E(t) \geq E^*$ and $C^A(E,t) > E(t) - X$ for $E(t) < E^*$. One can now combine these arguments by stating the following "value matching" boundary condition for an American FX option:

(2.12) $\quad \lim_{E \to E^*} C^A(E,\tau) = E^* - X$.

A further boundary condition can be derived be examining the value of the American call on foreign currency as $\tau \to 0$:

(2.13) $\quad \lim_{\tau \to 0} C^A(E,\tau) = [(E - X)H(E^* - E)]^+$,

where $H(\cdot)$ is the Heavyside function. Equation (2.13) formalizes that, *conditional on* $E < E^*$, the premium of the American call converges to its payoff function as the maturity of the contract is reached.

Note that equations (2.12) and (2.13) are formulated in terms of the early exercise exchange rate threshold E^*. As the latter is not known before the

---

[14] This inequality cannot hold in the case of a European call option on a nondividend paying asset. As discussed, e.g., in Hull (1993), this implies that it is never optimal to exercise a corresponding American call option before the maturity of the contract. However, note that a similar argument does not apply in the case of an American put option on a nondividend paying asset. It might, thus, be optimal to exercise an American put option on a nondividend paying asset for $\tau > 0$.

problem has been solved but must instead be determined as an essential part of it, the pricing of American options is known as a *free boundary problem* (see, e.g., Wilmott et al. 1995: 55). Because the financial analyst has to determine this free boundary as part of the solution to the pricing problem, an additional condition is needed in order to close the model. This condition obtains by requiring that the expected value of holding the option another infinitesimal period of time is identical to the expected value of exercising the contract immediately as the exchange rate reaches the threshold E^*. This no-arbitrage argument can be implemented by forcing the option pricing function to satisfy

$$(2.14) \quad \lim_{E \to E^*} C_E^A(E^*,\tau) = 1.$$

If $C_E^A(E^*,\tau) > 1 \, (C_E^A(E^*,\tau) < 1)$, the expected value of holding the option during the next short period of time would be higher (lower) than the corresponding expected value of exercising the contract immediately. Hence, a rational investor would hold the American option a little bit longer for $C_E^A(E^*,\tau) > 1$ and would have already exercised it in a situation characterized by $C_E^A(E^*,\tau) < 1$. It follows that the optimal early exercise exchange rate threshold E^* has to satisfy the so-called *high-contact condition* formalized in equation (2.14).[15]

An unpleasant facet of the valuation of American options is that a solution to the free-boundary problem consisting of the fundamental contingent claim valuation equation (2.7) and the boundary conditions derived above does not exist in closed form.[16] This has challenged quite a few researchers to compute American option prices by resorting to numerical solution and analytical approximation techniques. Popular numerical solution techniques include the techniques introduced by Schwartz (1977) and Brennan and Schwartz (1978), who resort to a finite difference method to transform the parabolic partial differential equation given in (2.7) into a finite linear set of difference equations. This system of equations defines the American option value on a two-dimensional grid of realizations of the underlying asset price and the time-to-maturity. The difference equations can then easily be solved iteratively to determine the option value at

---

[15] For a discussion of high-contact conditions, see Dumas (1991).

[16] Closed-form solutions can, however, be derived if it is never optimal to exercise an American option before the contract expires. In this case, the American option degenerates to a European contract, so that an analytical solution is readily available. See Merton (1973) for the case of an American call on a nondividend paying asset. In the special case of discrete dividends, analytical solutions to the American option pricing problem have been derived by Roll (1977), Geske (1979a), and Whaley (1981). Johnson (1983) discusses some extreme situations in which simple solutions to the free-boundary problem can be derived.

the nodes of this grid. Another flexible and computationally efficient method of pricing American options numerically is the binomial tree approach introduced by Cox et al. (1979). The idea behind this approach is to model asset price fluctuations as a discrete time binomial stochastic process. The up and down ticks of the asset price are then used to construct a lattice. At every node of this lattice, it is possible to compare the payoff realized if the option is exercised with the payoff which obtains if the option is held another period of time. Assuming that investors act rationally, the larger of the two values obtained for an individual node is chosen as the premium of the American option at that node. Starting at the maturity of the option and going backward in time allows then the present value of the American option to be determined.

An alternative with which to solve for American option values numerically is to employ an analytical approximation technique. A popular and computationally efficient analytical approximation technique has been suggested by Barone-Adesi and Whaley (1987).[17] The central insight underlying the Barone-Adesi and Whaley technique is that the premia of both European and American call options satisfy the fundamental contingent claim valuation equations provided in equation (2.7).[18] Consequently, the early exercise premium of the American call option must follow the same partial differential equation. Restricting the analysis to either very short-term or rather long-term contracts, the time derivatives that show up in this fundamental valuation equation can be neglected. In this case, the early exercise premium of the American call option obtains as the solution to a second-order ordinary differential equation that can be easily solved, e.g., by the method of undetermined coefficients. The undetermined coefficients characterizing the solution are the roots of the characteristic quadratic equation of the ordinary differential equation obtained for the early exercise premium. For this reason, the Barone-Adesi and Whaley (1987) approach to the pricing of American-style option contracts is also known as a "quadratic approximation technique." Finally, the boundary conditions discussed above can be used to determine the numerical value of two constants of integration and of the early exercise threshold.

---

[17] Their work extends ideas already formulated in MacMillan (1986).

[18] An alternative approximation technique can be found in Geske and Johnson (1984), who use an infinite series of compound options to express the value of an American option analytically. Compound options, i.e., options on options, have been introduced into the literature by Geske (1979b). Though interesting from an economic point of view, the tractability of this approach is hampered by the fact that it requires the evaluation of multivariate normal density functions. In a recent contribution, Kim (1990) derives a pricing expression as the limit of a valuation formula for American calls. This formula applies in those cases where the contract might be exercised before expiry at a finite number of points in time.

Using either one of the numerical or analytical approximation techniques discussed in the literature, the following comparative static results summarizing the impact of various parameters important in option pricing theory on the early exercise premium $\Theta(E,\tau)$ can be derived:[19]

- The higher the domestic riskless interest rate as compared to its foreign counterpart, the smaller the incentive to exercise the American FX call before the maturity of the contract. The economic intuition behind this result is that exercising the option renders it possible to receive the continuous leakage from the foreign investment at the expense of losing the interest on X. Thus, the opportunity costs of early exercise are an increasing function of the domestic interest rate. Consequently, the function $\Theta(E,\tau)$ is adversely affected by movements in the instantaneous domestic risk-free interest rate.
- The early exercise premium $\Theta(E,\tau)$ is increasing in the moneyness of the option. The positive impact of the moneyness on the early exercise premium can best be understood by recognizing that the chance that the GK European call price will settle below its intrinsic value is an increasing function of the moneyness of the option. An alternative interpretation (Bodurtha and Courtadon 1987b: 21) is that an increase in the exchange rate raises the moneyness of a call and, thus, increases the delta of the contract. This, in turn, raises the capital costs borne to hedge the option and makes it relatively more attractive to exercise the contract early.
- The early exercise premium of out-of-the money American FX calls is an increasing function of the diffusion parameter of the exchange rate process. In contrast, the early exercise premium of the corresponding in-the-money calls reaches a maximum if the volatility of the exchange rate process is very low. The underlying economic intuition for this is that, for a rather small diffusion term, the GK European call price converges to its lower boundary provided in equation (2.22). In this situation, the early exercise premium of its American counterpart must rise in order to rule out riskless arbitrage profits.
- The early exercise premium for in-the-money contracts is an inverse function of the time-to-maturity of the American call option contract. As the option reaches its expiry, the foregone interest that could be realized upon exercising the contract immediately tends to outweigh the rapidly decreasing time value of the option. Consequently, early exercise becomes more attractive as the maturity of the call declines.

---

[19] See Bodurtha and Courtadon (1987b: 20) and Fastrich and Hepp (1991: 462) for an analysis of the comparative static properties of the premia of American options.

2.2   Risk-Neutral Valuation

The point of departure of the risk-neutral valuation technique pioneered by Cox
and Ross (1976) and further examined by Harrison and Kreps (1979) is the
observation that the "fair" price of a European option on foreign currency, given
by the function $C(E,\tau)$ introduced in Section 2.2.1, is both arbitrage-free and
preference-free. As the fundamental contingent claim valuation equation (2.7)
does not involve terms capturing economic agent's preferences toward exchange
rate uncertainty, it should be perfectly valid to price options *as if* economic
agents were risk-neutral. The price of the option obtained in a risk-neutral setting
should be equal to the premium resulting in an environment with risk-averse
option traders. In a risk-neutral economy, however, it would be much more convenient to price contingent claims. The reason for this is that in such an economy
the expected returns on holding a risky asset would have to be equal to the interest accrued by investing in the risk-free opportunity. In a risk-neutral international economy it would thus be possible to write

$$(2.15) \quad \mathbb{E}_t\left\{d\left[\exp(-(r-r^*)t)E(t)\right]\right\}= 0,$$

$$(2.16) \quad \mathbb{E}_t\left\{d\left[\exp(-rt)C_i(E(t),\tau)\right]\right\}= 0,$$

with $\mathbb{E}_t$ being the expectations operator conditional on time t information. The
risk-neutral valuation approach to option pricing exploits this implication and
examines whether the current premium of a European-style derivative security
$C_i(E(t),\tau)$ can alternatively be expressed as the expected value of its terminal
payoff discounted at the risk-free rate of interest.[20] If the derivative security
under investigation is a European FX call, this can be formalized as:

---

[20]   Cox and Ross (1976) have argued that equation (2.17) can be used to value European
options as long as options can be priced by constructing a hedge portfolio. Harrison
and Kreps (1979) discuss the general conditions under which equation (2.17) applies.
Specifically, they have demonstrated that the equivalent martingale measure used to
compute the conditional expectations in equation (2.17) can be used if it is assumed
that the economy under investigation is arbitrage-free. Note, however, that the
existence of this measure does not necessarily include its uniqueness. The uniqueness
of the martingale measure is closely related to the completeness of the modeled
security market. See, e.g., the discussion in Zimmermann (1998: Chapter 4); see also
Björk (1996: 61–65). Even if the martingale measure is not unique, the existing
equivalent martingale measures can still be utilized to price derivative securities by
taking into account the respective factor risk premia (see lemma 4 in Cox et al.
1985a: 380). Under the assumptions of the GK model, the martingale measure exists
and is unique.

(2.17) $\quad C(E(t),\tau) = \mathbb{E}_t\left[\exp(-r\tau)(E(T) - X)^+ | E(t)\right]$

$$= \exp(-r\tau)\int_0^\infty (E(T) - X)^+ \tilde{g}(E(T), E(t), T, t)dE(T),$$

where $\tilde{g}(E(T), E(t), T, t)$ denotes the density function of $E(T)$ conditional on the current exchange rate realization $E(t)$. To demonstrate how the risk-neutral valuation technique works in the case of a European FX call option, it is necessary (i) to verify the validity of the approach by proving that equation (2.17) satisfies the contingent claim valuation equation (2.5) *and* the boundary conditions formalized in equation (2.6), and, (ii) to show how to find the risk-neutral probability measure $\tilde{g}(E(T), E(t), T, t)$. [21]

Differentiating under the integral with respect to the current exchange rate and substituting the resulting partial derivatives into equation (2.5) yields

(2.18) $\quad \int_0^\infty \exp(-r\tau)(E(T) - X)^+ \left[0.5\sigma^2 E^2 \tilde{g}_{EE} + (r - r^*)E\tilde{g}_E + r\tilde{g}_E + \tilde{g}_t\right]dE(T) = 0.$

The bracketed term in equation (2.18), which involves partial derivatives of $\tilde{g}(E(T), E(t), T, t)$, can be identified as the Chapman–Kolmogorov backward equation for the conditional density of a geometric Wiener process with drift $(r - r^*)E$ and diffusion parameter σE. [22] As this shows that this expression is identically equal to zero, it follows that equation (2.17) is a solution to equation (2.5).

The backward equation can be utilized to solve for the probability density $\tilde{g}(E(T), E(t), T, t)$ defining in a risk-neutral environment. Specifically, note that equation (2.18) implies that the risk-neutral exchange rate process is given by $dE = (r - r^*)Edt + \sigma Ed\tilde{W}$, where the process $\{\tilde{W}_t, t \geq 0\}$ is a standard Brownian motion with $\mathbb{E}(d\tilde{W}) = 0$ and $\mathbb{E}(d\tilde{W}^2) = dt$. [23] The crucial point to note is that this Brownian motion is run by employing the probability measure $\tilde{g}(E(T), E(t), T, t)$ characterizing in a risk-neutral world rather than the objective measure, $g(E(T), E(t), T, t)$ characterizing the process formalized in equation (2.1). [24] Equation (2.18) reveals that this change in the density function allows

---

[21] The proof outlined below follows Ingersoll (1987: 364).

[22] See Dixit (1993) for a derivation of the Chapman–Kolmogorov equation and a discussion of some of its applications in economics.

[23] Note that equation (2.18) is consistent with the definition of the exchange rate risk premium defined in equation (2.3). In a risk-neutralized world, it must hold that $\gamma = 0$, so that equation (2.3) gives $\mu = r - r^*$. Replacing the drift in equation (2.1) with this expression yields equation (2.18).

[24] The probability measure $\tilde{g}(E(T), E(t), T, t)$ is the continuous-time analogue to the risk-neutralized state prices in the binomial option pricing model of Cox et al. (1979).

the drift of the exchange rate process to be switched from μE to $(r - r^*) E$ but leaves the volatility structure of the process unchanged.[25]

The process $\{\tilde{W}_t, t \geq 0\}$ obtains by noting that equations (2.15) and (2.16) require the asset price processes discounted at the risk-free rate of interest to be martingales under the measure $\tilde{g}(E(T), E(t), T, t)$. For example, equation (2.15) states that under $\tilde{g}(E(T), E(t), T, t)$ the geometric Gauss–Wiener process $dE = \mu E dt + \sigma E dW$ used in the GK currency option pricing model will be transformed into a martingale. To examine under which conditions this holds, utilize Ito's lemma to compute the differential of $\exp(-(r - r^*)t)E(t)$ and let the differential of the process $\{\tilde{W}_t, t \geq 0\}$ be given by $d\tilde{W} = dW + dZ$. The above semimartingale will be transformed into a martingale that satisfies equation (2.15) if and only if the condition $dZ = [(\mu - (r - r^*))/\sigma] dt$ is imposed (Neftci 1996: 311–317). The economic intuition behind this restriction is that, in a real-world speculative market populated by economic agents with arbitrary degrees of risk-aversion, the process $\{\tilde{W}_t, t \geq 0\}$ will allow for $\mathbb{E}_t\{d[\exp(-(r - r^*)t)E(t)]\} = 0$ if and only if the exchange rate risk premium is internalized by introducing the drift adjustment factor dZ.

To check that equation (2.17) is indeed equal to the GK option premium, it is necessary to analyze whether the risk-neutral pricing formula also satisfies the boundary conditions that apply in the case of a European FX call. First note that for $X = 0$, one has $C(E(t), \tau) = E(t) = \exp(-r\tau) \mathbb{E}_t(E(T))$. Consequently, it must hold that $C(E(t), \tau) \leq E(t)$ for all $X \geq 0$. This shows that equation (2.17) satisfies the third boundary condition in equation (2.6). As regards the absorbing barrier at $E = 0$, it must hold that $\tilde{g}(E(T), 0, T, t) = \delta^D(E(T))$, with $\delta^D(\cdot)$ denoting the Dirac delta function. This implies $C(0, \tau) = 0$, which is the second side condition stated in equation (2.6). Similarly, at expiry of the contract $\tilde{g}(E(T), E, T, T) = \delta^D(E(T) - E)$, so that $C(E, 0) = [E_T - X]^+$, which is the first boundary condition in equation (2.6). Thus, the risk-neutral valuation approach satisfies both the fundamental contingent claim valuation equation (2.5) and the boundary conditions that apply in the case of a European FX call. Consequently, the option premium computed by resorting to the GK framework and by employing the Cox–Ross valuation technique must also be identical. This, in turn, implies that the two approaches are equivalent to each other.

---

[25] This is an application of Girsanov's theorem. See Baxter and Rennie (2000: Chapter 3) for a treatment of the conditions under which this theorem applies. See also Neftci (1996) for a discussion of the relevance of the Girsanov theorem to the pricing of financial derivatives. See also Zimmermann (1998: 134–167).

The possibility of pricing options by resorting to the risk-neutral pricing technique formalized in equation (2.17) has three far-reaching implications which are important for the valuation of derivative securities in practice:

- The first implication concerns the probability measure $\tilde{g}(E(T),E(t),T,t)$. If it is possible to pin down the functional form of this measure, which prevails *in a risk-neutral world,* it is also a straightforward exercise to evaluate the integral on the right-hand side of equation (2.17) and, thus, to compute the premium of the derivative security $C_t(E(t),\tau)$. Moreover, the risk-neutral valuation approach does not require the measure $\tilde{g}(E(T),E(t),T,t)$ to be of a specific functional form. The functional form of the measure $\tilde{g}(E(T),E(t),T,t)$ might even not be known a priori but might instead be approximated by running Monte Carlo simulations. In fact, the practical importance of the risk-neutral valuation approach stems from the fact that it provides the financial analyst with the theoretical results needed to justify this approach to computing option premia. This result will be exploited in Chapter 3.
- The second implication concerns calculating the probability measure $\tilde{g}(E(T),E(t),T,t)$ by means of Monte Carlo simulation techniques. Such calculations require the formulation of a specific stochastic process for the underlying asset price. In applied work, observed exchange rates series can be used to estimate the parameters of such a process. An alternative approach is to resort to the risk-neutral valuation techniques to infer the a priori unknown equivalent measure $\tilde{g}(E(T),E(t),T,t)$ from observed option prices. Using the risk-neutral valuation approach, the measure $\tilde{g}(E(T),E(t),T,t)$ implicit in real-world options data obtains by evaluating the second derivative of equation (2.17) with respect to the strike price $C_{XX}(E(t),\tau)\exp(r\tau) = \tilde{g}(E(T),E(t),T,t)$ at $E(t) = X$ (Breeden and Litzenberger 1978).[26] Thus, if a financial analyst observes trading in a sufficiently large number of options with different strike

---

[26] Note that the second derivative of the European call-pricing function with respect to the strike price corresponds to a "butterfly spread" consisting of calls with infinitesimally small differences in strike prices. A butterfly spread can be composed by going long on two calls with strike prices $X \pm u$, $u > 0$ and going short on a corresponding call with strike price X (see, e.g., Kolb 1997: Chapter 2) for a comprehensive review of this and related option trading strategies). In the limit when $u \to 0$, the payoff function of the butterfly spread resembles a Dirac delta function. Implementing a butterfly spread with $u \to 0$, thus, amounts to pricing Arrow–Debreu securities (Arrow 1964; Debreu 1959), which pay off \$1 if $E(T) = X$. This, in turn, explains why it is possible to interpret numerical values obtained from $\tilde{g}(E(T),E(t),T,t)$ as risk-neutralized state prices. See Breeden and Litzenberger (1978) for a discussion on this line of argumentation. See also Zimmermann (1998: 241–250).

prices and the same time to maturity on the same underlying asset price, he can exploit these data to estimate the risk-neutral probability density function utilized by option traders to price these contracts. The implied probability density function can then be used to assess market participants sentiments regarding the variability, skewness, and kurtosis of exchange rate returns over the remaining time to expiry of the options. For alternative quantitative techniques that allow the equivalent martingale measure to be estimated from real-world option data, see Jackwerth and Rubinstein (1996), Rubinstein (1994), Melick and Thomas (1997), Ait-Sahalia and Lo (1998), and Malz (1996, 1997) and the references cited therein.

– The third implication concerns the payoff function that characterizes the financial instrument $C_i(E(t),\tau)$. In its most general form, equation (2.17) does *not* depend upon the specific payoff structure of the derivative security under investigation. The approach can, thus, be used not only to determine the premia of the type of options examined in the GK model, but also to price a broad range of related financial derivatives including, e.g., Asian options, knockout options, and other exotic options with complicated payoff functions.[27]

2.3 Models with a Variable Diffusion Term

Motivated by the empirical shortcomings of the first-generation FX option valuation model, many attempts have been made to explain observed pricing errors theoretically by modifying the stochastic environment underlying the basic Garman and Kohlhagen (1983) model. The point of departure of most of the various approaches to extending and to refining the GK model is the observation that the characteristic, more or less symmetric U-shaped functional relationship between implied volatilities and the moneyness of currency options harmonizes with the empirical finding that the unconditional distribution of daily and weekly foreign exchange rate returns can typically be shown to exhibit fat tails (de Vries 1994). Compared with the normal distribution, such a probability density function allocates more probability mass to the center and the tails of the distribution. Because a larger probability mass in the tails of the empirical exchange rate distribution directly increases the chance that out-of-the-money calls or puts will

---

[27] See Zhang (1996) for detailed analyses of exotic options. For an application of the risk-neutral valuation technique to the valuation of exotic options, see also Dufresne et al. (1996).

end up in-the-money, these contracts are traded at higher prices in real-world FX option markets than predicted by the first-generation currency option valuation models. This, in turn, raises volatility quotes implicit in these options and produces the characteristic smile effect in the volatility strike structure.

One way of accounting for the fat tails of the distributions of exchange rate returns is to price FX options by employing a currency option valuation model with a variable diffusion term. This section discusses two popular FX option pricing models featuring such a flexible diffusion term. The first model, which is discussed in Section 2.3.1, is the constant elasticity of variance model tracing back to Cox and Ross (1976). The model retains the assumption of the GK model that the volatility parameter is constant but incorporates an additional parameter capturing the elasticity of the instantaneous volatility of exchange rate returns with respect to the level of the exchange rate. In Section 2.3.2, the analysis turns to the second type of model, namely the stochastic volatility models. The assumption underlying models belonging to this class of option pricing setups is that the asset price and the volatility of the underlying are governed by separate but possibly correlated stochastic processes. An early example of a stochastic volatility model is the model developed by Hull and White (1987a). This model will be reviewed in Section 2.3.2.1. A drawback of the Hull–White model in its most general form is that it does not allow the option premium to be expressed in terms of elementary mathematical functions. This contrasts with the approach more recently suggested by Heston (1993). Heston utilizes the characteristic functions of the conditional probabilities that the option expires in-the-money to obtain an analytical solution for option premia under stochastic volatility. The implications of Heston's model for the pricing of FX options will be discussed in Section 2.3.2.1.

2.3.1   Constant Elasticity of Variance Models

The constant elasticity of variance (CEV) model has been developed by Cox and Ross (1976). Further studies of this model include MacBeth and Merville (1980) and Emanuel and MacBeth (1982). Peterson et al. (1988), Scott and Tucker (1989), and Melino and Turnbull (1991) have utilized the CEV model in empirical work on foreign currency options. Retaining all other assumptions made to construct the GK option pricing model, the CEV model is predicated on the assumption that the exchange rate process is given by the following stochastic differential equation (see, e.g., Emanuel and MacBeth 1982):

(2.19) $dE = \mu E dt + \sigma E^{v/2} dW.$

The constant parameter v represents the elasticity of the instantaneous volatility of exchange rate returns with respect to the level assumed by the exchange rate. For $v = 2$, the model degenerates into the classical GK setup. When $v = 0$, the volatility of the stochastic process provided in equation (2.19) is inversely proportional to the level of the exchange rate and the CEV model transforms into a so-called absolute diffusion model. For $v = 1$, equation (2.19) describes a square-root process (Cox and Ross 1976). In the general case of $v \neq 2$, the CEV model implies that the relation between the level of exchange rate volatility and the level of the underlying is asymmetric. For $v < 2$ ($v > 2$), the instantaneous variance of returns on holding foreign currency declines (increases) as the domestic currency depreciates. This implies that the model should be particularly suited to accounting for skewness effects in the volatility strike structure.

As exchange rate risk is the only source of uncertainty allowed for in the model, the no-arbitrage argument employed by Garman and Kohlhagen (1983) and Black and Scholes (1973) and Merton (1973) can also be applied to price FX options in the context of the CEV model. The fundamental contingent claim valuation equation is (Melino and Turnbull 1991: 255):

$$(2.20) \quad 0.5 C_{EE}\sigma^2 E^v + (r - r*)EC_E - rC = C_\tau.$$

The particular solution describing the premium of a European FX call obtains by invoking the boundary conditions in equation (2.6). The general functional form of the solution to this boundary value problem depends upon the numerical value assumed by the elasticity parameter v. Cox and Ross obtain a solution to the CEV model for the case of $v < 2$. Emanuel and MacBeth (1982) extend the model and present an analytical solution for $v > 2$. Though the resulting formulas for the premium of a European FX option mimic the GK solution, the involved expressions are relatively complex and are not reproduced in the present study. This complexity arises because in the CEV model the premium of a European-style currency option is computed by replacing the standard normal distribution functions of the GK option pricing formula with terms involving the cumulative distribution function of the noncentral chi-square distribution. A comprehensive treatment of the technical details of the solution can be found in Schroder (1989). In this section, I provide a graphical analysis of the implications of CEV type models for the pricing of FX options. For the sake of brevity, I follow the empirical work of Melino and Turnbull (1991) and confine the analysis to the case of $v < 2$.

Utilizing the results derived in Schroder (1989), Figure 2.1 plots the difference between CEV European foreign currency call option prices and the cor-

Figure 2.1: Implications of the Absolute Diffusion Model for the Pricing of FX Options

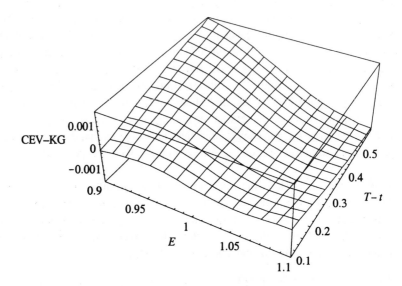

Note: Option premia were computed using the following numerical values for the other parameters of the valuation models: $X = 1$, $r = 0.1$, $r^* = 0.07$, and $\sigma = 0.1$.

responding premia obtained by implementing the GK formula. The surface exhibited in the figure is based on the assumption $v = 0$, which corresponds to the absolute diffusion model of Cox and Ross (1976). The figure shows that the CEV model produces higher option premia than the GK model for out-of-the-money calls and lower option premia for in-the-money calls when the elasticity of the instantaneous volatility of exchange rate returns assumes values $v < 2$. Moreover, it can be seen in Figure 2.1 that this effect becomes more pronounced as the time-to-expiry of the contract is increased. The economic intuition behind these results is that the CEV model does not invoke the assumption underlying the GK approach that the volatility of exchange rate returns is invariant to changes in the moneyness of the option. In foreign exchange markets characterized by $v < 2$ $(v > 2)$, the volatility of exchange rate returns declines (increases) as the domestic currency depreciates and the moneyness of the contract is raised (depressed). Consequently, the relative pricing difference between the CEV and the GK call option model which obtains in the case of $v < 2$ exhibits a positive (negative) sign for out-of-the-money (in-the-money) options.

This discussion indicates that CEV type models can be utilized to theoretically reproduce a variety of deviations of actual option prices from the corresponding premia predicted by the GK model. Empirical evidence, however, suggests that the increased flexibility of this theoretical model reflected in the additional parameter v does not suffice to fully account for observed pricing errors in actual FX options markets. For example, Melino and Turnbull (1991) implement a CEV model for Philadelphia Stock Exchange (PHLX) currency options using data for five major currencies and find that this model does not perform particularly well. As regards the predictive power of volatility quotes inferred from option prices, Scott and Tucker (1989) and Peterson et al. (1988) report that the forecasting power of implied volatilities implicit in CEV models does not shadow the performance of GK forecasts. Their sample includes data for the world's most important currencies over the period from 1982 to 1986.

Taking the perspective of an economic theorist, a further drawback of CEV type models is that they have primarily been designed for stock options. In the case of stocks, the additional parameter v renders it possible to model an inverse relationship between the level of the stock price and the volatility of the investment. Such an inverse relation results in the case of $v < 2$. A CEV model, thus, makes it possible to account for a possible systematic impact of the leverage effect (Christie 1982) on the perceived riskyness of the stock in the pricing of the corresponding options. In contrast to stocks, however, it is economically rather difficult to motivate the leverage argument underlying CEV models in the case of currencies (Bates 1996a). All in all, the empirical and theoretical shortcomings of the CEV model thus indicate that it is worthwhile to focus attention on an alternative class of FX option pricing models with a variable diffusion term, namely stochastic volatility models.

2.3.2 Stochastic Volatility Models

The only input parameter of the GK currency option valuation formula not directly observable in actual financial markets is the volatility coefficient of the underlying exchange rate process. Consequently, observed pricing errors of the GK model are typically discussed in terms of volatilities implicit in option prices. Visual inspections of time series of implied volatilities typically reveal that this parameter is not constant over time. To provide an example that illustrates the time-varying nature of volatility quotes implicit in foreign currency options, Figure 2.2 depicts volatilities inferred from at-the-money US dollar/

Figure 2.2: The Time-Varying Nature of Annualized Volatilities Implicit in At-the-Money Forward US/DM and Yen/DM Options (time to expiry: one month)

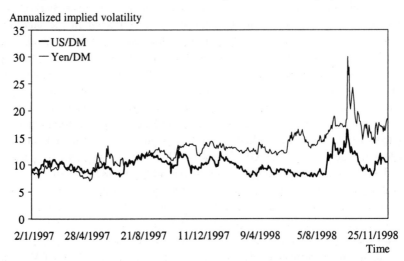

deutsche mark and yen/deutsche mark options with a time to maturity of one month.[28]

The data presented in Figure 2.2 cover the period January 1997–December 1998. It can be seen from the figure that the time-invariance property of the co-efficient σ needed to derive the GK model does not hold for volatilities implicit in real-world currency option contracts. All in all, the plotted time series indicate that the volatility used by market participants to price FX options is a highly unstable parameter which might even exhibit sudden and substantial outbursts. Given this erratic behavior of options' implied volatilities, a leading candidate for the pricing of options on foreign currency is pricing models that are applicable to options on assets with a stochastic volatility.

2.3.2.1   The Model of Hull and White

Hull and White (henceforth abbreviated as HW) (1987a) were among the first to develop an option pricing model featuring an asset price process with a stochastic volatility.[29] The model is predicated on the assumption that financial markets

---

[28]   The Deutsche Bundesbank kindly provided the implied volatility series.

[29]   Other "first-generation" studies of the stochastic volatility option pricing problem include Wiggins (1987), Johnson and Shanno (1987), Finucane (1989), Scott (1987), Dothan (1987), Chesney and Scott (1989), and Hull and White (1988).

are frictionless, that domestic and foreign default-free interest rates are constant, and that trading takes place continuously. The stochastic processes for the exchange rate and its variance are given by the following set of equations (Hull and White 1987a: 282):[30]

(2.21) $dE = (r - r^*)E dt + \sqrt{V} E dW^E$,

(2.22) $dV = \mu V dt + \xi V dW^V$,

where the drift coefficient of the exchange rate process has already been replaced by the international interest rate differential and where the standard Wiener processes $\{W_t^E, t \geq 0\}$ and $\{W_t^\sigma, t \geq 0\}$ are possibly correlated with $dW_E dW_\sigma = \rho\, dt$.[31] The coefficients μ and ξ are assumed to be constants.

In order to derive the fundamental contingent claim valuation equation that applies in this economy, the first step is to form a portfolio $\tilde{\Omega}$ consisting of a short position in one European FX call option $C(E, V, \tau)$ and a long position in C_E units of the underlying E. Holding C_E constant during an infinitesimal period of time, the change of the value of the portfolio can be expressed as

(2.23) $d\tilde{\Omega} = -\big(C_V dV + C_t dt + 0.5 C_{EE}(dE)^2 + 0.5 C_{VV}(dV)^2 + C_{EV} dE dV\big)$
$\qquad\qquad + r^* E C_E dt.$

The presence of the term $C_V dV$ in equation (2.23) demonstrates that the evolution of the value of the portfolio is still subject to stochastic shocks caused by the innovation term of the variance equation (2.22). In sharp contrast to the baseline GK currency option pricing model, the composed portfolio $\tilde{\Omega}$ is, thus,

---

[30]   Strictly speaking, the dynamics of the variance, rather than those of the standard deviation of exchange rate returns, are modeled in the Hull and White (1987a) model and in the model advanced by Heston (1993) discussed in the next section. Notwithstanding, it will often be convenient to employ the term "volatility" to discuss the properties of the models.

[31]   For a model in which the standard deviation of exchange rate returns follows a geometric Brownian motion, see Johnson and Shanno (1987). The process introduced in Johnson and Shanno resembles the stochastic differential equation utilized in CEV models. The advantage of selecting a geometric Wiener process to model stochastic fluctuations in the exchange rate volatility/variance is that such a specification assures that the volatility parameter will always assume a positive numerical value. The major economic shortcoming of this modeling strategy is that it implies that the volatility process is not stationary. Stationarity of volatility can be achieved by utilizing a mean-reversion process to model the dynamic behavior of volatility. Models with a mean-reverting stochastic volatility have been analyzed by Melino and Turnbull (1990), Chesney and Scott (1989), Scott (1987), Stein and Stein (1991), Ball and Roma (1994), and Heston (1993). Heston's model will be analyzed in the following section.

not risk free even over the infinitesimally short period of time dt. From this it follows that, as long as economic agents require a positive risk premium to bear volatility risk, the expected returns on holding this portfolio will not be equal to the interest earned by investing the amount $\tilde{\Omega}$ into risk-free domestic discount bonds. The reason for this is that a portfolio consisting only of an option and an investment in the underlying asset does not suffice to completely cover the risk fostered by the two different sources of uncertainty dW^E and dW^V. The complication introduced by modeling a stochastically evolving exchange rate variability is that volatility is not a traded asset, so that it is not possible to eliminate the residual uncertainty dW^V from the stochastic differential in (2.23) by incorporating a third "volatility based" security into the replicating portfolio $\tilde{\Omega}$. This, in turn, implies that some further assumptions regarding the market price of volatility risk need to be invoked in the stochastic volatility economy under investigation. The most general strategy is to utilize a general equilibrium asset pricing framework to determine the premium required to bear the risk caused by a stochastically evolving exchange rate variance.[32] For example, in the consumption-based intertemporal asset pricing framework analyzed by Breeden (1979) this risk premium $\tilde{\lambda}$ can be expressed as $\tilde{\lambda} = \hbar \mathrm{Cov}(dV, dc/c)$, with $\hbar \equiv -c \cdot U_{cc}/U_c$ being defined as the relative risk-aversion parameter of the utility function $U(c)$, and $\mathrm{Cov}(dV, dc/c)$ denoting the conditional covariance of variance changes and the rate of change of the aggregate consumption flow c. This equation shows that if the process driving V is uncorrelated with aggregate consumption, then the risk premium is zero. If, in contrast, the conditional covariance operator is different from zero, then further assumptions regarding the utility function of the representative agent and the evolution of the stochastic state variables of the economy are necessary to determine the risk premium. For example, Heston (1993) uses a consumption process which can be derived in the Cox et al. (1985a) general equilibrium framework to motivate a risk premium of the format $\tilde{\lambda} = \lambda V$, with λ representing a constant.

Employing equation (2.23), adjusting the expected returns on holding the portfolio $\tilde{\Omega}$ for the risk premium $\tilde{\lambda} = \lambda V$, noting that the investor is short in the option, and setting the resulting expression equal to the return on a correspond-

---

[32] Another technique discussed in the literature to tackle this problem is to presume continuous trading in an asset driven by an innovation term which is instantaneously perfectly correlated with the stochastic volatility process. In this case, it would be possible to make the replicating portfolio $\tilde{\Omega}$ riskless by investing a fraction of financial wealth into this asset (Johnson and Shanno 1987). Yet another alternative is to construct a riskless replicating portfolio by relying on the existence of a second call option with a different time to maturity (Scott 1987). The problem with this approach is that one has to price the option so that it will hardly be possible to use a second option of the same type to price the first contract.

ing investment in risk-free discount bonds results in the following fundamental contingent claim valuation equation (Hull and White 1987a: 283):

$$(2.24) \quad 0.5 V E^2 C_{EE}(E,V,\tau) + 0.5 \xi^2 V^2 C_{VV}(E,V,\tau) + \rho \xi V^{3/2} EC_{EV}(E,V,\tau)$$
$$+ (r - r^*) EC_E(E,V,\tau) + (\mu - \lambda) V C_V(E,V,\tau) - rC(E,V,\tau) = -C_t(E,V,\tau).$$

This bivariate partial differential equation corresponds to equation (31) (Theorem 3) of Cox et al. (1985a) for an economy with two stochastic state variables. In the case of a European call on foreign currency $C(E,V,\tau)$, the set of boundary conditions employed to identify a particular solution to this fundamental valuation equation consists of the set of standard equations in (2.6) and two additional boundary conditions that account for the stochastic nature of exchange rate volatility (Heston 1993: 330):

$$(2.25) \quad \lim_{V \to \infty} C(E,V,\tau) = E,$$

$$(2.26) \quad (r - r^*) EC_E(E,0,\tau) + (\mu - \lambda) V C_V(E,0,\tau) - rC(E,0,\tau) + C_t(E,0,\tau) = 0.$$

Hull and White do not provide a closed-form solution to the boundary value problem (2.6), (2.24)–(2.26). However, they demonstrate that interesting insights into the valuation problem might be gained by imposing some further assumptions. In order to tackle the stochastic volatility problem analytically, they set $\mu = 0$, $\rho = 0$, and $\tilde{\lambda} = 0$. Thus, the drift term of the variance process assumes the value zero, exchange rate and exchange rate volatility innovations are instantaneously uncorrelated, and the conditional covariance between the variance of the spot rate and the aggregate consumption flow is zero. Agreeably, these assumptions are restrictive and it would be economically far more appealing to have a stochastic volatility option pricing setup that would allow some or all of these additional technical conditions to be relaxed. In fact, the valuation framework developed by Heston (1993) is such a model and provides financial analysts with the necessary technical tools to accommodate a nonzero drift of the process specified to describe the dynamics of V, a nonzero instantaneous correlation coefficient ρ, and a nonzero risk premium. Despite these recent advances in options research, analyzing the HW framework remains interesting insofar as it provides market participants with a relatively simple approximation formula for European options on assets with a stochastic volatility.

Having invoked the above-mentioned additional assumptions, Hull and White show that if the state variables of the model follow the diffusion processes in equations (2.21) and (2.22), the distribution of the exchange rate at the expiry of the contract conditional on the current realization of this asset price and the current value assumed by its variance is lognormal. This, in turn, implies that the stochastic volatility FX call price is equal to the expected GK price, with expectations calculated using the conditional distribution $h^V(\overline{V}|V(t) = V)$ of the average variance $\overline{V}$. This result can be formalized as follows (Hull and White 1987a: 286):[33]

(2.27) $C(E,V,\tau) = \int_0^\infty C^{GK}(E,\overline{V},\tau)h^V(\overline{V}|V)d\overline{V}.$

Having computed the moments of the distribution $h^V(\overline{V}|V(t) = V)$, Hull and White utilize a third-order power-series expansion of the Garman and Kohlhagen currency option price around $\overline{V}$ to reformulate equation (2.27) in terms of elementary mathematical functions. This power-series approximation formula can then be implemented to shed light on the consequences of a stochastic exchange rate volatility on the pricing of European options on foreign currency.

Figure 2.3 plots the pricing difference between the HW and the GK model as a function of the moneyness of a European call and its time to expiry. The surface depicted in the figure reveals that allowing the volatility of the exchange rate to fluctuate stochastically depresses the prices of at-the-money options and increases the price of out-of-the money and in-the-money options. These effects tend to be exaggerated as the time to maturity of the contract is increased. The economic reasoning behind this "butterfly" phenomenon can be read off Figure 2.4. It depicts the sensitivity of the GK option premium with respect to the volatility parameter; that is, the graph plots the vega of the GK option formula (Table 2.1). It can be seen that the call premium is a convex function of volatility for out-of-the-money and in-the-money options. Near-the-money contracts, in contrast, turn out to be concave in exchange rate volatility. Because of Jensen's inequality, rising uncertainty with respect to volatility then implies that the expected value of the GK option price computed for near-the-money contracts by using the conditional variance density $h^V(\overline{V}|V)$ is an inverse function of the variability of the underlying asset price (Hull and White 1987a). Consequently, allowing for a stochastically evolving exchange rate volatility depresses the price of near-the-money options and increases the prices of out-of-the-money and in-the-money options. As the uncertainty regarding the future behavior of (average) volatility is an increasing function of the time to expiry of the contract, the "butterfly" effect becomes more pronounced as $T-t$ assumes larger numerical values.

---

[33] Note that the economic interpretation of the variance/volatility parameter in the HW model is different from that of the volatility coefficient in the GK model. In the HW model, the volatility parameter denotes the average expected volatility over the remaining time to maturity of the contract. In the GK model, in contrast, this parameter reflects the instantaneous volatility of the exchange rate (Abken and Nandi 1996: 31).

Figure 2.3: Stochastic Volatility and the Premia of a European Call on Foreign Currency

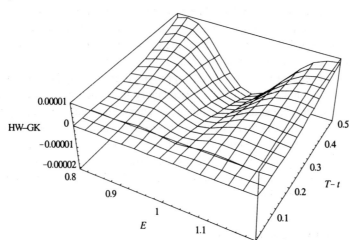

Note: The figure was computed by using the following set of parameter values to numerically set up the model of Hull and White (1987a): $r = r^* = 0.07$, $V(t) = \xi = 0.15$, and $X = 1$.

Figure 2.4: The Vega of the Garman and Kohlhagen Option Premia

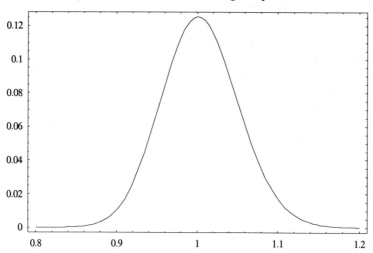

Note: The figure plots the vega of the Garman and Kohlhagen (1983) option price ($\equiv \partial C^{GK}/\partial \sqrt{V}$) on the vertical axis as a function of the exchange rate on the horizontal axis. For numerical parameter values see Figure 2.3.

The major shortcoming of the HW model is that it is not possible in this model to derive a closed-form solution to the most general form of the stochastic volatility option pricing problem. The power-series expansion used by Hull and White allows option premia to be approximated only under rather restrictive assumptions regarding the properties of the stochastic spot rate and instantaneous volatility processes and the market price of risk $\tilde{\lambda}$. Furthermore, nothing in the model guarantees that the power-series approximation used by Hull and White to express the option value in terms of elementary mathematical functions indeed converges. In theoretical analyses, this is, of course, not really a binding restriction, as the economic theorist is always free to base simulations of the model on a numerical parameter constellation that assures convergence of the HW series expansion. Convergence problems with the power-series approximation might, however, cause some trouble when the model is fitted to real-world option data (see, e.g., Gesser and Poncet 1997).

2.3.2.2 The Approach of Heston

The major contribution of Heston's (1993) analysis to the literature on the stochastic volatility option valuation problem is that his framework renders it possible to express option premia in closed-form and, thus, serves to overcome the most important shortcoming of the HW model. In contrast to the series expansion of Hull and White, this closed-form solution can also be computed when both the instantaneous correlation between exchange rate and volatility innovations and the market price for bearing the risk caused by a stochastic spot rate variance are not equal to zero. Rather than figuring out the option premium by tackling a boundary value problem of the format (2.6), (2.24)–(2.26) directly, Heston's idea was to compute the characteristic functions of the conditional probabilities that the option expires in-the-money and then to use an inverse Fourier transformation technique to obtain an analytical solution for option premia under stochastic volatility.[34] The list of contributions to the option pricing literature adapting this technique to tackle the stochastic volatility option pricing problem includes Koch (1992), Bates (1996b), Bakshi and Chen (1997), and Bakshi et al. (1997).

---

[34]   In the option pricing literature, inverse Fourier transformations have also been used by Stein and Stein (1991). However, the results presented in this paper are incomplete insofar as the innovations of the asset price and volatility processes are not allowed to be instantaneously correlated.

The basic building block of Heston's model is formed by the following set of stochastic differential equations for the exchange rate and its variance (Heston 1993: 328–329):

(2.28) $\quad dE = \mu E dt + \sqrt{V} E dW^E$,

(2.29) $\quad dV = \kappa(\theta - V)dt + \xi \sqrt{V} dW^V$,

with $dW^E dW^V = \rho dt$. The exchange rate is assumed to follow a geometric Brownian motion and the dynamics of its variance are captured by the kind of mean reverting square-root process introduced by Cox et al. (1985a, 1985b). Instantaneous interest rates are constant, trading takes place continuously, and markets are frictionless.

Given the stochastic processes for the state variables formalized in equations (2.28)–(2.29), the no-arbitrage argument already employed to price derivative securities in the HW economy leads to the following fundamental contingent claim valuation equation (Heston 1993: 329):

(2.30) $\quad 0.5VE^2 C_{EE}(E,V,\tau) + 0.5\xi^2 VC_{VV}(E,V,\tau) + \rho\xi VEC_{EV}(E,V,\tau)$

$\qquad + (r - r^*)EC_E(E,V,\tau) + (\kappa(\theta - V) - \lambda V)C_V(E,V,\tau) - rC(E,V,\tau)$

$\qquad = -C_t(E,V,\tau)$,

where the risk premium $\tilde{\lambda}$ has been specified as $\tilde{\lambda} = \lambda V$. The premium of a European call on foreign currency obtains upon solving equation (2.30) subject to the boundary conditions in equations (2.6), (2.24)–(2.26), where (2.26) is slightly modified to account for the fact that the variance of the exchange rate now follows a square-root process.

Exploiting the analogy to the analysis of Garman and Kohlhagen, the starting point of Heston's strategy to find a solution to this boundary value problem is to guess that the functional form of the option pricing formula can be expected to be of the format:

(2.31) $\quad C(E,V,\tau) = E\exp(-r^*\tau)Q^1 - X\exp(-r\tau)Q^2$.

The economic interpretation of equation (2.31) is that the current premium of the FX call should be equal to the present discounted value of the terminal payout of the option weighted by the respective probabilities that the option will end up in-the-money. As the risk-free interest rates are utilized to perform the discounting exercise, Q^1 and Q^2 can be interpreted as the equivalent martingale probabilities that $E(T) - X > 0$ at expiry of the contract. Solving the stochastic volatility model, thus, amounts to determining the functional forms of Q^1 and

Q^2. In the GK model, it is known that these probabilities are given by the standard normal distribution function.

To determine Q^1 and Q^2, the first step taken by Heston (1993) is to substitute the conjectured solution formula provided in equation (2.31) into the fundamental contingent claim valuation equation (2.30). Carrying out this exercise gives a set of bivariate partial differential equations in Q^1 and Q^2. Unfortunately, the probabilities Q^1 and Q^2 are not directly available from these equations in closed form. However, Heston's main insight is that the characteristic functions $cf^j(e,V,\omega,\tau)$, $j = 1,2$ of Q^j again satisfy a similar set of partial differential equations subject to the terminal condition

$$(2.32) \quad cf^j(e,V,\omega,0) = \mathbb{E}_t[\exp(\text{IM}\,\omega e(T))], \qquad j = 1,2,$$

with **IM** denoting the imaginary number and e symbolizing the natural logarithm of the spot exchange rate. Using a separation of variables argument, it can be verified that $cf^j(e,V,\omega,\tau)$ can be stated in terms of a set of separable functions which, in turn, can be expressed analytically by successively solving a set of nonlinear first-order *ordinary* differential equations. Compared with tackling the partial differential equation (2.30) directly, it is a relatively straightforward exercise to solve such a system.[35] Equipped with the resulting closed-form expressions for the characteristic functions, the probabilities Q^1 and Q^2, and the premium of the FX call under stochastic volatility can be determined by applying a Fourier inversion formula (Heston 1993: 331). In a final step, the formulas obtained for Q^1 and Q^2 can then be plugged into equation (2.31) to compute premia of options on assets with a stochastically evolving volatility numerically.

The most interesting feature of Heston's model is that it renders it possible to elaborate on the impact of the correlation between exchange rate and volatility innovations on option prices. Coding up the model numerically, Heston (1993) shows that a negative (positive) coefficient of correlation $\rho < 0$ ($\rho > 0$) between the innovation terms of the equations capturing the exchange rate and the volatility dynamics allows an asymmetric smile effect in the volatility strike structures implicit in the simulated option premia to be reproduced theoretically. For example, implementing the model for $\rho < 0$, it can be shown that the assumption of a negative correlation coefficient results in a decrease in the value of out-of-the-money contracts and raises the price of in-the-money contracts. In

---

[35] The lengthy expressions for the solutions to these equations involve only elementary mathematical functions and can be found in Heston (1993: 331). In the interest of brevity, they are not reproduced here.

particular, out-of-the-money and in-the-money options tend to be asymmetrically affected by varying ρ : the premia of out-of-the-money contracts tend to be an increasing function of the negative correlation coefficient, and in-the-money options turn out to be inversely related to ρ. It can also be verified that, similar to the relative impact of stochastic volatility on option premia reported in Hull and White (1987a), the absolute value of the percentage price bias induced by varying ρ declines as the moneyness of the option is increased.

The economic intuition behind these results is that allowing for a nonzero correlation coefficient destroys the symmetry of the exchange rate returns distribution (Heston 1993: 336–339). Assigning a negative numerical value to the parameter ρ implies that exchange rate volatility tends to be high when the domestic currency appreciates. This, in turn, increases the fatness of the left tail of the probability density function of the returns of this asset price. The left-skewed shape of the density of exchange rate returns increases both the probability of significant negative and the probability of above-average realizations of exchange rate returns. In the case of out-of-the-money (in-the-money) options, the first (second) effect dominates and the increased probability of large negative realizations of exchange rate returns (the shift of the mode of the returns density to the right on the real axis) results in a decline (rise) in the premia of out-of-money (in-the-money) contracts. A negative correlation coefficient, therefore, amplifies (contracts) the increasing impact of stochastic volatility on premia of in-the-money (out-of-the-money) FX calls found in the HW model. Opposite results can be obtained when the correlation coefficient is within the interval $0 < \rho \leq 1$.

To summarize, the Heston (1993) model provides financial analysts with a tractable and powerful framework with which to value and hedge European options on assets with a stochastic volatility. The model has a closed-form solution and, thus, allows for an efficient and speedy computation of option premia. Furthermore, the model allows the pricing of options in environments characterized by a nonzero volatility risk premium and by a nonzero correlation between the stochastic processes driving the asset price and its volatility. A nonzero correlation between the Wiener processes of the exchange rate and the volatility equation implies that the impact of volatility fluctuations on the premia of out-of-the-money options differs from their effect on corresponding in-the-money options. This, in turn, renders it possible to employ the model to theoretically reproduce skewness effects in the volatility strike structure.

2.4   Models Featuring Discontinuous Exchange Rate Paths

An alternative to resorting to stochastic volatility approaches to modeling a leptokurtic and possibly skewed probability density function of exchange rate returns and the resulting smile and smirk effects in the volatility strike structure is pure jump and jump-diffusion models. The incorporation of a jump component into the stochastic differential equation which describes exchange rate dynamics implies that the probability of a nonnegligible, disruptive movement of this asset price during an infinitesimal period of time becomes positive. Such a modeling strategy, therefore, makes it possible to discuss the implications of discontinuous exchange rate paths for the pricing of FX options. Jumps in the exchange rate process can be economically motivated, e.g., by the discrete arrival of unanticipated new information (see, e.g., Dornbusch 1976). The release of the latest data regarding important macroeconomic aggregates is an example of a discretely spaced "news" arrival process. The fundamental building blocks for option pricing with discontinuous asset returns have been developed by Cox and Ross (1976) and by Merton (1976). In the case of FX options, jump models for exchange rate dynamics have been employed by Jorion (1988), Borenzstein and Dooley (1987), and Malz (1996). Recently, Bates (1996b) and Bakshi et al. (1997) have adapted the Heston (1993) technique to solve option pricing models featuring asset price dynamics exhibiting both a jump-diffusion component and a stochastic volatility. In order to focus attention on the problems specific to option valuation frameworks with discontinuous asset returns, I follow Jorion (1988) and adapt the baseline jump-diffusion model suggested by Merton (1976) to the case of options on foreign currency.

In this jump-diffusion model, unanticipated exchange rate returns are assumed to evolve according to the following stochastic process:

$$(2.33) \quad \mathrm{d}E = (r - r* - \ell \, \mathbb{E}(J-1))E \, \mathrm{d}t + \sigma E \, \mathrm{d}W + E \, \mathrm{d}p,$$

where $\mathrm{d}W$ is a standard Gauss–Wiener process with an instantaneous standard deviation conditional on no jumps of σ. The term $\mathrm{d}p$ denotes an independent Poisson counting process with jump intensity $\mathrm{Prob}(\mathrm{d}p = 1) = \ell \, \mathrm{d}t$ and independently normally distributed jump size $J \sim \Phi'(\iota, \sigma_J^2)$. The symbol $\mathbb{E}$ denotes the expectations operator. Notice that equation (2.33) is already interpreted under a equivalent martingale measure. Subtracting the expected rate of change in the exchange rate arising if a jump takes place assures that the exchange rate martingalizes with respect to this measure (see, e.g., Neftci 1996: 116).[36]

As in the case of options on assets with a stochastic volatility, the additional sources of uncertainty introduced into the valuation framework by assuming the exchange rate path to exhibit unpredictable discontinuities of random size imply that it is not possible to price derivative securities by constructing an instantaneously risk-free dynamic replicating portfolio.[37] Though the innovation term driving the continuous part of the exchange rate process could be neutralized by composing a GK delta hedge portfolio, the returns on such a portfolio would still be stochastic due to the presence of a second source of randomness fostered by the Poisson jump component of equation (2.33). In order to derive a fundamental contingent claim valuation equation, it is therefore necessary to make some further assumptions regarding the nature of the exchange rate jump risk. Merton (1976) adopts the strategy of Black and Scholes (1973) and assumes that the capital asset pricing model (CAPM) holds.[38] Presuming further that the risk attributable to exchange rate jumps can be classified as "nonsystematic" in the context of this asset pricing framework implies that the beta of the GK hedge portfolio will be zero. In the case of stocks, this set of additional assumptions can then be used to derive a fundamental contingent claim valuation equation for an economy with a discontinuous asset price path by resorting to the ideas already used to derive equations (2.3) and (2.4). Unfortunately, in the case of FX options, a complication arises which has recently been pointed out by Dumas et al. (1995a).[39] The problem emphasized by these authors is that if both a domestic and a foreign investor simultaneously adopt the entire set of assumptions formulated above, the paradox of Siegel (1972) holds and the valuation equation for a domestic call on foreign currency will not be identical to the one describing the premium of a foreign put on the domestic currency. In other words, the situation is as if the law of one price did not hold and the value of a coin depended on which side of it the researcher is looking. Strictly speaking, this argument implies that exchange rate jump risk may not be presupposed to be diversifiable,

---

[36] The existence of the equivalent martingale measure is assured by assuming the economy under investigation to be arbitrage-free. However, as in the case of options on assets with a stochastic volatility, the presence of exchange rate jumps implies that this martingale measure is not unique.

[37] It should be mentioned, however, that in contrast to the stochastic volatility model the jump component of the stochastic process specified in (2.33) introduces *two* additional sources of uncertainty into the model: both the occurrence and the size of a jump are random variables (see also Neftci 1996 for a discussion).

[38] For the CAPM, see Sharpe (1964), Lintner (1965), and Mossin (1966).

[39] See also the discussion in Bardhan (1995) and Dumas et al. (1995c).

but rather should be derived from the type of general equilibrium considerations already adopted above to obtain an expression for the premium of taking the risk caused by a stochastically evolving exchange rate volatility. However, the numerical simulations performed by Dumas et al. (1995a) show that for many parameter values the bias introduced into the setup by assuming that it is possible for domestic and foreign investors to form a zero beta GK hedge portfolio might be rather small. This effect might thus be outweighed by the appreciated property of the jump-diffusion approach to reduce the mispricing associated with the first-generation FX option valuation model. For expositional purposes, I therefore follow the route conventionally taken in the literature and use the line of argumentation suggested by Merton (1976) to derive a fundamental contingent claim valuation equation.

Let the twice differentiable function $C(E,\tau)$ denote the premium of an FX option with time to expiry $\tau \equiv T-t, T \geq t$. Applying Ito's lemma for jump-diffusion models (Neftci 1996: 212–214), computing the expected rate of return and standard deviation on holding the option, and resorting to the usual no-arbitrage argument, the following contingent claim valuation equation obtains:

$$(2.34) \quad 0.5 C_{EE}\, \sigma^2 E^2 + (r - r^* - \ell\, \mathbb{E}(J-1)) E C_E - rC$$

$$+ \ell\, \mathbb{E}\{C(EJ,\tau) - C(E,\tau)\} = C_\tau.$$

Solving this equation subject to the boundary conditions in equation (2.6) yields the premium of a European call on foreign currency. Merton (1976) has demonstrated that the option premium that solves this boundary value problem can be written as the sum of Black and Scholes (1973) option prices which obtain if exactly $n \geq 0$ jumps occur over the remaining time to expiry of the contract weighted with the probability that n jumps occur.[40] In the case of foreign currency options, this proposition can be formalized as follows (see, e.g., Jorion 1988: 436):

$$(2.35) \quad C^{Jump}(E,\tau) = \exp(-r^*\tau) \sum_{n=0}^{\infty} \frac{\exp\left(-\ell\tau \exp(\iota + \sigma_J^2/2)\right)\left(\ell\tau \exp(\iota + \sigma_J^2/2)\right)^n}{n!}$$

$$\times C^{GK}(E,\tau, r - r^* + n(\iota + \sigma_J^2/2)/\tau - \ell(\exp(\iota + \sigma_J^2/2), \sigma^2 + n\sigma_J^2/\tau, X).$$

Equation (2.35) shows that the incorporation of a jump component into the valuation framework requires adjustment of the instantaneous interest rate differential and increases the overall variance utilized to price options from σ^2 in the pure diffusion model to $\sigma^2 + n\sigma_J^2/\tau$.

---

[40]   The formal proof can be found in Merton (1976: 141).

Figure 2.5 summarizes the implications of adding a jump component to the geometric Gauss–Wiener process underlying the GK model for the pricing of European options on foreign currency. The figure depicts the difference between the value of an FX call computed by implementing equation (2.35) and the corresponding premium obtained by coding up the GK pricing formula. In the numerical simulation, the jump intensity parameter has been chosen to be $\ell = 0.1$ and the mean jump amplitude of the Poisson process has been set equal to $\iota = 0.7$. These assumptions imply (i) that the probability that a jump will occur during the next infinitesimal period of time is nonzero, and, (ii) that if a jump occurs it is expected to result in a discontinuous depreciation of the domestic currency.

The figure shows that the higher exchange rate volatility used to price derivative securities raises the premium of the jump-diffusion European call relative to the price of its GK counterpart. Furthermore, a nonzero mean jump

Figure 2.5: Implications of Exchange Rate Jumps for Currency Option Prices and Hedge Ratios

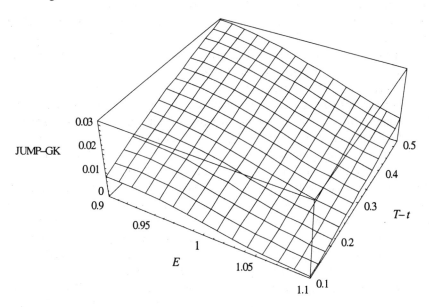

Note: The figure is based on the following set of parameter values: $r = 0.1$, $r^* = 0.07$, $\sigma = \sigma_J = 0.15$, $\ell = 0.1$, $\iota = 0.7$, and $X = 1$. As in Jorion (1988: 443), I set $n_{max} = 10$. Choosing a larger n only raised the computation time needed to construct the graph but did not affect the option premia significantly.

amplitude results in an asymmetric exchange rate distribution. The positive numerical value $\iota = 0.7$ for the mean jump size utilized in this example raises the probability of a large depreciation of the domestic currency during the next instant of time and, thus, enhances the chance that an option which is currently out-of-the money will end up in-the-money. As can be seen in the figure, this implies that the increasing effect exerted by extending the stochastic differential exchange rate equations to incorporate a jump component is relatively stronger for out-of-the-money contracts than for in-the-money FX calls. Of course, in the case a of negative mean jump amplitude the reversed version of this proposition holds.

The above review of the jump-diffusion model indicates that this valuation model allows a number of pricing errors of the first-generation currency option pricing models to be explained theoretically. In view of these appealing theoretical features of the setup, exchange rate models incorporating a jump component into the stochastic differential equation describing the dynamics of this asset price have often been used in empirical work on foreign currency options (see, e.g., Borenzstein and Dooley 1987; Jorion 1988). Recently, an interesting application of the jump-diffusion model has been suggested by Malz (1996), who uses a binomial version of the jump-diffusion model to estimate the equivalent martingale ex ante probability of a realignment of the pound sterling as implied in over-the-counter option prices during the run-up to the crisis of the European Monetary System (EMS) in September 1992.

Another strand of the literature uses the advances made in the pricing of options on assets with a stochastic volatility to construct mixed stochastic volatility jump-diffusion option pricing models. An elucidating example for this modeling approach is the setup developed by Bakshi et al. (1997). An application of this type of pricing models to FX options can be found in Bates's (1996b) analysis. He utilizes the Heston (1993) technique to construct a mixed jump-diffusion stochastic volatility model for Philadelphia Stock Exchange future options. He then proceeds to estimate the structural parameters of the model implicit in deutsche mark future options over the period 1984–1991. His analysis indicates that smile effects in the volatility strike structure implicit in these future options can best be explained by enriching a stochastic volatility model with a jump process for the underlying futures price. An interesting theoretical extension of the jump model has also recently been suggested by Naik (1993) who prices options under the assumption that the jump component enters into the volatility equation rather than into the asset price equation itself. So far, this model has not been subjected to empirical tests.

2.5   Summary

The preceding sections have been devoted to a survey of the baseline foreign currency option pricing framework and its extensions and refinements which have been introduced into the literature to account for its empirically observed pricing failures. Taking the GK model as a benchmark, the FX option pricing implications of constant elasticity of variance (CEV) models (Section 2.3.1), of stochastic exchange rate volatility frameworks (Section 2.3.2), and of jump-diffusion models (Section 2.4) have been analyzed.

The first-generation FX option valuation model tracing back to Garman and Kohlhagen (1983) is built on the assumption that exchange rate dynamics can be adequately described by an exogenously evolving constant volatility geometric Brownian motion. This assumption implies that exchange rates (returns) are lognormally (normally) distributed. Assuming further that trading takes place in continuous time, that transaction costs can be neglected, and that domestic and foreign risk-free interest rates are constant, the GK model allows analytical expressions for the arbitrage-free premia of European-style foreign currency options to be derived.

An important implication of the GK model is that the arbitrage-free FX option premium does not depend on the preferences of economic agents with respect to exchange rate risk. In the risk-neutral valuation approach developed by Cox and Ross (1976), this observation is exploited to express the current premium of a European-style derivative security as the expected value of its terminal payoff discounted at the risk-free rate of interest. This technique is of practical importance as it provides investors with the theoretical results needed to justify the implementation of Monte Carlo simulation studies to price FX options under nonstandard exchange rate and/or terminal payoff assumptions.

In Section 2.3, the analysis turned to an investigation of currency option valuation models with a variable diffusion term. Three models were selected to represent this class of option pricing setups: the constant elasticity of variance model and the stochastic volatility models of Hull and White (1987a) and of Heston (1993).

A technically appealing feature of the CEV model is that the assumption of a constant volatility parameter is retained. The distinguishing element of the model is that an additional parameter is introduced which captures the elasticity of the instantaneous volatility of exchange rate returns with respect to the level of the exchange rate. The CEV model can be used to reduce the pricing errors of the first-generation FX option valuation. From the viewpoint of economic theory, however, it is rather difficult to motivate the leverage argument employed as a theoretical underpinning of CEV stock option models in the case of currencies (Bates 1996a).

As an example of stochastic volatility option pricing models, the model of Hull and White (1987a) was discussed in Section 2.3.2.1. The model has been employed to show that a stochastic exchange rate volatility instantaneously uncorrelated with the innovation term driving the spot rate process implies that the baseline GK model tends to overprice (underprice) at-the-money (in- and out-of-the-money) options. The implications of correlated exchange rate and volatility innovations on FX option premia were discussed in Section 2.3.2.2 by resorting to a valuation model developed by Heston (1993). The model implies that a positive (negative) correlation between the exchange rate and the volatility process exerts a dampening (increasing) impact on the premia of out-of-the-money contracts and tends to inflate (depress) the prices of in-the-money options. In contrast to the model of Hull and White, the model originated by Heston (1993) can, thus, be employed to explain theoretically asymmetries in the volatility strike structure implicit in foreign currency options.

The jump-diffusion model tracing back to Merton (1976) was utilized to discuss the option pricing implications of discontinuous exchange rate paths in Section 2.4. Enriching the geometric Gauss–Wiener process underlying the GK model with a jump component inflates the variance of the asset price process and causes the exchange rate return distribution to exhibit fat tails. This leptokurtosis of the returns distribution implies that the GK model underprices out-of-the-money and in-the-money options, which, in turn, allows smile effects in the volatility strike structure to be theoretically explained. If the probability of an exchange rate jump in one direction is larger than the probability of a jump in the other direction, the model allows smirks rather than smiles to be generated when plotting volatilities implicit in options against the moneyness of the contracts. As stressed by Dumas et al. (1995a), a theoretical problem which arises when the jump-diffusion model is adopted to pricing FX options is that under the assumption of a diversifiable jump risk the premium of the contract depends on whether the perspective of a domestic or a foreign investor is taken when pricing the contract. While the resulting pricing differences might be small, this shortcoming of the model might nevertheless stimulate researchers in the future to discuss this issue in the context of general equilibrium jump-diffusion option pricing models.

The basic idea common to the various competing modifications of the GK foreign currency option valuation approach reviewed in this chapter is to price derivative contracts by resorting to stochastic asset price processes capable of reproducing the empirically observed leptokurtosis of unconditional exchange rate returns distributions. Though the refinements of the GK model discussed above do indeed contribute to explaining the deviations of actual FX option premia from those predicted by the baseline valuation model, a shortcoming common to all these valuation frameworks is that the exchange rate dynamics suggested as alternatives to the geometric Brownian motion used in the GK model are specified in a completely exogenous and ad hoc manner. For this reason, it is valid to claim that the models surveyed in the preceding sections offer a purely technical rather than an economic explanation of the empirically observed pricing errors associated with the first-generation foreign currency option pricing frameworks. As the stochastic exchange rate processes utilized to price derivative securities in these models are exogenously given, smile and smirk effects in volatility strike structures implicit in foreign currency options are exogenous phenomena. Thus, the extensions of the GK model reviewed above do not really provide an *economic* theory of the smile. Such an economic theory of the volatility strike structure, however, would help option traders, financial institutions, and policymakers alike to identify and to isolate the economic forces behind smiles and smirks. Only if one has an idea of the economic factors determining the overall shape of the volatility strike structure, it is possible to interpret the informational content implicit in smiles and smirks in economic rather than merely in technical terms.

3 Noise Trader Trigger Rates, FX Options, and Smiles

While the preceding chapters and sections have been utilized to survey important technical aspects emphasized in the existing literature on the pricing of foreign currency options, this chapter sheds light on the economics underlying FX option pricing theory. The basic idea is to develop a foreign currency option valuation model which allows the implications of *noise trading* in the spot market for the pricing of FX contingent claims to be highlighted. Following Hung (1997: 781), noise traders can be characterized as "investors whose demand for currencies is influenced by beliefs or sentiments that are not fully consistent with economic fundamentals". In contrast to the modeling strategy adopted in the classical FX option pricing literature outlined in the preceding chapters, the model suggested in this chapter allows smile and smirk effects in the volatility strike structure to be derived endogenously. The material contained in the chapter draws on convincing recent results derived in the literature concerned with the micro-structure of FX markets which impressively demonstrate that the trading behavior of economic agents is an important determinant of the dynamics of exchange rates in general and of the volatility of these asset prices in particular. The model contributes to the growing and substantial literature emphasizing the importance of the trading behavior of economic agents in the spot market for the dynamics of exchange rates and, thus, for the pricing of foreign currency options.

The research outlined in this chapter is motivated by the well-known stylized fact that the volatility of exchange rates can hardly be attributed to fluctuations in macroeconomic fundamentals alone (see, e.g., Rose 1994; Flood and Rose 1995; Jeanne and Rose 1999). Confronted with the failure of classical fundamentals-based structural models of exchange rate determination to explain the erratic movements of real-world floating exchange rates at higher and medium-term frequencies (see Meese and Rogoff 1983; Boughton 1987), recent research in international economics has begun to elaborate on the microstructure of FX markets and on noise trading as a potential source of exchange rate volatility. Because the volatility structure of the underlying economy is a key factor in determining the premia of options on foreign currency, the impact of technical position-taking of traders in the spot market on exchange rate dynamics is also an issue of central importance for the pricing of FX options. I address this question by focusing on the implications of market-sentiment-induced implicit price barriers that separate different trading regimes in spot markets for the dynamic properties of exchange rates and for arbitrage-free premia of the corresponding foreign currency options.

In Section 3.1, a modified version of a continuous-time noise trader model of exchange rate determination originated by Krugman and Miller (1993) and by Krugman (1987) is set up to discuss theoretically how the market entry and exit of technical traders in FX markets at discretely spaced trigger thresholds affects actual and expected exchange rate fluctuations. To set up such a model, I exploit the fact that a particularly simple, powerful, and generally acknowledged technique to allow for heterogeneous trader groups in FX markets is to subdivide market participants into fundamentalists and chartists. Rather than being continuously present in the spot market, these two types of traders are assumed to enter (to exit) the market whenever the exchange rate reaches certain critical trigger thresholds. The fundamentalists are assumed to expect a reversion of the exchange rate towards a long-run target value. Chartists, in contrast, are assumed to rely on a type of extrapolative chart analysis. They believe that a current deviation of the exchange rate from an expected long-run level will become even larger in the next instant of time. If either a nonnegligible number of spot market participants adheres to such nonfundamental trading rules or the technically motivated order flow reacts sufficiently sensitively to technical traders expectations regarding subsequent exchange rate changes, a large amount of technically motivated selling or buying orders reaches the market whenever the exchange rate crosses certain implicit trigger levels and technical traders are induced either to enter or to exit the market for domestic assets. Rational traders anticipate the impact of this type of nonfundamental FX trading on the exchange rate path and this, in turn, affects both the volatility of the current spot rate and the international interest rate differential even before the exchange rate hits an implicit trigger point resulting from the specific timing of orders by technical traders.

Utilizing this model of analysis, I examine how the effect of technical trading in the spot market on the dynamics of the exchange rate translates into the arbitrage-free prices of foreign currency options. Results obtained by implementing a Monte Carlo simulation approach indicate that implicit exchange rate thresholds due to the shifts in the spot market structure caused by the market entry or exit of technical traders can give rise to the type of smile and smirk effects in the volatility strike structure often observed in real-world FX options markets. Thus, the model to be developed in Section 3.1 offers an economically attractive explanation for the pricing errors resulting when the baseline FX option valuation models are implemented to price real-world foreign currency options.

The second part of the chapter is devoted to a closer examination of one of the empirically testable implications of the theoretical model. The model predicts that volatilities implicit in FX options premia reflect that the instantaneous variability of exchange rates increases (decreases) as the distance of the exchange rate to destabilizing (stabilizing) implicit threshold spot rates at which a non-negligible number of technical traders enter (exit) the market declines. Starting from this central insight of the theoretical study, two alternative volatility-based quantitative tests are utilized to test for implicit price barriers and implicit adjacent trading regimes in actual foreign exchange markets. The volatility-based tests render it possible to determine whether implicit trading-induced price barriers are present in spot markets and also render it possible to detect the perceived sign of the impact of nonfundamental FX trading on the anticipated volatility of exchange rates in actual foreign currency markets. Thus, the empirical tests employed in the empirical part of this chapter render it possible to directly address the questions whether market-sentiment-induced implicit trading barriers separating different trading regimes exist and whether such thresholds are perceived to stabilize or to destabilize exchange rates. Moreover, as the theoretical analysis presented in Section 3.1 underscores that noise traders' implicit trigger rates can exert a significant impact on foreign currency option premia and can even account for smiles and smirks in the volatility strike structure, the empirical tests provide further insights into the issue of whether or not taking care of the microstructure of the spot market can help firms and financial institutions to hedge currency risks more efficiently.

The first empirical research strategy adopted to determine implicit trading triggers in real-world FX markets is discussed in Section 3.2. In this section, ideas presented in Donaldson and Kim (1993) and De Grauwe and Decupere (1992) are drawn upon and a modified version of a volatility-based empirical methodology recently suggested by Hogan et al. (1997) and Cyree et al. (1999) is used to test for the presence of an implicit grid of price barriers in actual foreign exchange markets. The testing procedure is designed to uncover generally not immediately observable implicit trigger exchange rates at which a nonnegligible number of traders are perceived either to buy or to sell foreign currency. The testing procedure uses a time-series model to trace out a time-varying conditional exchange rate volatility and then examines the behavior of exchange rate volatility near potential trading-induced implicit price barriers. One drawback of this test for implicit trigger rates in FX markets is that it is only capable of detecting trading thresholds on a rather rigid grid of prespecified price barriers assumed to hold special significance for market participants. Furthermore, the test does not take into account the current strength or weakness of a currency relative to longer-term trends characterizing the spot rate path. This latter aspect, however, might be important for noise traders trying to extract buy or sell signals by comparing the current spot rate with medium-term swings in the relative value of a currency.

In Section 3.3, I therefore extend the empirical test and use an alternative volatility-based testing technique for implicit trigger rates which separate different trading regimes in spot markets for foreign currency. The test uses the prediction of the theoretical model suggested in the theoretical part of this chapter that the instantaneous volatility of the spot rate is positively (inversely) related to the distance of the current spot rate from the market entry or exit triggers of destabilizing (stabilizing) trend chasers (fundamentalists). To operationalize this notion, I first utilize the moving average of the exchange rate as a benchmark to assess the position of the currently prevailing spot rate relative to a longer-term target value. I then exploit the idea that the probability that a substantial number of trend-based mechanical orders are executed should increase as the distance of the current spot rate from the moving average representation of the exchange rate increases. Using this insight, I measure the inverse of the distance of the prevailing spot rate from noise traders' market entry or exit thresholds by using the absolute deviation of the current FX rate from its moving average representation. This test for implicit trading regimes in FX markets then examines whether the level of the instantaneous volatility of the spot rate increases whenever this figure exceeds certain critical threshold levels. Alternative time-series models allowing a time-varying conditional exchange rate volatility and parametric as well as nonparametric test statistics are used to implement the new volatility-based test for adjacent implicit trading regimes in actual foreign currency markets.

Motivated by the results of the empirical analysis and the fact that the model introduced in Section 3.2 does not allow option premia to be expressed in terms of elementary mathematical functions, I also discuss the impact of noise trading on the prices of contingent claims within the context of a watered-down FX option valuation model. Using a noise trader model of exchange rate determination introduced into the literature by Frankel (1996), I use a valuation approach in the tradition of the frameworks originated by Heston (1993), Scott (1997), and Bakshi and Chen (1997) to study the influence of noise trading on the prices of options on foreign currency. These latter frameworks allow closed-form expressions for FX option premia to be derived.

The main ideas formulated in this chapter and the results of the theoretical and empirical analyses conducted here are summarized in Section 3.5. This section is also utilized to offer suggestions for future research and to shed some light on the implications of the analyses with respect to the interpretation of the informational content of volatility quotes implicit in foreign currency options by authorities conducting monetary and exchange rate policy.

3.1   Implicit Price Barriers, Exchange Rate Dynamics, and Smiles

The stochastic continuous-time economies laid out in Chapter 2 of this study can be utilized to compute a wide array of possible shapes for the volatility strike structure and the term structure of implied volatilities. The general idea underlying the various approaches discussed is to calculate theoretical option premia which allow the empirically observed cross-sectional pricing biases of the baseline GK foreign currency option valuation model to be eliminated. In general, this is achieved by composing the stochastic environment so that the dynamics of the spot rate match important statistical properties of real-world foreign exchange rate returns. With the exception of general equilibrium option pricing models (Bick 1987; Bakshi and Chen 1997; Nielson and Saá-Requejo 1993), however, the stochastic differential equations suggested for generating spot rate dynamics which give rise, for example, to a U-shaped volatility strike structure are most often specified in a rather ad hoc manner. The analysis contained in this chapter departs from this modeling strategy. A foreign currency option valuation model featuring nonfundamental FX trading is constructed which renders it possible to interpret the pricing errors produced by the first-generation foreign currency option valuation model in an economically meaningful way.

In a first step, a stylized noise trader model of exchange rate determination advanced by Krugman and Miller (1993) is modified to shed light on the consequences of implicit trading thresholds in FX markets for the valuation of foreign currency options. In the model of Krugman and Miller discretely spaced implicit trading thresholds show up in the exchange rate path when a nonnegligible group of FX market participants tends to rearrange the share of imperfectly substitutable domestic and foreign assets in their portfolios infrequently at certain prespecified spot rate levels.[41] The modeling strategy adopted in this section

---

[41]   The model of Krugman and Miller (1993) stands in the tradition of models developed by Grossman (1988), Brennan and Schwartz (1989), and Gennotte and Leland (1990).

departs from this approach in that heterogeneous trader groups are introduced into FX markets by subdividing market participants into continuously trading spot market traders with model-consistent expectations and technical traders who adhere either to a fundamentalist or to a chartist investment philosophy which is derived from extrapolating trends. Technical traders enter (exit) the market for domestic assets whenever the spot rate reaches certain critical trading triggers. Fundamentalists are assumed to trade on a reversion of a weak (strong) currency towards a medium-term or long-run value. Chartists, on the contrary, are assumed to perceive that a current depreciation or appreciation of the domestic currency will even gain momentum during the next instant of time. From an empirical point of view, an advantage of such a modeling approach is that the implications of this type of technical trading for exchange rate volatility are more in line with the empirical results documented in the second part of this chapter than those of the original Krugman and Miller (1993) model.

A similar modeling approach has been utilized by Frankel and Froot (1988, 1990) to demonstrate that the presence of chartists can force the exchange rate to deviate substantially and for a long time from its intrinsic value. De Grauwe et al. (1993) introduce fundamentalists and chartists into otherwise standard macroeconomic models of exchange rate determination to show how the interaction of such FX trader groups can result in very complex and even chaotic exchange rate dynamics. Similar models can be found in De Grauwe and Dewachter (1992), Geiger (1996), Frenkel (1997), and Kempa and Nelles (1994). The latter also modify the model developed by Krugman and Miller (1993) to examine the impact of chartism on exchange rate dynamics in exchange rate target zones. However, as they model technical trading by means of a continuous, fundamentals-based trend-chasing trading rule, their model only generates linear free-float exchange rate paths. Thus, it does not serve to examine the type of nonlinearities arising in the model discussed below in which the entire real line forms the domain of the spot rate process and the nonlinear shape of the exchange rate function is caused by the state-contingent nature of trend-based technical spot trading.

The findings reported in the above-mentioned studies underline that the trading behavior and the interaction of fundamentalists and chartists in FX markets can help to theoretically explain the high level of exchange rate volatility observed in actual foreign exchange markets. The capability of the noise trader approach to the modeling of financial markets to generate even time-varying

---

The main objective behind these theoretical models is to shed light on the consequences of program trading and portfolio insurance for the returns and the volatility of asset prices.

variances of asset price returns and volatility clusters in financial markets documented in Lux (1997), Lux and Marchesi (2000), and Youssefmir and Huberman (1997) indicates that this line of research might be particularly relevant to the discussion of the empirical regularities observed in the quantitative option pricing literature. This impression is further corroborated by the empirical evidence reported in Allen and Taylor (1990, 1992), Menkhoff (1997), and Frankel and Froot (1990). The results documented in these contributions to the empirical noise trading literature suggest that chartism and trend-chasing behavior might be important driving forces behind the price formation process in real-world FX markets.

The spot rate process utilized in the option pricing model to be developed below is derived by setting up a stochastic version of the continuous-time flex-price monetary model of exchange rate determination with heterogeneous trader groups. As in the models originated by Krugman and Miller (1993) and Krugman (1987), one implication of the model is that market participants' rational expectations regarding the timing of the market entry (exit) and the trading behavior of technical traders alter the dynamics of the spot rate even before the exchange rate reaches a level which triggers technical traders to enter or to exit the market. Assuming that the members of the chartist (fundamentalist) trader group dominate at the entry and exit thresholds and that chartists sell domestic interest-bearing securities when the domestic currency price of foreign currency rises (falls) above (below) a certain critical level, it can be shown that the presence of technical traders makes exchange rates excessively volatile as compared to economic fundamentals (see also, e.g., Balduzzi et al. (1997) and Balduzzi et al. (1995)). The functional form of the nonlinear exchange rate function solving the model implies that the endogenously determined stochastic volatility of the spot rate process raises as the exchange rate reaches such a destabilizing trading-induced implicit price barrier.

With respect to the trading pattern in actual foreign exchange markets, De Grauwe and Decupere (1992) find empirical evidence in favor of such implicit price barriers in the US dollar/yen but not in the US dollar/deutsche mark spot rate. Skeptical notes regarding the existence of implicit price barriers in stock market data can be found in Ceuster et al. (1998) and in Ley and Varian (1994). Other empirical studies, including Donaldson (1990), Donaldson and Kim (1993), Koedjik and Stork (1994), and Cyree et al. (1999), however, document evidence supporting the hypothesis of market sentiment-induced psychological price barriers in stock market data. The results reported in these studies indicate that the option valuation model developed below might not merely be a fruitful instrument to explain smile and smirk effects implicit in FX options but might also contribute to a better understanding of the shapes of volatility strike structures implicit in options on stocks and stock indices.

In the second step in the theoretical analysis, the implications of rational investors' anticipation of technical traders market entry (exit) for the endogenously computed stochastic exchange rate volatility are used to construct a foreign currency option valuation model. It is argued that the FX option valuation framework laid out below can be utilized to generate the smile and smirk effects most often characterizing real-world implied volatility strike structures. However, rather than pointing to purely technical arguments, the FX option valuation framework provides a rich setting which renders it possible to interpret a smiling volatility strike structure economically. Results obtained by simulating the model numerically indicate that important factors influencing the specific shape of the *endogenously* derived volatility smiles and smirks implicit in FX option premia are the width of the interval of inaction of technical traders, the proportion of market participants adhering to a nonfundamental asset allocation rule, and the aggressiveness with which the market participants following technical trading strategies implement their investment plans. Moreover, the noise trader FX option valuation model predicts that the convexity of the volatility smile depends upon the distance between the exchange rate levels which induces technical traders to enter (to exit) the market for domestic assets. The model can also be employed to generate volatility strike structures which resemble a skewed smirk rather than a symmetric smile. Such a smirk arises if, for example, chartists tend to bet more aggressively against a weak than in favor of a strong domestic currency. The central insight motivating these findings is that a variation of one or more of the variables mentioned alters the overall shape of the nonlinear exchange rate function, which, in turn, is a main factor in determining the volatility of the stochastic spot rate process utilized to price foreign exchange contingent claims.

Contrasting the assumptions made to compose the stochastic volatility models discussed in the second chapter of this study, an important aspect of the FX option pricing framework is that the volatility of the spot rate and the differential between domestic and foreign interest rates are derived endogenously. Hence, rather than exogenously introducing a separate stochastic differential equation for the volatility of the exchange rate, the formation of exchange rate expectations and the concomitant trading behavior of spot market participants are utilized to figure out the dynamics of the exchange rate and of its volatility. This important feature implies that the model can be compared to recent contributions to the options pricing literature which stress the role of feedback effects from hedging (actually existing or synthesized) derivatives for the dynamics of the price of the underlying financial security. Examples of this area of the noise trader literature can be found in Frey and Stremme (1997), in Sircar and Papanicolaou (1998), and in Platen and Schweizer (1998). Setting up micro-economic equilibrium models (see also Föllmer and Schweizer 1993), all authors analyze the impact of technical demand induced by option traders implementing dynamic delta hedging strategies for the evolution of the underlying financial security. Program traders are assumed to rely on a fictitious reference model given by the Black and Scholes (1973) model for European options to figure out the hedge ratios required to implement this dynamic trading strategy. The consequences of this trading behavior for the stochastic volatility of the underlying asset price are derived endogenously upon invoking a market clearing condition. It is shown that the endogenously determined volatility of the price of the underlying security is inflated for far-from-the-money options due to the fact that the gamma of the fictitious reference model shows up in the denominator of the endogenous diffusion term of the stochastic differential equation driving the asset price. Platen and Schweizer (1998) show that this class of models can be employed to theoretically generate smile and smirk effects in the volatility strike structure. The volatility smile arises due to the fact that the feedback effects from option hedging amplify asset price volatility as the underlying moves away from its at-the-money level. Skewness in the smile arises if out-of-the-money options are more heavily traded than in-the-money options, and vice versa.

The model contained in this section differs from the model suggested by Platen and Schweizer (1998) in (at least) two important respects:

(1) Exchange rate dynamics in my noise trader options pricing model are influenced by the presence of discretely spaced implicit price barriers due to rational traders' anticipation of the market entry or exit of technical traders rather than by feedback effects from the hedging of (actual or synthesized) derivatives. Furthermore, the model draws attention to other factors which might be important in influencing the shape of real-world volatility strike structures. The model suggested by Platen and Schweizer (1998) relies on the quantitative importance of feedback effects from options hedging and on the relative trading volume of options with a different moneyness. While their model also features reference traders, as, e.g., modeled by Föllmer and Schweizer (1993), the structure of the modeled economy implies that only feedback effects from options hedging account for the characteristic convexity of the volatility smile. The model outlined in this section, in contrast, emphasizes the role of the width of the band of inaction of technical traders, the functional form of the technical trading strategy dominating in FX markets, and the parameters capturing the sensitivity of the technical asset demand or supply with respect to the deviation of the

current spot rate from the medium-term equilibrium value estimated by technical traders.

(2) A critical assumption underlying the model of Platen and Schweizer (1998) is that option writers resort to a fictitious reference model formed by the Black and Scholes (1973) model to compute hedge ratios needed to implement dynamic portfolio insurance strategies. This option pricing formula is derived by assuming that the underlying asset price is driven by an exogenously given geometric Brownian motion. The impact of feedback effects from options hedging, however, implies that this assumption does not hold for the endogenously derived asset price process in the model of Platen and Schweizer (1998). Therefore, the decision to resort to the baseline option valuation function to model program traders' hedging behavior is somewhat arbitrary.[42] As the noise trader option pricing model outlined in this section does not feature feedback effects from options hedging, I do not need to invoke this critical assumption to derive smile and smirk effects in the volatility strike structure.

The theoretical model contained in this section is also related to a recent study conducted by Grossman and Zhou (1996). Like Platen and Schweizer (1998), these authors construct a closed-economy continuous-time general equilibrium pricing model with utility maximizing agents which allows the implications of the interaction of portfolio insurers and noninsurers for the volatility of asset prices to be traced out. Portfolio insurers implement a convex dynamic risk control technique which prevents their terminal wealth from falling below a certain fraction of the amount initially invested. These authors show that the impact of this type of trading pattern on the variability of the underlying financial security can give rise to asymmetric smirk effects in the volatility strike structure implied in the corresponding options contracts.

The theoretical model contained in this chapter differs from the model used by Grossman and Zhou (1996) in several respects. *Firstly*, I do not examine the implications of the type of nonlinear program trading rules for the shape of the volatility strike structure examined by Grossman and Zhou (1996). Instead, I

---

[42] As discussed in Platen and Schweizer (1998), the ideal solution to account for feedback from options hedging would be to follow a three-step procedure: (i) First employ the market-clearing exchange rate process to derive an option pricing model for a given hedging function. (ii) Proceed to use this new option valuation model to neatly modify market participants hedging plans. (iii) Search for a kind of rational expectations equilibrium by trying to find the point of convergence (provided it exists) of this algorithm. Such a procedure, of course, gives rise to complex theoretical problems. For this reason, Platen and Schweizer (1998) prefer to invoke the simplifying assumption that program traders resort to the baseline option valuation framework when implementing dynamic trading strategies.

analyze how the anticipation of the market entry (exit) of fundamentalists and chartists can give rise to smile and smirk effects when volatilities implicit in foreign currency options are plotted as a function of the moneyness of the contracts. Resorting to this alternative modeling strategy renders it possible to pay attention to other factors which might be important in influencing the shape of the volatility strike structure characterizing real-world FX option markets. My assumption regarding the state-contingent trading behavior of technical investors acting in the spot market for foreign currency further implies that in the present model, chartists synthesize an implicit long call when the domestic currency is relatively weak and a long put when the domestic currency is relatively strong. In the model of Grossman and Zhou (1996), in contrast, portfolio insurers always try to replicate the payoff of a long put option. *Secondly*, Grossman and Zhou (1996) are concerned with a one-sided portfolio insurance strategy. Consequently, their asset pricing model can be employed to theoretically simulate asymmetric volatility smirks implicit in options prices. While analyzing a one-sided investment strategy is a natural point of departure for constructing a portfolio insurance framework for stock markets, the model discussed below features a different form of noisy spot trading which also allows symmetric volatility smiles to be interpreted in an economically meaningful way. *Thirdly*, in the model of Grossman and Zhou (1996) technical traders are permanently present in the spot market and the proportion of traders belonging to each of the trader groups is time-invariant. In the model suggested below, fundamentalists and chartists are assumed only to be involved in the trading of foreign currency when the spot rate settles in certain intervals of the domain of the exchange rate process. This has the important implication that in the model discussed below the *anticipation* of the market entry or exit of noise traders accounts for the existence of the volatility smile implicit in FX option contracts, whereas in the contributions pioneered by Grossman and Zhou (1996) or Platen and Schweizer (1998) the *actual* trading behavior of noise traders is employed to explain the volatility strike structure.

Drawing on a modified version of the Krugman and Miller (1993) and Krugman (1987) models of exchange rate determination, my noise trader FX option pricing model is also related to the model suggested by Dumas et al. (1993, 1995b). These authors use a homogenous agents monetary model of exchange rate determination to develop valuation models for contingent claims under regulated asset price processes. My model differs from the models developed in these contributions in several respects. I depart from the representative agents assumption and price FX options in a heterogeneous agents economy featuring continuously trading rational investors and noise traders who implement state-contingent technical investment strategies. Even more important from a technical point of view, fundamentals follow an unregulated stochastic process in the model discussed below, and, thus, the exchange rate process is not restricted to fluctuating within a certain exogenously determined fluctuation interval. This has the important implication that the fundamental contingent claims valuation equation has to be solved subject to a different set of boundary conditions. Changing the boundary conditions, of course, implies that a different type of option pricing function can be extracted from the theoretical model. As will be demonstrated in Section 3.1.3, an important implication of this facet of the following model is that it allows convex volatility strike structures to be endogenously generated. This is in contrast to the models of Dumas et al. (1993, 1995b), which can only be used to compute a certain, empirically far less relevant type of hump-shaped inverted volatility smile.

The analysis is organized as follows. The underlying model of exchange rate determination and the implications of implicit trading-induced price barriers for the dynamics of the spot rate and its volatility are discussed in Section 3.1.1. Section 3.1.2 is devoted to the presentation of the foreign currency option valuation model. As it is not possible to derive closed-form analytical expressions for FX option premia, the model is solved numerically by resorting to Monte Carlo simulation techniques. These techniques have often been used in the options pricing literature. Section 3.1.2 therefore also provides a brief description of the principles on which this technique for simulating option premia rests. In Section 3.1.3, the results of the performed numerical simulations are discussed and the implications of the theoretical model for the shape of the volatility strike structure are elucidated.

3.1.1   Implicit Price Barriers and Exchange Rate Dynamics

The flex-price monetary model formulated in continuous time, t, stipulates that the logarithm of the exchange rate, $e(t)$, defined as domestic currency units expressed in terms of a foreign currency unit is equal to the sum of a set of general economic fundamentals, $f(t)$, and the differential between the domestic, r, and the foreign, r^*, risk-free interest rates premultiplied by the interest-elasticity of money demand, υ :

(3.1) $e = f + \upsilon(r - r^*)$.

Economic fundamentals are assumed to evolve according to a driftless stochastic differential equation:

(3.2) $\mathrm{d}f = \sigma \,\mathrm{d}W,$

with σ denoting a constant diffusion coefficient and $\mathrm{d}W$ symbolizing the differential of a standard Gauss–Wiener process with expected value zero and unit variance.

The differential in international rates of interest is assumed to be determined by the logarithmic version of the condition of uncovered interest rate parity. This no-arbitrage condition stipulates that any differential between domestic and foreign interest-bearing assets must be offset by corresponding aggregate exchange rate expectations. To reach a formal expression for these aggregate exchange rate expectations, it is assumed that the foreign exchange market is populated by two groups of price-taking agents. The first group of price-taking agents consists of a continuum of continuously speculating agents with rational expectations. The second trader group is formed by a nonnegligible number of technical traders engaged in nonfundamental FX trading. Taking into account the results of the empirical studies mentioned in the introductory section, technical traders are assumed to follow either an extrapolative (chartist) or a contrarian (fundamentalist) investment strategy. To focus attention on the basic channel through which state-contingent noise trading affects the shape of the volatility strike structure, it is further assumed that fundamentalists and chartists do not engage in spot FX trading simultaneously.

Instead of rebalancing the composition of their asset holdings continuously, the members of the technical trader group enter and exit the foreign exchange market only if the spot rate reaches one of the boundaries of a prespecified band of inaction. The threshold exchange rates triggering the market entry and exit of technical traders are denoted by $(\underline{e}, \overline{e})$ with $\underline{e} < \overline{e}$. Chartists are assumed to start (to stop) betting against the domestic currency whenever the exchange rate reaches the trigger point $\overline{e}$ $(\underline{e})$ from below (above), and vice versa for fundamentalists. Thus, technical traders tend to engage in spot trading whenever the domestic currency has already either depreciated or appreciated by a sufficient amount and a psychological trading barrier has been reached (see also Siebert 1994: 343). One way to motivate this assumption economically is to resort to a line of argumentation suggested by Frenkel (1997: 16) and to presume that technical traders do not observe the actual stochastic process driving economic fundamentals.[43] Acting in such an environment, these traders extract signals to participate or to refrain from FX trading only by observing the exchange rate

---

[43]   Frenkel (1997: 16) considers only the case of a state-dependent contrarian investment rule. In this section, Frenkel's line of argumentation is adopted to model the investment behavior of both fundamentalists and trend-chasers.

path itself. Under this interpretation, the assumption regarding the specific timing of technical traders investment decisions introduced above expresses that these relatively uninformed agents will only decide to exercise their "option to trade" by stepping into the market if the entry signals are sufficiently strong and convincing.

Before turning to the formal analysis, it should once again be underscored that it is not assumed that technical investors enter or exit the spot market only once. This assumption implies that all trigger points continue to exist even when the exchange rate has already hit one of the trigger thresholds, $(\underline{e}, \overline{e})$, and technical traders have been induced either to enter or to exit the spot market for foreign currency.

Equipped with these assumptions, I am now in a position to express the aggregate exchange rate expectations required to formally set up the condition of uncovered interest rate parity as a state dependent weighted average of the spot rate expectations of rational traders and of technical investors. Let the conditional expectations operator that applies under the objective probability measure g be given by $\mathbb{E}_t^g$. The expected rate of depreciation of the domestic currency over the infinitesimally small interval of time dt computed by continuously trading rational agents can then be formalized as $\mathbb{E}_t^g(de)$. Assume further that technical investors' trading elasticity with respect to the deviation of the actual exchange rate from an exogenously specified target value, e_0, is symbolized by the time-invariant parameter ϕ. Under measure g the expected aggregate rate of change of the spot rate, $\tilde{\mathbb{E}}_t^g(de)$, can then be expressed as

$$(3.3) \quad \tilde{\mathbb{E}}_t^g(de)/dt = \Im^1 \mathbb{E}_t^g(de)/dt + \Im^2 \phi(e - e_0),$$

where the indicator functions $\Im^j$, $j = 1,2$ partition the domain of the exchange rate process into three nonoverlapping trading regimes.[44] These trading regimes summarize whether or not technical investors are involved in the trading process taking place in the spot market. Denote the market share of rational investors who participate continuously in FX spot trading by α. The indicator functions, $\Im^j$, are then given by

---

[44] This type of weighting procedure is commonly used in the noise trader literature to aggregate the expectations of heterogeneous groups of FX market traders. Discrete-time noise trader models of exchange rate determination using this aggregation technique can be found in De Grauwe et al. (1993), Frenkel (1997), and Pierdzioch and Stadtmann (2000). For a continuous-time model of spot rate dynamics using similar weighting schemes, see, e.g., Kempa and Nelles (1994) and Frankel and Froot (1990).

(3.4) $\mathfrak{I}^1 = \begin{cases} \alpha \text{ if } \underline{e} \leq e(t) \leq \overline{e} \\ 1 \text{ otherwise} \end{cases}$ with $0 < \alpha < 1,$

(3.5) $\mathfrak{I}^2 = \begin{cases} 1-\alpha \text{ if } e(t) < \underline{e} \text{ or } e(t) > \overline{e} \text{ and chartists are in the market} \\ -(1-\alpha) \text{ if } e(t) < \underline{e} \text{ or } e(t) > \overline{e} \text{ and fundamentalists are in the market} \\ 0 \text{ otherwise.} \end{cases}$

To solve the model, define a continuous, twice differentiable function, $e(f)$, to express the logarithm of the exchange rate as a deterministic function of economic fundamentals. Focusing first on the case $\underline{e} \leq e(t) \leq \overline{e}$ and applying the rules of stochastic calculus, the following inhomogenous second-order ordinary differential equation describing the dynamics of the exchange rate obtains:

(3.6) $\hat{e} = f + \upsilon\sigma^2 \hat{e}_{ff},$

where $\hat{e}(t)$ denotes the spot rate function that applies in technical traders no-trade range $\underline{e} \leq e(t) \leq \overline{e}$. Resorting to the method of undetermined coefficients, the general solution to equation (3.6) can be pinned down as

(3.7) $\hat{e} = f + A_1 \exp(\lambda_1 f) + A_2 \exp(\lambda_2 f)$ with $\lambda_{1,2} = \pm\sqrt{\dfrac{2}{\upsilon\sigma^2}},$

where A_1 and A_2 are constants of integration which can be determined by imposing appropriate boundary conditions and where $\lambda_1 < 0 < \lambda_2$ are the positive and negative roots of the characteristic equation (3.6).

While equation (3.7) already constitutes the complete solution of the model for $\underline{e} \leq e(t) \leq \overline{e}$, it remains to trace out the exchange rate functions that apply in the noise trader regimes $e(t) < \underline{e}$ and $e(t) > \overline{e}$. Following the same steps as outlined above, the respective spot rate functions can be identified as

(3.8) $e = \dfrac{\tilde{f}}{1 - \mathfrak{I}^2\upsilon\phi} + \dfrac{\alpha\upsilon\sigma^2}{2(1 - \mathfrak{I}^2\upsilon\phi)} e_{ff},$ where $\tilde{f} \equiv f + \mathfrak{I}^2\upsilon\phi e_0,$

and where the implicit assumption is that the parameters of the model satisfy the strict inequality $1 > \mathfrak{I}^2\upsilon\phi$. The functional form of the solution to the above equation depends on the realizations of the indicator functions, $\mathfrak{I}^j$, and, thus, on the position of the exchange rate relative to the trading thresholds $\overline{e}$ and $\underline{e}$. Denoting the exchange rate function that applies in the case of $e(t) > \overline{e}$ by $\breve{e}(t)$, equation (3.8) can be solved to obtain:

(3.9) $\breve{e} = \dfrac{\tilde{f}}{1 - \Im^2 \upsilon \phi} + B_1 \exp(\lambda_3 f) + B_2 \exp(\lambda_4 f)$

with $\lambda_{3,4} = \pm \sqrt{\dfrac{2(1 - \Im^2 \upsilon \phi)}{\alpha \upsilon \sigma^2}}$.

Similarly, the exchange rate function $\hat{e}(t)$ that characterizes the spot rate path in the complementary case of $e(t) < \underline{e}$ is given by

(3.10) $\hat{e} = \dfrac{\tilde{f}}{1 - \Im^2 \upsilon \phi} + D_1 \exp(\lambda_3 f) + D_2 \exp(\lambda_4 f)$.

As in equation (3.7), the sets $\{B_1, B_2\}$ and $\{D_1, D_2\}$ contain constants of integration and $\lambda_3 < 0 < \lambda_4$ denote the roots of the respective characteristic polynomials of equations (3.9) and (3.10).

It remains to specify an appropriate set of boundary conditions which render it possible to determine the functional form of the constants of integration and, thus, to recover a unique solution to the above noise trader model of exchange rate determination.

To formalize a suitable set of boundary conditions, the first step is to invoke transversality conditions stipulating that the exchange rate converges to its intrinsic value once the spot rate has settled sufficiently far outside the interval $(\underline{e}, \overline{e})$ and the probability that technical traders will exit the FX market during the next instant of time becomes negligibly small. Upon imposing these side conditions and utilizing the definition of the noise trader augmented fundamentals $\tilde{f}$, it follows that the strategy-dependent exchange rate functions for $e(t) < \underline{e}$ and $e(t) > \overline{e}$ must satisfy

(3.11) $\lim\limits_{f \to \infty} \breve{e} = \left(f + \Im^2 \upsilon \phi e_0 \right)\left(1 - \Im^2 \upsilon \phi \right)^{-1}$, $\lim\limits_{f \to -\infty} \hat{e} = \left(f + \Im^j \upsilon \phi e_0 \right)\left(1 - \Im^2 \upsilon \phi \right)^{-1}$.

Given the notational conventions regarding the characteristic roots of the exchange rate functions $\breve{e}(f)$ and $\hat{e}(f)$, it follows immediately that the transversality conditions provided in equation (3.11) require $B_2 = 0$ and $D_1 = 0$.

Two additional boundary conditions obtain by recognizing that continuously trading rational investors will anticipate the impact of technical traders' market entry and exit on the path of the spot rate. Rational investors' awareness of the behavior of technical investors rules out the occurrence of discrete step-jumps in the exchange rate at the boundaries of the implicit range of inaction of non-fundamentally orientated market participants. To see this, suppose that the spot rate reaches the market entry trigger $\overline{e}$ from below. In this case, investors with rational expectations will anticipate that, during the next infinitesimal instant of time, movements in fundamentals will either induce a small step in the exchange along the continuous spot rate function in the direction of the central parity of its implicit fluctuation band $(\underline{e},\overline{e})$ or a discrete nonnegligible shift of the spot rate due to the change in the market structure caused by nonfundamental FX traders' market entry. Clearly, the resulting asymmetric magnitude of the potential infinite rate of trading profits, as opposed to the limited size of appreciation losses, would stimulate investors to go short in domestic assets. The additional supply of domestic assets would drive up the exchange rate until no further "bets" with limited downside risk are traded in FX markets and the exchange rate function no longer exhibits a discrete jump at the edges of the interval $(\underline{e},\overline{e})$. Taking this line of argumentation into account, it is possible to invoke the following set of boundary conditions (Krugman and Miller 1993):

$$(3.12)\quad \hat{e}(\overline{f}) = \breve{e}(\overline{f}), \qquad \hat{e}(\underline{f}) = \breve{e}(\underline{f}),$$

where $\overline{f}$ and $\underline{f}$ are the realizations of economic fundamentals at which the spot rate reaches the trading-induced price triggers $\overline{e}$ and $\underline{e}$.

The set of boundary conditions formalized in equations (3.11) and (3.12) allows four out of six unknown constants of integration to be determined. To deduce the functional form of the remaining two boundary conditions, assume once again that the spot rate has just reached the entry threshold $\overline{e}$ from below. In such a situation, rational investors will realize that during the next infinitesimal period of time, a shock that hits economic fundamentals will push the exchange rate either back into technical traders' range of inaction, $(\underline{e},\overline{e})$, or into the region where noise traders participate in spot trading. From the set of boundary conditions provided in equation (3.9), rational investors already know that the shift in the market structure implied by a shock to fundamentals will not result in a discrete step-jump in the exchange rate. If, however, the slope of the exchange rate function governing the dynamics of the spot rate in the noise trader regime is greater (smaller) than the slope of the exchange rate function within technical traders' band of inaction, rational investors can still expect to generate positive excess profits by taking short (long) positions in domestic-currency-denominated assets. To clarify the economic intuition behind this argument, assume that economic fundamentals have settled in the vicinity of $\overline{f}$ and rational investors observe that $\breve{e}_f(\overline{f}) > \hat{e}_f(\overline{f})$. Because of Jensen's inequality, this apparent "excess" convexity of the exchange rate function would imply that the potential profits accumulated in the case the domestic currency should depreciate would dominate the losses caused by an appreciation of a comparable size. In such a situation, rational investors would begin to trade against the domestic currency and the slope of the spot rate function in the region $(\underline{e}, \bar{e})$ would increase until the expected profits from taking long and short positions in domestic-currency-denominated assets would be equal to each other. It is, thus, possible to close the model by introducing the following set of sufficient conditions for the absence of arbitrage opportunities in the foreign exchange market:[45]

$$(3.13) \quad \hat{e}_f(\bar{f}) = \breve{e}_f(\bar{f}), \qquad \hat{e}_f(\underline{f}) = \bar{e}_f(\underline{f}).$$

The transversality conditions and the no-jump and smooth-transition boundary conditions can now be utilized to express the six unknown constants of integration in terms of elementary mathematical functions. From the invoked boundary conditions, it follows that these functions depend upon the levels of economic fundamentals at which the exchange rate passes the trading-induced implicit trigger prices $\bar{e}$ and $\underline{e}$. Resorting to the definitions $\bar{e} = e(\bar{f})$ and $\underline{e} = e(\underline{f})$, either two of the three functions $\hat{e}(t)$, $\breve{e}(t)$, and $\bar{e}(t)$ can be numerically inverted (Newton's method typically took only a few iterations to converge) to compute an explicit numerical value for the respective critical realizations $\bar{f}$ and $\underline{f}$ of fundamentals. Upon substituting the resulting figures into the expressions obtained for the constants of integration, a unique particular function describing the evolution of the exchange rate across the set of three different trading regimes considered in the present analysis obtains:

---

[45] A similar set of boundary conditions is commonly used in the literature with regard to irreversible investment decisions under uncertainty to merge valuation functions applying in no-investment and in investment regimes. See, e.g., Dixit and Pindyck (1994). Also note that these boundary conditions do not force the slope of the exchange rate function to tend to infinity (zero) at the respective market entry and exit thresholds of chartists (fundamentalists). This property of the model guarantees that the equivalent martingale measure used to price the contingent claims below always exists. To illustrate the argument, assume that fundamentalists enter (exit) the FX market at an arbitrarily given price threshold. As this price threshold does not constitute a reflecting barrier, the spot rate function does not attain a local maximum at this trading trigger. It immediately follows that the sufficient condition for a local maximum will be violated at the market entry threshold of fundamentalists. The only remaining possibility would be to conclude that the spot rate function reaches a saddle at the implicit trading-induced price barrier. For this reason, the second derivative of the exchange rate with respect to fundamentals evaluated at the implicit trading trigger would be zero, too. However, for this condition to be satisfied, the constants of integration of $\breve{e}(f)$ and $\hat{e}(f)$ would have to be zero. Given the functional form of the derived exchange rate function, this result constitutes a contradiction of the initial hypothesis that the slope of the spot rate function at fundamentalists' trading thresholds is equal to zero.

$$(3.14) \quad e(f) = \begin{cases} \bar{e}(f) \text{ if } \overline{f} < f \\ \hat{e}(f) \text{ if } \underline{f} \leq f \leq \overline{f} \\ \check{e}(f) \text{ if } f < \underline{f}. \end{cases}$$

Figure 3.1 illustrates the exchange rate function resulting in this extended version of the Krugman and Miller (1993) model. The figure plots the logarithm of the exchange rate on the vertical axis as a function of economic fundamentals, f, on the horizontal axis. Ruling out extrinsic bubbles, the function ee_0 depicts the solution to the model for all exchange rate realizations if technical traders are in general absent from FX markets.[46] In such an economy, rational foreign exchange traders recognize that the stochastic process chosen to depict the dynamics of economic fundamentals does not feature a predictable component and thus they form static expectations regarding future changes of the exchange rate. This, in turn, implies that the constants of integration in equation (3.7) are identically equal to zero and that the model degenerates to the baseline stochastic representative agent monetary model of exchange rate determination.

The linear function $ee_{c,1}$ represents the intrinsic value of the exchange rate applying in a noise trader world which comes into existence whenever the spot rate has reached the upper (lower) threshold rates, $\bar{e}$ $(\underline{e})$, from below (above) and agents adhering to a trend-chasing asset allocation strategy have been motivated to enter the FX market. For simplicity, the linear function $ee_{c,1}$ has been derived by setting the antilog of the reference exchange rate level used by chartists to form exchange rate expectations equal to unity. The slope of the linear function $ee_{c,1}$ is an increasing function of the market share of chartists, of the interest elasticity of money demand, and of the elasticity of noise traders exchange rate expectations with respect to the deviation of the current spot rate from the implicit target level e_0. The linear function $ee_{f,1}$ summarizes the symmetric scenario of a clockwise rotation of the intrinsic exchange rate path caused by the market entry of contrarian traders induced either by $e(t) \geq \bar{e}$ or by $e(t) \leq \underline{e}$.[47]

---

[46]   See Siebert (2000a) for a textbook exposition of the theory of rational bubbles. For a comprehensive discussion of policy issues raised by financial market bubbles and asset price inflation, see Siebert (2000b).

[47]   The result that the presence of noise traders alters the linear intrinsic relation between the spot rate and economic fundamentals and, thus, affects the sensitivity of this asset price to fluctuations in fundamentals is well-known in the noise trader literature. For example, Jeanne and Rose (1999), Kempa and Nelles (1994), and Frankel (1996) derive similar results in flex-price monetary models. Buch et al. (1998) discuss this effect in the context of the Dornbusch (1976) sticky-price model. For an analysis of

Figure 3.1: State-Contingent Market Entry and Exit of Technical Traders and Exchange Rate Dynamics

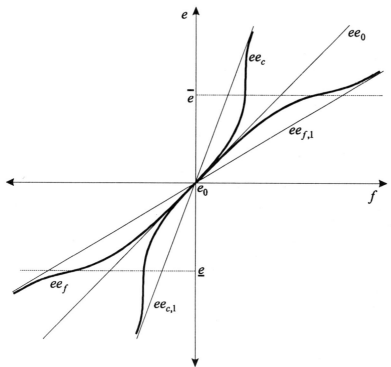

While the functions $ee_{c,1}$ and $ee_{f,1}$ resemble the representative rational agent solution ee_0 of the baseline monetary model of exchange rate determination insofar as the intrinsic spot rate turns out to be a linear function of fundamentals, the most interesting exchange rate dynamics obtain when the implications of rational traders' anticipation of noise traders' implicit trigger prices on the dynamics of the spot rate are taken into consideration. To present an equilibrium exchange rate solution applying in such an economy, the nonlinear function ee_c (ee_f) gives an example of a spot rate path applying in an FX market exhibiting infrequent market entries and exits of trend-chasing (contrarian) investors. To explain the specific shape of this function capturing exchange rate dynamics in FX markets with heterogeneous agents, suppose that the process driving eco-

---

the impact of technical trading on exchange rate dynamics in a model with sluggish goods market adjustment, see also Levin (1997).

nomic fundamentals forces the exchange rate to reach chartists' (fundamentalists') implicit trading trigger $\bar{e}$ from below. Continuously trading agents rationally recognize that this development increases the probability that technical traders will execute their investment strategies during the next infinitesimal instant of time. Rational traders embed this information in current exchange rate expectations by weighting the depreciation (appreciation) pressure on the domestic currency resulting from this simultaneous taking of short (long) positions in domestic-currency-denominated assets carried out by a nonnegligible group of FX market participants with the increased probability of such an event. These depreciation (appreciation) expectations are taken into consideration by rational agents when currently pricing foreign exchange. As can be seen by checking equation (3.3), this implies that for any given realization of economic fundamentals in the upper half of the implicit exchange rate fluctuation band the depreciation of the domestic currency is always an edge stronger (weaker) than the corresponding depreciation observed in a world without noise traders. As the exchange rate approaches the trading trigger $\bar{e}$ from below, continuously trading FX market participants bit up (down) the spot rate until the resulting additional supply (demand) of (for) domestic assets is large enough to rule out a discrete jump of the exchange rate function at the upper boundary of technical traders' no-trade interval. Also note that the state-dependent nature of the exchange rate path shown in Figure 3.1 requires a smooth transition of the spot rate from the no-noise trading regime to the region where technical traders are involved in the trading of foreign exchange. Thus, the exchange rate path is not only required to be continuous at $\bar{e}$ and at $\underline{e}$ as in the model of Krugman and Miller (1993) but also continuously differentiable. Of course, the situation is just reversed as the spot rate reaches the trading trigger $\bar{e}$ from above. In this situation, rational investors' additional demand (supply) for (of) domestic assets puts a strong appreciation (depreciation) pressure on the domestic currency. This, in turn, rules out arbitrage opportunities in FX markets by eliminating the possibility of a one-time discrete jump of the exchange rate function at chartists' (fundamentalists') trading threshold and by guaranteeing a smooth transition as the exchange rate crosses the critical realization $\bar{e}$ separating the different trading regimes. As can be seen by scrutinizing the exchange rate functions plotted in Figure 3.1, similar effects take place at the lower implicit trading trigger $\underline{e}$ fixed by technical investors.

3.1.2 The Foreign Currency Option Valuation Model

In this Section, a valuation model is developed which allows the implications of infrequent noise trading and implicit price barriers in FX spot markets for the pricing of foreign currency options and, thus, for the shape of the volatility strike structure implicit in these price contingent contracts to be discussed. The model applies in the case of European-style options. I focus on call options and denote the premium of this financial security by a continuous valuation function, $C(E,t)$, twice-differentiable in the antilog E of the exchange rate and once in t.

The first step in the analysis of the model is to apply the rules of stochastic calculus to trace out the process driving the antilog of the spot rate under measure g. Noting that

$$(3.15) \quad de = \frac{1}{2} e_{ff} \sigma^2 dt + e_f \sigma dW,$$

one obtains for $E \equiv \exp(e)$ the stochastic process:

$$(3.15)' \quad dE = \frac{1}{2} \left(e_f^2 + e_{ff} \right) \sigma^2 E dt + e_f \sigma E dW.$$

Two features of the stochastic differential equation derived in equation (3.15)' are worth mentioning. *Firstly*, both the drift rate and the diffusion term of the exchange rate process are state-dependent functions of technical investors' trading behavior. *Secondly*, the instantaneous volatility of the antilog of the spot rate is an increasing function of the first derivative of the natural logarithm of the exchange rate with respect to economic fundamentals. In a world without noise traders, this derivative assumes the value one. With noise traders present in the spot market, exchange rate volatility will, in general, differ from the volatility of fundamentals. While the market entry of fundamentalists tends to depress the variability of the spot rate, the trading strategy of chartists serves to amplify the instantaneous volatility of the exchange rate. If only chartists (fundamentalists) participate or are perceived to be involved in spot trading, one obtains, as highlighted in Figure 3.1, in the baseline scenario for the slope of the exchange rate function, the inequality $e_f \geq 1$ $(e_f \leq 1)$. Economically speaking, this formal result shows that the presence of a nonnegligible group of trend-chasing (contrarian) traders entering or leaving the market for domestic-currency denominated assets at certain trigger thresholds inflates (dampens) the instantaneous volatility of exchange rates. Moreover, the shape of the function $e(f)$ implies that the impact of technicians on the volatility of the exchange rate tends to become stronger as the spot rate moves closer to the trigger rates fixed by nonfundamental FX traders. As will be shown when discussing the results of numerical simulations of the model, it is this latter property of the present valuation model which plays a crucial role for the shape of the volatility strike structure implicit in foreign currency options.

Let μ_C and σ_C denote the expected rate of return and standard deviation of holding a European FX call. Applying the rules of stochastic calculus to $C(E,t)$, it follows that

$$(3.16) \quad \mu_C C = \frac{1}{2} C_E \left(e_f^2 + e_{ff} \right) \sigma^2 E \, dt - C_\tau \, dt + \frac{1}{2} C_{EE} \left(e_f \sigma E \right)^2 dt \quad \text{and}$$

$$(3.17) \quad \sigma_C C = C_E e_f \sigma E.$$

The premium on holding a European FX call can be expressed as

$$(3.18) \quad \gamma = \frac{\mu_C - r}{\sigma_C}.$$

Applying the standard no-arbitrage argument, the fundamental contingent claims valuation equation can be derived as

$$(3.19) \quad \frac{1}{2} C_{EE} \sigma^2 e_f^2 E^2 + \left(\frac{1}{2} \Im^1 e_{ff} \sigma^2 + \Im^2 \phi (e - e_0) \right) \left[E C_E - \left(\frac{r}{r - r^*} \right) C \right] = C_\tau,$$

where $\tau \equiv T - t$ denotes the time to expiry of the contract. From now on, the price of domestic discount bonds is fixed at unity. Upon resorting to the underlying structural exchange rate model to reexpress the differential between domestic and foreign interest rates, it is then possible to rewrite equation (3.19) as:

$$(3.20) \quad \frac{1}{2} C_{EE} \sigma^2 e_f^2 E^2 + \left(\frac{1}{2} \Im^1 e_{ff} \sigma^2 + \Im^2 \phi (e - e_0) \right) E C_E = C_\tau,$$

which must be solved subject to the standard set of terminal and boundary conditions applying in the case of European plain vanilla call options:

$$(3.21) \quad C(E,0) = [E - X]^+$$

$$(3.22) \quad \lim_{E \to 0} C(E,\tau) = 0$$

$$(3.23) \quad C(E,\tau) \leq E.$$

The European call option valuation model formalized in equations (3.20) to (3.23) degenerates to the GK model when the band of inaction defined by noise traders becomes infinitely large.

In an arbitrage-free international setting, FX options are priced under an equivalent martingale measure $\tilde{g}$. The spot rate process discounted for the forward report/discount martingalizes under this measure. Upon utilizing Ito's lemma, the exchange rate process which applies under the equivalent martingale measure can be expressed as:

$$(3.24) \quad dE = -r^*E\,dt + e_f\sigma\,d\tilde{W}.$$

The Wiener process $\{\tilde{W}(t), t \geq 0\}$ is a martingale under measure $\tilde{g}$, while the Wiener process $\{W(t), t \geq 0\}$ martingalizes with respect to measure g. The two processes are related through

$$(3.25) \quad d\tilde{W} = dW + dZ \quad \text{with} \quad dZ = \frac{\left(e_f^2 + e_{ff}\right)\sigma^2 - \left(\Im^1 e_{ff}\sigma^2 + 2\Im^2\phi(e - e_0)\right)}{2e_f\sigma}\,dt.$$

Also note that the change of the probability measure has not altered the structure of the diffusion term of the exchange rate process. Thus, the Radon–Nikodym derivative $\tilde{G} \equiv d\tilde{g}/dg$ linking the measures $\tilde{g}$ and g is specified by the geometric likelihood ratio process $d\tilde{G} = -\tilde{G}(dZ\,dt^{-1})dW$.

Under the equivalent martingale measure, the expected yield per period of time dt on holding the option must be identical to the yield which had been accrued upon investing the corresponding amount in the risk-free opportunity. The Radon–Nikodym derivative, thus, shows that (3.20) is indeed the correct fundamental partial differential valuation equation for price-dependent derivative securities in the present noise trader contingent claim valuation model.

Equation (3.24) is used in Monte Carlo simulations performed to numerically calculate FX currency option prices in the presence of noise traders and implicit price barriers in foreign exchange markets. The Monte Carlo valuation technique has been introduced into the options pricing literature by Boyle (1977). The technique is particularly useful for addressing options pricing problems which cannot be solved in terms of elementary mathematical functions or for verifying that closed-form option pricing formulas utilized in numerical simulations have been coded up correctly. A comprehensive discussion of the ideas underlying various alternative designs of Monte Carlo simulations can be found in Hammersley and Handscomb (1964). An analysis of these techniques in the context of options pricing theory is provided by Schäfer (1993). A discussion of recent applications can be found in Boyle et al. (1997).

To illustrate the central idea motivating the application of Monte Carlo techniques to address options pricing problems, recall from the discussion of the risk-neutral valuation model that the current premium of a European-style foreign currency option can be expressed as the expected terminal payout of the contract discounted at the risk-free rate of interest. Expectations are taken under the equivalent martingale measure $\tilde{g}$. Noting that the price of domestic discount bonds has been fixed at unity, this result can be translated into a mathematical language by writing:

$$(3.26) \quad C(E(t),\tau) = \mathbb{E}_t^{\tilde{g}}\left[(E(T) - X)^+|E(t)\right]$$

$$= \int_0^\infty (E(T) - X)^+ \tilde{g}(E(T), E(t), T, t)\,\mathrm{d}E(T).$$

Equation (3.26) states that the current value of the European FX call is equal to the area under the risk-neutral probability density function of the terminal exchange rate considered for all $E(T) \geq X$. A frequently encountered central problem when applying the risk-neutral valuation technique to value price contingent claims is that it is often not possible to derive closed-form analytical expressions for the integral appearing on the right-hand side of equation (3.26). The important value-added of the Monte Carlo approach to the pricing of European-style FX options is that this simulation methodology provides technically elegant instruments allowing this integral and, thus, the premium of the derivative security to be calculated numerically.

To compute the unbiased estimate $\hat{C}(E(t),\tau)$ of $C(E(t),\tau)$, the discrete time analogue of the exchange rate process provided in equation (3.24), obtained by subdividing the time to maturity τ of the option into $m - \tau/\Delta t$ disjoint sub-intervals of length Δt, is simulated n times. In the following analysis, an Euler approximation is utilized to obtain a discretization of the stochastic differential equation describing the evolution of the spot rate. A number of n sampled values is drawn from the probability density function of the terminal exchange rate $E(T)$. Following Hammersley and Handscomb (1964: 51–53), the respective estimate $\hat{C}(E(t),\tau)$ and the variance of the sampling distribution of this estimator are calculated by computing:

$$(3.27) \quad \hat{C}(E(t),\tau)= \frac{1}{n}\sum_{i=1}^n C(E_i(T),0) = \frac{1}{n}\sum_{i=1}^n\left[(E(T) - X)^+|E(t)\right]$$

$$(3.28) \quad \hat{C}^2(E(t),\tau)= \frac{1}{n-1}\sum_{i=1}^n\left(C(E_i(T),0) - \hat{C}(E(t),\tau)\right)^2.$$

To generate confidence bounds for the estimate of the option price, Boyle (1977: 325) suggests replacing $n-1$ in (3.28) by n and exploiting the result that, due to the central limit theorem, the standardized variable

$$\left[\hat{C}(E(t),\tau)-C(E(t),\tau)\right]/\sqrt{\hat{C}^2(E(t),\tau)/n}$$

converges to a standard normal distribution if the number of performed simulation runs is reasonably large.

For a given number of simulation runs, the standard deviation of the estimate of the option price can be reduced by implementing one of the variance reduction techniques discussed in Hammersley and Handscomb (1964) and in Boyle et al. (1997). However, enriching the programs used to simulate the present noise trader FX option valuation model by coding up one of these techniques, in general, inflates the computer time needed to obtain an estimate of the option price. To take this into consideration, it is common to evaluate the efficiency of variance reduction techniques not only by comparing the widths of the confidence bounds of the estimates of the option premia obtained by carrying out a more complex experiment with those produced by applying the crude Monte Carlo method described above. One also has to take into account the additional amount of processing time required when option prices are estimated by resorting to a more advanced Monte Carlo simulation technique (see, e.g., Hammersley and Handscomb 1964: 51). A variance reduction technique often utilized by researchers involved in options pricing research for its computational efficiency is the so-called antithetic variates approach (see, e.g., Hull and White 1987a). The general idea behind this technique is to attenuate the confidence bounds of a Monte Carlo estimate by recognizing that the variance of the arithmetic mean of two random variables will be smaller than the sum of the individual variances provided the random variables under investigation are negatively correlated. To generate such random variables, the first step is to store the m random shocks used to generate an individual simulation run of the model. In a second step, one changes the sign of each of the m shocks of each of the n sequences generated in the simulation. Each of these random sequences will be perfectly negatively correlated with its corresponding counterpart utilized in the original simulation run. With the new random series, a second estimate of the option value $\hat{C}_2(E(t),\tau)$ is calculated. Having stored the option premium $\hat{C}_1(E(t),\tau)$ based on the original simulation runs, the arithmetic average $\left[\hat{C}_1(E(t),\tau)+\hat{C}_2(E(t),\tau)\right]/2$ is formed to obtain new estimates of option prices showing smaller variances than those computed by resorting to the crude Monte Carlo technique. The variance of the estimate is reduced because the number of simulation runs is doubled and the antithetic variates are negatively correlated

(Campbell et al. 1997: 388–390). The confidence bounds of the volatility smiles presented in the next section have been computed by applying the antithetic variates approach.

3.1.3   Implicit Trading Regimes and the Volatility Strike Structure

The following paragraphs are devoted to the discussion of the results of the numerical simulations of the valuation model laid out in the preceding section. The results demonstrate that the presence of noise traders and implicit trading regimes can give rise to the kind of smile and smirk effects most often exhibited by real-world volatility strike structures implicit in foreign currency options premia.

Figure 3.2 plots an example of an endogenously determined volatility strike structure. The figure depicts volatility quotes implicit in simulated foreign currency option premia on the vertical axis as a function of the exchange rate/strike price ratio on the horizontal axis. In this scenario, technical traders' orders start to reach the FX market at the bounds of a symmetric band of inaction $\underline{e} = -\overline{e}$. In the simulation, it was assumed that noise traders adhere to an extrapolative chartist investment technique. The resulting symmetric exchange rate function utilized to price FX contingent claims therefore resembles the linear function ee_c depicted in Figure 3.1. To start the simulation, it was assumed that the natural logarithm of the current exchange rate has settled in the middle of the implicit spot rate band, $\left(\underline{e}, \overline{e}\right)$.

Inspection of Figure 3.2 shows that volatilities implicit in near-the-money and far-from-the-money options tend to be higher than volatility quotes inferred from at-the-money options. The implied volatility function reaches a minimum for at-the-money contracts and rises as the exchange rate/strike price ratio moves closer to the critical spot rate realizations inducing technical traders either to enter or to exit the market for domestic assets. Furthermore, the function $(E/X) \mapsto \sigma_{implied}$ is almost perfectly symmetrically spaced around the at-the-money point $(E/X) \approx 1$. Figure 3.2 thus demonstrates that the noise trader FX option pricing model utilized in the present analysis is capable of producing the type of smile effects in the volatility strike structure also generated by the stochastic volatility models of Hull and White (1987a) and of Heston (1993). Note, however, that my noise trader FX option pricing model discussed in the preceding section departs from these more standard stochastic volatility option valuation models in that my model allows these characteristics of options prices to be derived endogenously. This feature of the model renders it possible to interpret the volatility smile in

Figure 3.2: Noise Trading and a U-Shaped Implied Volatility Strike Structure

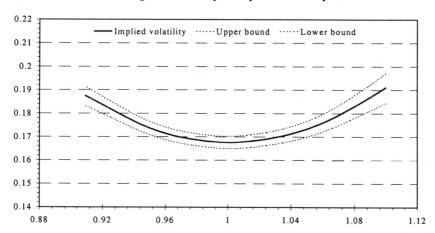

Note: The figure plots volatility quotes implicit in simulated foreign currency option premia on the vertical axis as a function of the exchange rate/strike price ratio on the horizontal axis. The figure is based on the following set of numerical option parameter values: $\sigma = \upsilon = 0.15$, $\bar{e} = -\underline{e} = 0.1$, $e(0) = 0$. The time to maturity of the option is one month. The trading behavior of noise traders is captured by the following set of parameter values: $\alpha = 0.5$, $\phi = 4$, $e_0 = e(0)$. The interest rate elasticity of money demand was set to $\lambda = 0.1$. The Monte Carlo estimates of option premia are based on 5,000 simulation runs. The Euler approximation of the stochastic differential equation describing the dynamics of the underlying spot rate was constructed by subdividing the remaining time-to-expiry of the contract into 150 equidistant subintervals. The upper and lower bounds are used to visualize the 90 percent confidence interval for simulated implied volatilities.

economic terms rather than in terms of a superimposed volatility of volatility or an exogenously prespecified correlation between the innovation terms driving exogenously specified stochastic processes for the underlying asset price and its volatility.

To understand the economic intuition behind these findings, note that continuously trading rational spot market participants anticipate the market entry of chartists as the exchange rate reaches the implicit trading trigger $\bar{e}$ ($\underline{e}$) from below (above). The expectations that the intrinsic relation between economic fundamentals and the exchange rate changes when a nonnegligible number of noise traders enter the spot market at these critical exchange rate realizations enlarges traders' information set. Traders acting in a competitive environment take the information regarding the present discounted value of the impact of the demand or supply of technical traders on the level of the exchange rate into account when currently trading foreign exchange. In contrast to the GK case of linear-homogenous agents, the resulting spot rate function mimics an inverted S and the endogenously determined volatility of the exchange rate increases as the stochastic system moves closer to one of the trigger rates associated with shifts in the trading behavior of technical traders. This rise in the instantaneous variability of the exchange rate exerts an increasing impact on the premia of options on this asset price. Because the volatility of the underlying increases as the spot rate reaches chartists' critical trading triggers $\underline{e}$ and $\overline{e}$, the premia of in-the-money (out-of-the-money) options tend to increase (decrease) by more (less), compared to the GK case, than at-the-money contracts. The result is the convex volatility strike structure depicted in the figure. Also note the figure unearths the presence of a Jensen's inequality effect which requires that volatility quotes inferred from strictly at-the-money FX options slightly exceed their GK homogenous trader counterparts due to the convex shape of the function relating the instantaneous volatility of the underlying spot rate to the moneyness of the derivative contract.

The moderate asymmetry of the mean smile for far-from-the-money options can be attributed to the fact that in the setting used here the international interest rate differential is closely related to rational investors exchange rate expectations. In the upper (lower) half of the implicit exchange rate band $(\underline{e}, \overline{e})$, the likelihood that noise traders will begin to bet on a further weakening of the domestic currency is larger than the likelihood of a portfolio reallocation in the opposite direction. This fosters economic agents' depreciation (appreciation) expectations that must be covered by a corresponding positive (negative) interest rate differential. From this, it follows that the price of foreign discount bonds expressed in terms of the price of their domestic counterparts increases for $(\overline{e} - \underline{e})/2 \le e(t)$, and vice versa. It is known from the baseline foreign currency option valuation models that this, in turn, implies that the premia of FX options as forward-looking instruments are stimulated to increase (to decline) if the contract is currently in-the-money (out-of-the-money). Thus, the interest rate effect explains the slight asymmetry of the volatility smile, as depicted in Figure 3.2, arising in the case of relatively far-from-the-money options.

Figure 3.3 serves to examine the impact of increasing the distance between the current exchange rate realization and noise traders' implicit trading triggers on the shape of the volatility strike structure. As can be seen by inspecting the graph, the function $(E/X) \mapsto \sigma_{implied}$ plotted in the figure is less convex than its counterpart shown in Figure 3.2. Thus, the impact of trend-chasing noise trading in the spot market on the curvature of the smile declines as the current exchange rate wanders farther away from technical traders' trigger thresholds. This finding

Figure 3.3: Distant Technical Trading Thresholds and the Convexity of the Volatility Smile

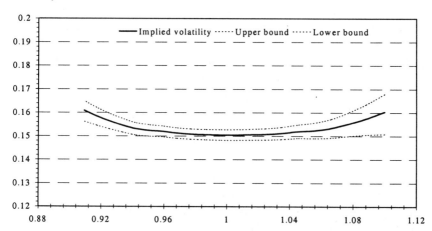

Note: The figure plots volatility quotes implicit in simulated foreign currency option premia on the vertical axis as a function of the exchange rate/strike price ratio on the horizontal axis. The trading thresholds of noise traders following an extrapolative investment strategy have been set equal to $\bar{e} = -\underline{e} = 0.2$. All other parameters are the same as in Figure 3.2.

reflects that the present discounted value of the anticipated impact of the execution of technically motivated buy or sell orders submitted by agents belonging to the group of traders following a trend-extrapolating investment strategy on the spot rate shrinks as the distance $\bar{e} - e$ is increased. As compared to the economy depicted in Figure 3.2, the likelihood of a further depreciation (appreciation) of the domestic currency caused by technical traders entering the spot market at the trading trigger $\bar{e}$ ($\underline{e}$) is set on the decrease and this, in turn, abates the pressure on the domestic currency tracing back to the trading behavior of continuously acting FX market participants. Consequently, the endogenously determined instantaneous exchange rate volatility implied by the underlying structural noise trader exchange rate model increases less rapidly than in Figure 3.2 as the exchange rate moves in the direction of the critical entry and exit thresholds placed by technical traders. This lowers the correlation between movements of the spot rate and its instantaneous volatility and results in the mildly smiling volatility strike structure depicted in Figure 3.3.

It should also be recognized that the figure reveals that the widening of the exchange rate interval in which technical investors do not participate in spot trading allows volatility quotes implicit in at-the-money FX options to converge to the level of the instantaneous exchange rate volatility inserted into the first-generation GK valuation formula utilized to calculate FX option premia in the representative agent rational expectations no-bubbles scenario. The economic reasoning motivating this finding can be traced out by pointing out that the less pronounced convex functional relation between the prevailing spot rate and its instantaneous variability results in a weaker Jensen's inequality effect. This, in turn, implies that the minimum of the volatility strike structure observed for at-the-money contracts can be found in the vicinity of the instantaneous spot rate volatility which obtains in the baseline homogenous trader GK model.

To further highlight the impact of noisy spot trading and implicit trading regimes on the shape of the smile, I have examined the implications of increasing the trading elasticity of technical investors ϕ with respect to the deviation of the actual exchange rate from its medium-term target value for the shape of the volatility strike structure. To simulate such a scenario, I have assigned a numerical value to this parameter twice as large as the trading elasticity used to generate the smiles depicted in the above figures.

The results of this exercise are summarized in Figure 3.4. As can be seen in the figure, raising the sensitivity of chartists with respect to deviations in the spot rate from its medium-term target value exerts a magnifying effect on the convexity of the volatility strike structure. As compared to the baseline scenario depicted in Figure 3.2, increasing the numerical value ascribed to the parameter ϕ implies that continuously trading rational agents anticipate that the market entry of noise traders results in a relatively steeper exchange rate function that captures the intrinsic relation between the exchange rate and economic fundamentals. This, in turn, implies that any movement of the exchange rate in the direction of either one of the trading triggers placed by technical investors results in a strong increase in the endogenously determined instantaneous volatility of the spot rate. The magnitude of this rise in the instantaneous volatility of the exchange rate is an increasing function of the parameter ϕ and, thus, of the sensitivity of noise traders with respect to the gap between the prevailing spot rate and its expected longer-term base level. The result is that the convexity of the volatility strike structure is directly related to the aggressiveness with which chartists begin to build up or to dissolve their positions in domestic assets once the spot rate has reached the critical trading triggers $\underline{e}$ and $\overline{e}$. This finding indicates that in the present model not only the quantitative importance of noise traders summarized by the nonnegligible fraction of investors following such an investment strategy but also qualitative features of the trading behavior of agents adhering to technical trading rules play an important role in the overall shape of the volatility strike structure.

Figure 3.4: The Aggressiveness of Noise Traders and the Shape of the Volatility Strike Structure

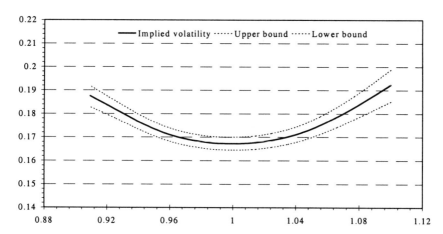

Note: The figure plots volatility quotes implicit in simulated foreign currency option premia on the vertical axis as a function of the exchange rate/strike price ratio on the horizontal axis. The trading thresholds of noise traders following an extrapolative investment strategy have been set equal to $\bar{e} = -\underline{e} = 0.2$. The trading behavior of noise traders is captured by the following set of parameter values: $\alpha = 0.5$, $\phi = 8$, $e_0 = e(0)$. All other parameters are the same as in Figure 3.2.

So far, the numerical analysis of the noise trader model of FX option pricing has been used to create endogenously convex volatility strike structures symmetrically spaced around the point at which FX options are just at-the-money. The next figure, in contrast, depicts a skewed volatility smirk obtained upon fixing the implicit investment thresholds of noise traders such that $\underline{e} = -2\bar{e}$. In this scenario, the distance of the prevailing spot rate from the upper market entry trigger of chartists is smaller than its distance from the lower trading threshold of chartists. Such a numerical parameter constellation captures a situation in which it takes a comparatively small (large) depreciation (appreciation) of the exchange rate to stimulate noise traders to begin to build up short (long) positions in domestic-currency-denominated assets.

Figure 3.5 highlights the implications of the asymmetric spacing of the trading triggers placed by trend-chasing chartists for the volatility strike structure implicit in foreign currency options. The figure demonstrates that the present noise trader FX option pricing model, like the related closed-economy model pioneered by Grossman and Zhou (1996), can be employed to theoretically

Figure 3.5: Asymmetrically Spaced Trading Thresholds and Skewness in the Smile

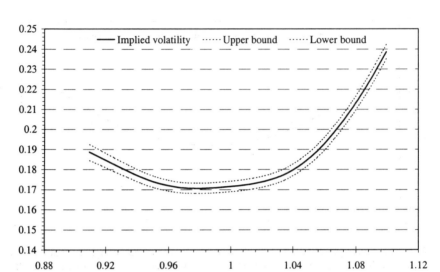

Note: The figure plots volatility quotes implicit in simulated foreign currency option premia on the vertical axis as a function of the exchange rate/strike price ratio on the horizontal axis. The trading thresholds of noise traders following an extrapolative investment strategy have been set equal to $\overline{e} = 0.1$ and $\underline{e} = -2\overline{e}$. All other parameters are the same as in Figure 3.2.

generate a skewed volatility strike structure. The skewness of the smile reflects on the assumption made in the numerical simulations that the upper and lower implicit trading thresholds of trend-chasing noise traders are asymmetrically spaced relative to the prevailing spot rate. From this observation, it follows that a change of the position of the current exchange rate relative to the investment triggers of technical agents will, in general, alter the degree of asymmetry exhibited by the volatility smile. Given that the exchange rate follows a stochastic process, this line of argumentation indicates that for a set of fixed implicit trading triggers, the noise trader FX option pricing model can be utilized to produce time-varying skewness in the smile. From an empirical point of view, this is an interesting implication of the FX option valuation model discussed in the preceding section. It has been emphasized by Bates (1996a: 599) that the empirically observed fluctuations in the sign of implicit skewness observed in options on currencies (and on other underlyings as well) require "models of time-varying skewness to complement our existing models of time-varying volatility."

In the above numerical examples, the model was simulated by assuming that program traders implement a trend-chasing investment strategy and thereby exert a destabilizing rather than a stabilizing impact on the dynamics of the exchange rate. It immediately follows from the discussion of the shape of the exchange rate in Figure 3.1 that the results of the simulation experiments are reversed in an economy in which technical traders adhere to a state-dependent contrarian rather than a trend-extrapolative trading philosophy. In such a scenario, continuously trading spot market traders anticipate the appreciation (depreciation) pressure on the domestic currency that arises as the exchange rate is driven in the direction of the implicit trading trigger $\bar{e}$ ($\underline{e}$) and the current spot rate $\underline{e} \leq e(t') \leq \bar{e}$ already incorporates these stabilizing exchange rate expectations. Starting in the interior of the implicit band $(\underline{e}, \bar{e})$, this, in turn, implies that the instantaneous volatility of the spot rate decreases as the stochastic system forces the exchange rate to move in the direction of one of the thresholds that induce technical traders to reallocate financial wealth. As a consequence, FX option premia now tend to decline as the exchange rate reaches program traders' implicit stabilizing trigger points, so that the volatility strike structure observed in such an economy mimics a frown rather than a smile or a smirk. Similar frown effects have also been reported by Dumas et al. (1995b) and by David and Veronesi (1999), albeit in differently motivated papers. While such frowns are an interesting phenomenon from a theoretical point of view, the empirical evidence reported in the empirical finance literature strongly indicates that real-world volatility strike structures show a convex rather than a concave shape. As discussed in detail above, the present model of analysis allows convex volatility strike structures to be computed if it is assumed that technical traders follow a state-dependent trend-chasing rather than a contrarian noise trading strategy.

All results considered, the numerical simulations underscore that the foreign currency option valuation model outlined in Section 3.1.2 contributes to the strand of research aiming at explaining empirically observed shapes of volatility strike structures implicit in FX options premia theoretically. The curvature of the volatility strike structure is explained by focusing attention on the width of the interval of inaction of technical traders, the position of the prevailing spot rate relative to the trading triggers placed by noise traders, and the trading elasticity of technical traders with respect to the deviation of the prevailing spot rate from a medium-term target value. A central finding is that the volatility quotes inferred from the simulated foreign currency option premia embed valuable information regarding implicit trading regimes in FX spot markets. The simulated volatilities implicit in foreign currency options tend to increase (decrease) as the underlying exchange rate moves in the direction of a destabilizing (stabilizing) trigger threshold reflecting the extrapolative (contrarian) trading of a non-negligible fraction of market participants.

The interpretation of the results of the various numerical simulations further indicates that the *endogenously* derived predictions of my noise trader contingent claim valuation model for the premia of foreign currency options tend to resemble those obtained from more classic stochastic volatility and jump-diffusion models. As discussed in detail in Chapter 2, FX option pricing settings belonging to these classes of price-contingent claim valuation models resort either to an *exogenously* specified stochastic exchange rate volatility or to an *exogenously* given discontinuous spot rate process to generate a leptokurtic exchange rate returns distribution. Despite the fact that the implications for the pricing of foreign currency options are similar to each other, the noise trader FX contingent claim valuation model discussed in this section differs from the well-established stochastic volatility and jump-diffusion models in at least one important respect. While in standard jump-diffusion and stochastic volatility models *exogenously* given stochastic differential equations are employed to describe discontinuous exchange rate dynamics and the evolution of the instantaneous volatility of the spot rate, my option valuation model allows the dynamics of the underlying spot rate and, thus, smile and smirk effects in the volatility strike structure to be derived *endogenously*. Rather than relying on a superimposed formal mathematical interpretation, the model renders it possible to interpret regularities in the volatility strike structure documented in the empirical literature in terms of the trading behavior of economic agents in the spot market. For this reason, the noise trading approach to option pricing discussed in this chapter complements the models presented in Platen and Schweizer (1998) and Grossman and Zhou (1996) in that it also offers an economically attractive explanation for the pricing errors that result when the baseline FX option valuation models are implemented to price real-world foreign currency options.

The results of the theoretical analysis also indicate that both the instantaneous volatility of the spot rate and volatilities embedded in FX options might help to identify implicit price barriers and trading regimes in actual foreign currency spot markets. In Sections 3.2 and 3.3, these issues will be discussed in more detail and simple volatility-based empirical tests for implicit support or resistance thresholds and adjacent trading regimes in real-world FX markets will be implemented.

3.2   Implicit Trading Triggers and Exchange Rate Volatility: The Traditional View

The noise trader foreign currency option pricing model laid out in Section 3.1 section stipulates that discretely spaced implicit trigger spot rate levels at which a substantial fraction of agents executing nonfundamental-based trading strategies either enters or exits the spot market are an important determinant of the shape of the volatility strike structure implicit in FX options premia. The core intention of the empirical analyses contained in this and the following section is to analyze whether such generally not immediately observable trading-induced implicit trigger exchange rates exist in real-world foreign exchange markets. As the theoretical analysis presented in Section 3.1 predicts that implicit trigger rates can exert a quantitatively substantial impact on foreign currency option prices, the empirical analysis conducted here helps to verify whether real-world exchange rate data do or do not support the barriers hypothesis of the volatility strike structure. The empirical analysis utilizes the main result derived in Section 3.1, namely that the instantaneous volatility of spot rates reflects the impact of noise trading on the dynamics of the underlying exchange rate process.

Early tests for implicit price barriers in financial markets can be found in Donaldson and Kim (1993) and De Grauwe and Dewachter (1992).[48] The central idea underlying the testing approach used in these studies is to subdivide the real line between asset price levels suspected to hold special significance for investors into a certain number of disjoint subintervals. Upon constructing a unique mapping between these subintervals and the level of the asset price under investigation, the authors then examine whether either the relative frequency distributions of the categorized returns or asset price series show a shape in line with the predictions of models of asset pricing under regulated fundamentals. Consistent with the implications of, for example, the model of Krugman and Miller (1993), a hump-shaped functional form of the respective relative frequency distributions is interpreted as evidence for the presence of destabilizing price barriers in the market. The formal reasoning underlying this line of argumentation exploits the argument that the existence of trading-behavior-induced price barriers in real-world FX markets requires that spot prices will spend less time near the barriers and will, therefore, be found significantly less frequently in those subintervals closest to the respective implicit price thresholds.

---

[48] For empirical studies using a similar testing approach, see Donaldson (1990), Ley and Varian (1994), and Koedjik and Stork (1994).

While Donaldson and Kim (1993) and De Grauwe and Dewachter (1992) resort to the relative frequency distribution of categorized returns and asset prices to test the barrier hypothesis, the central feature of the new empirical testing approach recently suggested by Hogan et al. (1997) and Cyree et al. (1999) is that time-varying conditional volatilities of the returns of financial market prices are estimated. While Cyree et al. (1999) use the volatility-based test to examine potential links between implicit price barriers and the volatility of stock market returns, Hogan et al. (1997) use an error correction model with conditionally heteroskedastic disturbances to study the impact of program trading on cash and future stock market volatility.

The intention behind the present analysis is to study whether systematic patterns in the volatility of major exchange rates point to the existence of trading-induced thresholds in the respective spot markets. To accomplish this task, I modify the testing approach suggested by Hogan et al. (1997) and Cyree et al. (1999) to account for the statistical properties of the exchange rate returns series under investigation and to ensure that my results are comparable to the ones presented by De Grauwe and Decupere (1992) in an earlier study on implicit price barriers in FX markets. Inspired by the predictions of the noise trader model outlined above, I use the test to categorize exchange rates between certain reference values and to test whether the estimated conditional volatility of exchange rate returns in those classes close to the suspected barriers is significantly higher or lower than the conditional volatility in the other classes. Using volatilities to perform tests for implicit price barriers is convenient as these data provide an economically intuitive terminology to examine (i) whether implicit price barriers exist in real-world FX spot markets, and, (ii) whether such price barriers can be perceived to stabilize or destabilize exchange rates.[49]

A technical advantage of the volatility-based tests for implicit price barriers is that such quantitative research techniques allow a critical facet of relative fre-

---

[49]   An alternative, rather different empirical approach would be to resort to options-implied volatilities rather than to estimated conditional exchange rate volatilities to conduct tests for the stabilizing or destabilizing properties of potential implicit price barriers or trading regimes in FX markets. Such a strategy has been adopted by Ackert et al. (1997) to examine the impact of circuit breakers in stock markets on expected stock price volatility. Campa and Chang (1998) have used a similar approach to test for the effect of publicly known bounds on the dynamics of EMS exchange rates. See also Dumas et al. (1995b: 1539–1540) for a discussion of the theoretical considerations motivating such a testing approach. Note also that these studies examine the impact of institutionally or politically defined and, thus, exogenously given and publicly known price barriers on expected exchange rate volatility. The present analyses, in contrast, contribute to the area of research concerned with the identification of potential systematic links between the volatility of spot rate returns and not directly observable implicit trading-induced price barriers.

quency distribution-based testing strategies stressed by Ceuster et al. (1998) and also noted in Ley and Varian (1994) to be circumvented. The former show that the assumption underlying the tests conducted by Donaldson and Kim (1993) and De Grauwe and Dewachter (1992), namely that, under the null hypothesis of no implicit price barriers, the trailing digits' distribution of the asset price under investigation should resemble a uniform distribution, is not correct. Thus, testing for implicit price barriers by plotting the relative frequencies of price realizations against categorized asset prices and testing whether or not the obtained mapping approaches a uniform distribution can lead to spurious results. Volatility-based testing approaches do not rely on the frequency distributions of categorized asset prices and are therefore not subject to the criticism of Ceuster et al. (1998).

The remainder of this section is organized as follows. Section 3.2.1 introduces an empirical test for implicit price barriers in FX markets. The empirical model implemented to trace out the impact of implicit trading thresholds on the time-varying conditional volatility of exchange rates is formalized in Section 3.2.2. The data used in the empirical analysis are described in Section 3.2.3. The results of implementing the volatility-based test for implicit price barriers in exchange rates are reported and discussed in Section 3.2.4.

3.2.1 Identification of Potential Trading Triggers in FX Markets

The first step in setting up a volatility-based test for implicit price barriers in FX markets is to identify a set of potential exchange rate trading triggers which are suspected to hold special significance for market participants. The financial press and the investor guides published by large financial institutions propound that agents involved in FX trading might perceive such trading thresholds whenever exchange rates reach certain rounded numbers. For example, reflecting on profitable FX strategies, Merrill Lynch (2000) explains that "The US dollar is close to a 10 year high against the Deutschemark and DEM 2.00 is proving to be a tough barrier...." (p. 5) and, in the same booklet, it is emphasized that the "Euro/yen has the potential for a significant recovery and after failing to breach the 110 level in early January" (p. 7). Taking this anecdotal evidence into consideration, the traditional approach taken in the empirical finance literature when elaborating on implicit price barriers in asset markets is to test whether or not the last trailing digits of the price of a currency hold special significance for agents participating in spot market trading. Using this concept, I analyze whether or not the volatility-based testing technique laid out below provides evidence for the presence of implicit price barriers at specific rounded exchange rate realizations ending with zero at the second and third digit after the decimal point. To offer an example, I examine whether an implicit price barrier can be detected at a spot rate of 1.800 deutsche mark/US dollar or, in the reverse case, at a ratio of 0.700 US dollar/deutsche mark. In a similar vein, I test whether implicit trading trigger thresholds are reached when the yen/US dollar parity is in the neighborhood of 1.600 or when the reverse parity moves toward 6.100.

Based on the theoretical analysis outlined in Section 3.1.3, the economic idea behind this volatility-based testing technique for implicit trading triggers in FX markets is to examine whether exchange rate volatility is significantly higher or lower in the neighborhood of such an implicit support or resistance barrier. Having defined a set of potential implicit exchange rate trading thresholds, the next step is therefore to identify the position of the spot rate relative to these suspected trading thresholds. To accomplish this step, the real line between two potential price barriers is subdivided into 100 disjoint intervals of the same length. Adopting the notation introduced by Donaldson and Kim (1993) and De Grauwe and Decupere (1992), the respective interval numbers are called M-values with $M = 1,...,100$. With this concept, it is possible to assign to every spot rate realization a unique interval number or M-value summarizing the distance of the current exchange rate from the two nearest potential trigger rates. Whenever the exchange rate can be found next to an implicit barrier price, its M-value is either very close to unity or to 100. Given this property, the M-values can be utilized to define the following set of dummy variables which allow for further operationalization of the proposition that an exchange rate can be found in the "neighborhood" of an implicit trading trigger:

$$(3.29a) \quad dummy_1 = \begin{cases} 1 \text{ if } M \in \{1,...,15,85,...,100\} \\ 0 \text{ otherwise,} \end{cases}$$

$$(3.29b) \quad dummy_2 = \begin{cases} 1 \text{ if } M \in \{1,...,20,80,...,100\} \\ 0 \text{ otherwise,} \end{cases}$$

$$(3.29c) \quad dummy_3 = \begin{cases} 1 \text{ if } M \in \{1,...,25,75,...,100\} \\ 0 \text{ otherwise.} \end{cases}$$

The three dummy variables are similar to those employed by De Grauwe and Decupere (1992) to define "neighborhood" intervals around the potential price barriers. This guarantees that the results reported in this chapter can be compared to those in the literature on implicit price barriers in FX markets. Moreover, given that the specific choice of the neighborhood of a potential trigger price is always to some extent arbitrary, utilizing three alternative different dummy variables to construct such intervals around an implicit price barrier provides an impression of the robustness of the results with respect to the definition of the "neighborhood" of implicit price barriers. The first dummy variable, *dummy*$_1$, provided in equation (3.29a), defines a relatively narrow symmetric interval around a potential implicit support or resistance level. In contrast, the dummy variable *dummy*$_3$, formalized in equation (3.29c), is equal to unity whenever an exchange rate settles in a relatively wide band around the suspected trigger rates. Finally, the variable named *dummy*$_2$, defined in equation (3.29b), can be employed to select a medium-sized range of *M*-values around the threshold spot rates suspected to hold special significance for FX spot market participants. Given the above definition of the dummy variables, roughly 1/3 (approximately 1/2) of the data can be found in the narrow (wide) interval placed around the potential implicit price barriers.

The set of dummy variables defined in equation (3.29) can now be utilized in a quantitative model of conditional asset price variability to test whether exchange rate volatility increases (or decreases) significantly as the distance of the exchange rate from a potential implicit spot market trading trigger tends to decline.

3.2.2 Modeling the Link between Trading Triggers and Exchange Rate Volatility

A variety of competing concepts have been proposed in the empirical literature to measure the variability of financial market prices (see Pagan and Schwert (1990) for a survey). Among the most popular models designed to estimate conditional financial market volatility are the numerous models belonging to the class of generalized autoregressive conditional heteroskedasticity (GARCH) models pioneered by Engle (1982) and extended by Bollerslev (1986). Surveys of the literature dealing with issues related to the construction and the estimation of these types of models include Bollerslev et al. (1992), Bera and Higgins (1993), and Diebold and Lopez (1995). Early evidence for autoregressive conditional heteroskedasticity in daily exchange rate data is reported in Hsieh (1988) and in Diebold and Nerlove (1989).

To construct a GARCH model of conditional exchange rate volatility, the first step is to define the rate of return, $\Delta \tilde{e}_t$, of the spot rate, E_t, from time $t-1$ to time t as:

(3.30) $\Delta \tilde{e}_t \equiv 100 \times [\ln(E_t) - \ln(E_{t-1})]$,

with $\tilde{e}_t$ being the natural logarithm of E_t and Δ denoting the first-difference operator. To rule out that possible systematic day-of-the-week effects distort the results of the volatility-based test for implicit price barriers in FX markets, the following regression for the conditional mean of the raw data is estimated:

(3.31) $\Delta \tilde{e}_t = \sum_{i=1}^{5} \beta_i \tilde{d}_{i,t} + \varepsilon_t$,

where $\tilde{d}_{i,t}$, $i = 1,...,5$ represent day-of-the-week dummies. Let the residuals obtained from estimating equation (3.31) by ordinary least squares be written as $\hat{\varepsilon}_t \equiv \Delta e_t$. Adopting a two-step methodology similar to the ones employed by Pagan and Schwert (1990), Amin and Ng (1997), and Alexander (1998), the input data employed in the estimation of the GARCH models used to trace out the time path of conditional exchange rate volatility are taken from the return series Δe_t. The general specification of a GARCH process of order $p \ge 1$ and $q \ge 1$, abbreviated as GARCH (p,q), can then be formulated as follows:

(3.32) $\Delta e_t = u_t$ with $u_t | \Omega_{t-1} \sim D(0, h_t)$,

(3.33) $u_t = \eta_t \sqrt{h_t}$ with $\eta_t \sim_{\text{i.i.d.}} D(0,1)$,

(3.34) $h_t = \omega + \sum_{i=1}^{p} \alpha_{p,i} u_{t-i}^2 + \sum_{i=1}^{q} \beta_{q,i} h_{t-i} + \delta \, dummy_{i,t}$,

where $D(0, h_t)$ is a density function with mean zero and variance h_t, Ω_{t-1} is the information set including the realizations of all relevant variables up to and including time $t-1$, and η_t is an independently identically distributed (i.i.d.) white-noise process independent of u_{t-i} with zero mean and unit variance density D. Equation (3.32) implies that the conditional and the unconditional mean of the serially uncorrelated exchange rate returns are equal to zero. The unconditional variance of the exchange rate returns is constant and finite provided the roots of the characteristic polynomial of difference equation (3.34) lie inside the unit circle (see, e.g., Bera and Higgins 1993).

Though not linearly related, the model in equations (3.32)–(3.34) implies that exchange rate returns are not statistically independent because the variance of the data-generating process conditioned on the information set Ω_{t-1} is given by $\mathbb{E}_t(\Delta e_t^2 | \Omega_{t-1}) = h_t$. It follows that the conditional variance, h_t, of exchange rate returns is a function of the information set Ω_{t-1} and is, thus, in general time-dependent. A sufficient condition ensuring that the conditional variance assumes only positive values is that $\omega > 0$, $\omega + \delta > 0$, $\alpha_i \geq 0$, and $\beta_j \geq 0$ for all $i = 1,...,p$ and $j = 1,...,q$. [50] According to this model, the time-dependent conditional variance of exchange rate returns depends on a constant mean level, ω, on the lagged squared residuals u_{t-i}^2, $i = 1,...,p$ from the mean equation, and on a set of past forecasted variances, h_{t-i}^2, $i = 1,...,q$ (GARCH terms). The GARCH model is equivalent to an ARCH model of infinite order featuring a rational lag structure with $p \to \infty$ and $\beta_q = 0$ for all q. The specific autoregressive functional form of the variance equation (3.34) implies that a volatility increase in a past period also raises the estimate of current volatility where the magnitude of the impact of a disturbance in period $t' < t$ on h_t declines geometrically in the distance $t - t'$.

The important economic feature of the empirical model formalized in equation (3.34) to capture the volatility dynamics of exchange rate returns is that the conditional variance, h_t, depends also on the position of the spot rate relative to the suspected implicit price barriers as measured by the variables $dummy_{i,t}$ defined in equation (3.29). The marginal significance of the coefficient δ allows whether implicit price barriers in FX markets do exist to be examined (see also Hogan et al. 1997 and Cyree et al. 1999). Moreover, as three different dummy variables have been defined, it is possible to examine the robustness of the findings regarding implicit price barriers in FX markets with respect to the specification of the width of the intervals defining the neighborhood of such a trading threshold.

To close the model formalized in equations (3.32) to (3.34), one has to select a specific functional form for the density D. In his seminal paper, Engle (1982) suggested allowing the disturbance term η_t to be standard normally distributed. This assumption implies that the innovation term u_t is conditionally normally distributed with conditional variance, h_t. In the context of the modeling of financial market data, however, the assumption of a normally distributed error term has often been found to be insufficient to account for the significant leptokurtosis characterizing the sample distributions of asset price returns in general and of daily and high-frequency returns data in particular. This finding is confirmed by the summary statistics offered in Table 3.2 for the daily exchange rate returns used in the empirical analysis below. For this reason, many authors including Baillie and Bollerslev (1989) and Hsieh (1989) have suggested resorting to a t-distribution to describe the properties of u_t in the context of the

---

[50] Though these conditions are sufficient, weaker conditions allowing individual coefficients of the variance equation to assume negative numerical values can be derived from the inverted representation of the conditional variance. See Nelson and Cao (1992) and Drost and Nijman (1993) for discussions.

modeling of exchange rate data. As an alternative, Lui and Brorsen (1995) have suggested the GARCH models featuring stable Paretian distributions introduced into the finance literature by Mandelbrot (1963) and Fama (1965). While Paolella (1999) provides further examples for models belonging to this strand of the ARCH literature, the focus of Hafner (1998) is on an application of alternative nonparametric GARCH frameworks to the modeling of the dynamics of the conditional volatility of (high-frequency) exchange rate returns.

In this study, a modeling strategy advanced by Nelson (1991) is adopted. Nelson proposed modeling asset returns with a GARCH model featuring the generalized error distribution $\eta_t \sim D(0,1,\overline{\kappa})$ normalized to have zero mean and unit variance. The positive parameter $\overline{\kappa}$ governs the thickness of the tails of the distribution. This parameter is not known in advance but must be estimated together with the other structural parameters of the model. In the case of $\overline{\kappa} < 2$ ($\overline{\kappa} > 2$), the distribution exhibits fatter (thinner) tails than the normal distribution. In the special case of $\overline{\kappa} = 2$, the generalized error distribution degenerates to the standard normal density (Hamilton 1994: Chapter 21; Box 1953; McDonald and Newey 1988). A discussion of the properties of the model for the special case of the exponential GARCH (EGARCH) specification for the conditional variance equation can be found in Nelson (1991). For a general discussion, see Hamilton (1994: 668). The density of the innovation term η_t is given by

$$(3.35) \quad D(0,1,\overline{\kappa}) = \frac{\overline{\kappa} \exp\left[-0.5\left|\eta_t/\overline{\omega}\right|^{\overline{\kappa}}\right]}{\overline{\omega} 2^{((\overline{\kappa}+1)/\overline{\kappa})} \Gamma(1/\overline{\kappa})} \quad \text{with} \quad \overline{\omega} = \left[\frac{2^{(-2/\overline{\kappa})} \Gamma(1/\overline{\kappa})}{\Gamma(3/\overline{\kappa})}\right]^{1/2},$$

where $\Gamma(\cdot)$ represents the gamma function

$$(3.36) \quad \Gamma(y) = \int_0^\infty \exp(-s)s^{y-1}ds, \quad y > 0.$$

The log-likelihood function is then given by (see Nelson 1991: 355):

$$(3.37) \quad LL = N\left\{\ln\left(\frac{\overline{\kappa}}{\overline{\omega}}\right) - \left(\frac{1+\overline{\kappa}}{\overline{\kappa}}\right)\ln(2) - \ln\left[\Gamma\left(\frac{1}{\overline{\kappa}}\right)\right]\right\} - \frac{1}{2}\sum_{t=1}^{N}\left|\frac{\varepsilon_t}{\overline{\kappa}\sqrt{h_t}}\right|^{\overline{\kappa}} - \frac{1}{2}\sum_{t=1}^{N}\ln(h_t).$$

The letter N denotes the number of observations. The procedure described in Berndt et al. (1974) is utilized to maximize the log-likelihood function over the set of structural parameters of the model.

3.2.3   Exchange Rate Data

To perform the volatility-based test for implicit price barriers in foreign exchange markets, I utilize daily spot rate quotes for the US dollar/deutsche mark (US/DM), the US dollar/yen (US/YEN), the deutsche mark/yen (DM/YEN), the US dollar/pound sterling (US/BP), and for the US dollar/Canadian dollar (US/CAN). The sample period covers eight years of spot trading in these markets and ranges from 2/1/1990 to 31/12/1997. The exceptional influences stemming from both the turmoil in foreign exchange markets during the so-called Asian crises and the preparations for the introduction of the euro in Europe led to the decision to exclude the year 1998 from the sample.

Table 3.1 provides information regarding the overall fluctuation range of the exchange rates observed over the sample period under investigation. The table further contains the respective number of exchange rate observations found in the three intervals around the potential implicit price barriers introduced in Section 3.2.1. The figures presented in the second column of the table show that roughly ⅓ of the observations can be found in the narrow interval (Interval 1) placed around the suspected implicit exchange rate thresholds. The figures summarized in the fourth column indicate that approximately ½ of the observations are an element of the widest interval (Interval 3) surrounding the potential implicit price barriers.

Before pushing on to present the results of the empirical study, I present some diagnostic statistics for the return series Δe_t in Table 3.2. The mean and the median of the series are approximately equal to zero. Furthermore, the returns data show a kurtosis larger than that implied by the normal distribution. The coefficient of skewness is approximately equal to zero for the DM/US returns and is very low for the CAN/US, the DM/YEN, and the BP/US returns series. Visual inspection of the YEN/US returns indicated that the slight negative skewness of the sample distribution of this time series can be attributed to a few influential outliers. To take account of these outliers, the day-of-the-week effect regressions in equation (3.27) were enriched in the case of YEN/US with a dummy variable forced to equal unity whenever the returns deviated more than four standard deviations from their sample mean. The results of conducting the portmanteau test developed by Ljung and Box (1978) provide no evidence for autocorrelation in the spot rate returns. However, the Lagrange multiplier tests formalized in Engle (1982) for ARCH effects in the squared returns series indicate that the null hypothesis of no conditional heteroskedasticity in second moments can be rejected at all commonly used significance levels. Both visual inspection of the autocorrelation and the partial autocorrelation functions of the

Table 3.1: Descriptive Statistics for the Levels of the Currency Pairs under Investigation

Currency pair	Interval 1	Interval 2	Interval 3	Maximum	Minimum	Observations
DM/US	672	887	1133	1.8822	1.3530	2088
US/DM	707	913	1171	0.7391	0.5313	2088
DM/YEN	475	658	877	0.0169	0.0104	2088
YEN/DM	617	839	1020	95.9360	59.3252	2088
US/YEN	572	756	956	0.0124	0.0063	2088
YEN/US	611	832	1034	159.6424	80.6322	2088
CAN/US	415	593	812	1.4395	1.1199	2088
US/CAN	271	426	627	0.8929	0.6947	2088
BP/US	494	671	890	0.7052	0.4983	2088
US/BP	631	841	1045	2.0067	1.4180	2088

Note: The column headed Interval 1 (Interval 2, Interval 3) presents for each currency pair the number of exchange rate realizations falling into the respective intervals around the potential implicit price triggers as defined in equation (3.29a) (equation (3.29b), equation (3.29c)).

Table 3.2: Diagnostic Statistics for the Returns of the Exchange Rates under Investigation

	DM/US	DM/YEN	YEN/US	CAN/US	BP/US
Mean	0.0000	0.0000	0.0000	0.0000	0.0000
Median	0.0150	−0.0074	0.0252	−0.0092	0.0098
Maximum	3.4939	3.4825	4.1958	1.2396	4.2407
Minimum	−3.5182	−3.6955	−5.4014	−1.4070	−3.3813
Std. deviation	0.6971	0.6745	0.6909	0.2701	0.6546
Skewness	0.0600	0.2310	−0.6790	0.1053	0.2499
Kurtosis	5.3385	5.1480	9.1740	5.2677	6.7227
Q(1)	0.0095	0.9679	2.5456	1.5963	0.0396
Q(4)	2.1715	3.0757	4.1076	2.1745	4.4636
ARCH(1)	18.5993	14.1517	9.2267	15.6835	10.8389
ARCH(4)	39.5799	3.0757	13.0390	2.1745	4.4636

Note: For a definition of exchange rate returns, see equation (3.31). Under the null of conditional homoskedasticity, the Ljung and Box (1978) $Q(k)$-statistic and the ARCH(k) test of Engle (1982) are asymptotically χ^2 distributed with k degrees of freedom.

squared series Δe_t^2 and tests for remaining ARCH effects in the residual series obtained by estimating the model suggested in equations (3.30) to (3.32) under the assumption that $p = q = 1$ indicated that a parsimonious GARCH(1,1) model suffices to account for the conditional heteroskedasticity in the daily exchange rate returns under investigation.

A final more institutional aspect which should be taken into consideration when specifying a model for the conditional volatility of BP/US returns is that the breakdown of the European Monetary System (EMS) in 1992 marked an important change in the exchange rate regime. Economically, this is equivalent to a change in the overall stance of monetary policy. As emphasized by Lastrapes (1989), neglecting such policy changes in setting up GARCH models implies that the variance equation is misspecified, resulting in a spuriously integrated conditional volatility process. To take this criticism into consideration, a dummy variable is included in the variance equations estimated to figure out the conditional volatility of BP/US and US/BP exchange rate returns. The dummy series assumes the value one before the EMS crisis and zero afterwards.

3.2.4 Conditional Exchange Rate Volatility and the Barriers Hypothesis

Table 3.3 presents the results of the volatility-based test for implicit price barriers in FX markets discussed above. The test is performed by analyzing whether or not conditional exchange rate volatility depends on the distance of the spot rate from the potential implicit price barriers. This issue is addressed by investigating the marginal significance of the coefficient δ in the variance equation of the empirical models employed to trace out the time-varying volatility of the spot rate returns under investigation.

The table presents the estimation results for three alternative models which differ from each other in the way the variable $dummy_i$, $i = 1,2,3$, is defined. Figures in parentheses below the estimated coefficients give the ratio of the respective parameters and their standard errors. For ease of exposition only, the dummy variable defined to account for the impact of the substantial widening of the EMS target zone on the volatility of the BP/US and the US/BP returns volatility is not presented in the table. The coefficient of the dummy series is significant in both cases.

Table 3.3 reveals that the coefficient δ is significant in the case of the US/BP and the CAN/US and borderline significant in the case of the DM/YEN and the US/CAN returns series. The coefficient of the trigger threshold dummy is insignificant in the frameworks estimated to model the conditional volatility of DM/US, YEN/US, and BP/US exchange rate returns. Furthermore, it can be seen in the table that the data provide only very weak evidence in favor of implicit trading triggers in the YEN/DM spot market. The respective barrier coefficient δ is significant at the 10 percent level only if the relatively narrow Interval 1 is used to define the neighborhood of potential trigger prices. The parameter is

Table 3.3: Implicit Price Barriers and Exchange Rate Volatility

	DM/US	US/DM	YEN/US	US/YEN	DM/YEN
	Model I: $dummy_1 = 1$ if $M_i \in \{1,...,15,85,...,100\}$ for $i = 1,...,N$ and zero otherwise				
ω	0.0030	0.0039	0.0093	0.0099	0.0092
	(1.5300)	(1.9403)	(2.1554)	(2.035)	(2.5134)
α	0.0347	0.0343	0.0327	0.00328	0.0521
	(4.2068)	(4.2621)	(3.5240)	(3.5038)	(4.8301)
β	0.9557	0.9586	0.9453	0.9453	0.9229
	(90.2120)	(94.5864)	(66.1831)	(60.9014)	(58.6352)
δ	*0.0056*	*−0.0007*	*0.0007*	*−0.0013*	*0.0112*
	(1.1664)	*(−0.3096)*	*(0.1998)*	*(−0.1192)*	*(1.7108)**
κ	1.1508	1.1535	1.1041	1.1040	1.2919
	(23.2827)	(22.8264)	(31.7439)	(31.7007)	(27.1536)
LL	−2044.61	−2045.21	−1945.97	−1945.99	−2019.35
	Model II: $dummy_2 = 1$ if $M_i \in \{1,...,20,80,...,100\}$ for $i = 1,...,N$ and zero otherwise				
ω	0.0029	0.0037	0.0089	0.0066	0.0090
	(1.3695)	(1.8879)	(2.2475)	(1.4363)	(2.2880)
α	0.0346	0.0346	0.0317	0.0301	0.05380
	(4.2025)	(4.2702)	(3.6460)	(3.6536)	(4.8329)
β	0.9566	0.9581	0.9485	0.9503	0.9212
	(92.47023)	(92.9112)	(68.1955)	(71.4675)	(56.9528)
δ	*0.0038*	*0.0001*	*−0.00001*	*0.0057*	*0.0091*
	(0.9802)	*(0.0420)*	*(−0.0046)*	*(0.5633)*	*(1.8113)**
κ	1.1512	1.1522	1.0623	1.0027	1.2937
	(23.2673)	(22.8879)	(31.0705)	(30.9069)	(26.8128)
LL	−2044.82	−2045.26	−1979.95	−1979.84	−2019.24
	Model III: $dummy_3 = 1$ if $M_i \in \{1,...,25,75,...,100\}$ for $i = 1,...,N$ and zero otherwise				
ω	0.0031	0.0039	0.010	0.0119	0.0087
	(1.2767)	(1.9267)	(2.3662)	(1.9258)	(2.1079)
α	0.0351	0.0343	0.0317	0.0331	0.05514
	(4.2691)	(4.2872)	(3.7014)	(3.6646)	(4.9002)
β	0.9570	0.9587	0.9485	0.9459	0.9200
	(92.9255)	(95.5949)	(69.5782)	(65.3708)	(56.7005)
δ	*0.0017*	*−0.0005*	*−0.0019*	*−0.0050*	*0.0074*
	(0.4762)	*(−0.2619)*	*(−0.6029)*	*(−0.5129)*	*(1.6720)**
κ	1.1521	1.1531	1.0621	1.0620	1.2943
	(23.2529)	(22.8698)	(31.2050)	(31.1439)	(26.5138)
LL	−2045.16	−2045.23	−1979.80	−1979.87	−2019.56

Table 3.3 continued

	YEN/DM	BP/US	US/BP	CAN/US	US/CAN
	Model I: $dummy_1 = 1$ if $M_i \in \{1,...,15,85,...,100\}$				
	for $i = 1,...,N$ and zero otherwise				
ω	0.0109	0.0019	0.0012	0.0006	0.0005
	(2.8328)	(1.82199)	(1.473)	(2.3839)	(2.0218)
α	0.0513	0.0374	0.0414	0.0408	0.0400
	(4.8843)	(4.4687)	(4.5009)	(4.7596)	(4.9023)
β	0.9295	0.9495	0.9473	0.9485	0.9526
	(60.4376)	(103.0950)	(90.1352)	(91.8329)	(100.540)
δ	–0.0058	0.0018	0.0059	0.0012	0.0010
	(–1.7298)*	(1.7614)	(1.9018)*	(2.0124)**	(1.7305)*
κ	1.2950	1.0484	1.0483	1.2119	1.2119
	(26.3836)	(24.5345)	(24.8164)	(26.0996)	(1.7305)
LL	–2019.74	–1779.66	–1778.32	–82.50	–83.89
	Model II: $dummy_2 = 1$ if $M_i \in \{1,...,20,80,...,100\}$				
	for $i = 1,...,N$ and zero otherwise				
ω	0.0111	0.00202	0.0016	0.0006	0.0004
	(2.8109)	(1.8487)	(1.3845)	(2.4270)	(1.9393)
α	0.0524	0.0378	0.0415	0.0408	0.0378
	(4.8776)	(4.4755)	(4.508)	(4.7436)	(4.7967)
β	0.9276	0.9544	0.9465	0.9473	0.9549
	(58.2437)	(101.6494)	(89.1968)	(88.9990)	(104.3984)
δ	–0.0039	0.0013	0.0053	0.0011	0.0008
	(–1.2634)	(0.8029)	(2.0181)**	(2.0954)**	(2.0317)**
κ	1.2923	1.0482	1.0486	1.2120	1.2133
	(26.8085)	(24.6037)	(24.7498)	(26.0722)	(26.2606)
LL	–2020.29	–1779.75	–1778.23	–82.20	–83.37
	Model III: $dummy_3 = 1$ if $M_i \in \{1,...,25,75,...,100\}$				
	for $i = 1,...,N$ and zero otherwise				
ω	0.0110	0.0021	0.0013	0.0006	0.0004
	(2.7520)	(1.8549)	(1.1214)	(2.4044)	(1.5861)
α	0.0530	0.0384	0.0422	0.0415	0.0389
	(4.8385)	(4.4744)	(4.501)	(4.7972)	(4.8847)
β	0.9256	0.9531	0.9447	0.9454	0.9544
	(56.3953)	(98.7271)	(87.3756)	(87.4032)	(102.9607)
δ	–0.0016	0.0015	0.0057	0.0011	0.0005
	(–0.5293)	(0.9159)	(2.3790)**	(2.3141)**	(1.7253)*
κ	1.2902	1.0485	1.0498	1.2139	1.2129
	(26.9747)	(24.5907)	(24.7717)	(25.9505)	(26.0205)
LL	–2020.85	–1779.65	–1777.51	–81.62	–84.19

Note: Figures in parentheses represent the ratio of the respective coefficient and its standard error. In the case of the coefficient δ, asterisks * (**) are utilized to denote significance at the 10 (5) percent level. The rows entitled *LL* give the maximized values of the log-likelihood function. The parameter δ captures the potential impact of implicit trading triggers on the conditional volatility of the exchange rate returns under investigation.

found to be insignificant in the competing models featuring wider bands around the suspected implicit price barriers. Thus, as regards the YEN/DM spot market, the results are rather sensitive to the concrete specification of the model and provide no strong support in favor of the barriers hypothesis.

The figures documented in Table 3.3 confirm the results of De Grauwe and Decupere (1992), who also find no clear-cut evidence for implicit price barriers in the US/DM exchange rate. Contrasting the findings of these authors, however, the results of this empirical study do not support the hypothesis of implicit barriers in the US/YEN spot rate, either.

In a nutshell, the results of the first volatility-based test for implicit price barriers in FX markets provide only rather weak support for the barriers hypothesis of the volatility smile implicit in foreign currency options. For many major exchange rates like, e.g., the US/DM and the US/YEN exchange rates, the traditional volatility-based test procedure fails to detect implicit trading triggers in FX markets. Given the fact that highly liquid options markets exist for these currencies and that smile and smirk effects typically can also be detected in the options contracts on these exchange rates, it seems that the noise-trading-induced barrier hypothesis of the smile does not help to explain the empirically observed pricing biases of the first-generation FX option pricing model. However, the results of an alternative volatility-based test for implicit trigger rates separating adjacent trading regimes in FX spot markets to be developed and implemented in the next section of this chapter cast doubt on this result.

Before proceeding with the economic interpretation of these results, it should be determined whether the estimated models provide an acceptable representation of the main features of exchange rate returns volatility. The outcomes of the various specification tests conducted are summarized in Table 3.4. For the sake of brevity, only the results for Model I are reported. Inspired by Nelson (1991: 361), the second, third, and fourth columns of the table have been reserved to present the results of three conditional-moments-based specification tests. The statistic M1 is used to test the null hypothesis that the estimated standardized residuals $\hat{\eta}_t$ have a mean of zero ($\mathbb{E}(\hat{\eta}_t) = 0$). Similarly, the figures presented in the column headed M2 summarize the findings of tests of the null hypothesis that the variance of the scaled residuals is not significantly different from unity ($\mathbb{E}(\hat{\eta}_t^2) = 1$). The intention behind the third test M3 is to check whether the standardized residuals are symmetrically distributed as required by the generalized error distribution ($\mathbb{E}(\hat{\eta}_t^3 / \sigma_{\hat{\eta}_t}^3) = 0$). The marginal significance levels reported below the respective test statistics indicate that for all currencies investigated, the null hypotheses of these misspecification tests cannot be rejected. To further challenge the estimated models for exchange rate

Table 3.4: Diagnostic Statistics for the Models of Implicit Price Barriers and Exchange Rate Volatility (Model I)

Currency pair	M1	M2	M3	ARCH(4)	Q(4)	KS
DM/US	−0.2011	2084.006	−0.3265	3.8740	2.3290	0.7668
	(−0.2011)	(0.4980)	(0.7441)	(0.4233)	(0.6755)	
US/DM	0.1608	2082.295	0.0985	3.4642	2.2871	0.7481
	(0.8722)	(0.4874)	(0.9216)	(0.4833)	(0.6831)	
YEN/US	−0.2915	2136.946	−0.0363	0.3137	2.2271	1.1760
	(0.7707)	(0.2095)	(0.9710)	(0.9889)	(0.6941)	
US/YEN	0.2955	2136.739	0.0320	0.3209	2.2517	1.1759
	(0.7676)	(0.2104)	(0.9745)	(0.9884)	(0.6896)	
DM/YEN	−0.177	2093.507	1.3033	7.3830	1.8365	1.3306
	(0.8592)	(0.4436)	(0.1926)	(0.1170)	(0.7658)	
YEN/DM	0.3136	2091.135	−1.1263	7.3624	1.2849	1.3377
	(0.7539)	(0.4581)	(0.2602)	(0.1179)	(0.8639)	
BP/US	−0.7108	2072.90	0.5282	2.6822	4.8099	1.2591
	(0.4773)	(0.4296)	(0.5974)	(0.6123)	(0.3074)	
US/BP	0.6867	2077.134	−0.5810	0.905	3.7829	1.2523
	(0.4923)	(0.4556)	(0.5613)	(0.9238)	(0.4361)	
CAN/US	−0.2606	2106.708	0.7549	3.0789	4.3408	1.9596
	(0.7944)	(0.3649)	(0.4504)	(0.3618)	(0.5447)	
US/CAN	0.2890	2107.399	−0.6495	4.1536	3.7040	1.9596
	(0.7726)	(0.3609)	(0.5161)	(0.3856)	(0.4476)	

Note: M1, M2, and M3 denote moment-based specification tests explained in the text (p. 94). ARCH(4) and LM(4) are Lagrange multiplier tests for remaining autocorrelation and ARCH effects in the standardized and the squared standardized residuals, respectively. Figures in parentheses represent marginal significance levels. The Kolmogorov–Smirnov statistic is presented in the column headed KS. Benchmark critical values for the Kolmogorov–Smirnov test under the assumption that the parameters of the distribution function under the null hypothesis are known are 1.22, 1.36, and 1.63 at the 10 (5, 1) percent significance level (see, e.g., DeGroot 1989).

returns, the fifth and sixth columns of Table 3.4 present the outcomes of tests for remaining autocorrelation and ARCH effects in the standardized and squared standardized residuals, respectively. As was the case with the moments-based specification tests, the results provide support for the proposed setups.

As a further test, the Kolmogorov–Smirnov statistic defined as the maximum of the absolute distance between the cumulative distribution functions of the fitted GED densities of the GARCH models (obtained by numerical integration) and the sample distribution of the standardized residuals weighted with the square root of the number of observations was computed (see, e.g., DeGroot (1989) for further comments on the KS test). Critical values (reported in the note to Table 3.4) for this test are available for the case that the parameters of the distribution function prevailing under the null hypothesis are known. As the parameter governing the thickness of the tails of the GED density assumed to describe the innovation term of the GARCH models was estimated, these critical values should not be taken literally but should be used as a first benchmark providing an impression of the overall fit of the model.

All in all, the results of the Kolmogorov–Smirnov test indicate that the model provides, at least for my purposes, a fairly acceptable representation of the distribution of the scaled residuals.[51] A remarkable exception arises in the case of the returns of the Canadian dollar/US dollar parity. However, in view of the magnitude of the estimated tail parameter, $\bar{\kappa}$, I suspected that the high values of the KS tests do not reflect a mismatch in the tails of the distributions of the scaled residuals and the estimated GED densities. This impression is confirmed by Figure 3.6, which compares the sample (F(x)_NRESIDS) with the estimated (F(x)_GED) cumulative distribution function of the standardized residuals (labeled NRESIDS_CANUS) for the CAN/US exchange rate. Eyeballing the graph reveals that the most pronounced differences between the sample and the estimated distribution function occur when the standardized residuals assume moderately negative numerical values. This suggests that, despite the high KS test result, the model still provides a reasonable characterization of the fat-tails property of daily CAN/US and US/CAN exchange rate returns. For this reason and in view of the fact that the other specification tests support the estimated models, I decided to stick to the relatively simple GARCH models as a tool to model the conditional volatility of the CAN/US exchange rate returns.

Finally, the maximized log-likelihood function of the above GARCH models have been compared with the log-likelihoods obtained under an integrated (I) GARCH restriction. The motivation to carry out this exercise was the observation that the figures provided in Table 3.4 indicate that the sum of α and β typically lies in the vicinity of unity, implying that exchange rate returns volatility is highly persistent. This finding might be interpreted to suggest that an IGARCH model in which the ARCH and the GARCH terms sum up to unity, so that conditional volatility exhibits a unit root, could be an alternative framework to capture the variability of exchange rate returns. The respective likelihood ratios, however, indicated that the baseline GARCH models are superior to their integrated alternatives. This result further corroborates the impression obtained

---

[51] Though beyond the scope of the present section, further insights into the ability of the GED assumption to accurately account for the shape of the respective exchange rate returns distributions could be obtained by comparing the results reported in Table 3.5 with KS test results obtained for competing models relying on alternative distributional assumptions. In the context of the modeling of returns of financial market prices, examples of model selection strategies involving this criterion can be found in, e.g., Mittnik and Rachev (1993) and Paolella (1999).

Figure 3.6: Actual versus Fitted Cumulative Distribution Function for the Standardized Residuals of the CAN/US Returns

by implementing and interpreting the results of the other specification tests, namely that the GARCH frameworks provide an acceptable representation of conditional exchange rate volatility.

Taken together, the findings of the empirical analyses indicate that the data provide some weak support for the barriers hypothesis in the case of the DM/YEN, the US/BP, and the CAN/US exchange rates. As regards the US/DM and the US/YEN spot markets, the results of the volatility-based test for implicit price barriers do not serve to support the notion that trading-induced implicit price barriers exist at the spot rate levels suspected to hold special significance for market participants in this empirical study. These findings, of course, do not allow one to reject the barriers hypothesis of the volatility smile per se. Indeed, the empirical findings only imply that such implicit price barriers presumably do not exist at the grid of trigger thresholds defined in Section 3.2.1. It would, therefore, not conflict with the results of the empirical study outlined above if a researcher or a practitioner claimed that trading-induced implicit price barriers might show up when spot rates reach other critical levels holding special significance for market participants. To examine this possibility in more detail, the next section is devoted to the development and the implementation of additional volatility-based tests for implicit price barriers and adjacent trading regimes in real-world foreign exchange markets.

3.3   Technical FX Trading and the Barrier-Smile Hypothesis: A Rival Empirical Model

The crucial step in setting up the volatility-based test for implicit trading triggers discussed in the preceding section is the identification of a certain set of exchange rates assumed to hold special significance for market participants involved in the spot trading of foreign exchange. The identification scheme advanced by Donaldson and Kim (1993), De Grauwe and Decupere (1992), and, in a modified version, also by Cyree et al. (1999) allows one to test whether or not such trading thresholds tend to show up whenever exchange rates reach certain rounded numbers. These spot rate values define a grid of critical exchange rate realizations. The position of the current exchange rate relative to the nearest elements of this grid is then used to identify the neighborhood of potential implicit trading thresholds in FX markets. As this implies that the procedure identifies an implicit trading trigger only if it coincides with one of the components of the prespecified set of critical exchange rate realizations, the test does not help to identify trading triggers not contained in this set. Thus, if the test routine fails to detect trading triggers in real-world exchange rate time series, this leaves open the possibility that such spot rate realizations that hold special significance for a nonnegligible fraction of market participants may show up whenever the exchange rate crosses other critical trading triggers not ending in a round number. Therefore, before offering a definitive answer to the question of whether or not the noise trading approach to the volatility smile implicit in foreign currency options provides an empirically valid description of the trading process taking place in actual spot FX markets, tests built on alternative identification schemes for potential trading triggers should be implemented. This impression is further corroborated by the fact that the volatility-based test for implicit trading triggers in FX markets employed in the previous section does not allow the researcher to take into consideration the current strength or weakness of a currency measured by the position of the prevailing exchange rate relative to a medium- or longer-term trend characterizing the spot rate path. Scrutinizing the trading rules surveyed in the literature on technical financial market analyses (see, e.g., Pring 1990) suggests that the relative strength of a currency may be important for noise traders trying to extract buy or sell signals by confronting the current spot rate with medium-term swings in the value of a domestic or foreign currency.

These observations motivate the design and the implementation of a modified test for implicit price barriers in spot FX markets separating adjacent trading regimes. As was the case with the modeling approach taken in Section 3.2, the alternative test routine exploits the prediction of the noise trader model outlined in Section 3.1, namely that the instantaneous volatility of the exchange rate increases (decreases) as the distance of the current spot rate from a destabilizing (stabilizing) trading trigger shrinks. Three steps are necessary to construct a quantitative research strategy which allows one to examine whether actual exchange rate time series data support this prediction of the theoretical model. In a first step, a benchmark rate is defined which can be utilized to gauge the position of the current spot rate relative to a medium-term target value used by noise traders. In a second step, it is assumed that the propensity of trend-based mechanical traders to enter the spot market tends to increase as the absolute gap between the current spot rate from its benchmark representation widens. Note that this assumption is also in line with the model of exchange rate determination discussed in Section 3.1. In a third and final step, the empirical validity of this presupposition is tested. An alternative test for implicit trading regimes in FX markets is used to examine whether the level of the instantaneous volatility of the spot rate is higher whenever the deviation of the exchange rate from its target level exceeds certain critical threshold levels. Formally paralleling the research strategy adopted in Section 3.1, these thresholds define the neighborhood of an implicit price barrier.

While the trailing-digits-based test for implicit trading triggers utilized a grid of critical exchange rate levels to define the neighborhood of an implicit price barrier, the test presented in Section 3.3.1 accomplishes this task by measuring the absolute distance between the current spot rate and its moving average representation. As further detailed in Section 3.3.1, this latter convention reflects on the assumption made in the theoretical part of this chapter that noise traders only enter or exit the market for domestic assets whenever the exchange rate reaches certain discretely spaced trigger rates. Taking the perspective of technical traders, these trigger rates indicate that the domestic currency is sufficiently weak (strong) as compared to a medium- or longer-term target value, e_0. In the context of the empirical work contained in this section, this latter reference value is represented by the moving average representations of the respective spot rate series.

As the distance of the prevailing spot rate from the rolling moving average of its past realizations is employed as a benchmark to assess the relative strength of a currency, the volatility-based empirical testing technique for implicit trading ranges in FX markets adopted in the following sections combines elements of both filter and moving-average-based investment rules.[52] This research strategy is motivated by observations made, for example, by Allen and Taylor (1992),

---

[52] Comprehensive descriptions of alternative strategies belonging to the toolkit of technical traders can be found in Feeny (1989), Dunis (1989), Geiger (1996: Chapter 4), Pring (1990), or Rosenberg (1996).

who report that many traders involved in FX trading extract buy and sell signals from historical spot rate series by implementing moving-average-based investment strategies. Moreover, moving-average-based trading investment strategies have also been used in a number of empirical studies examining the profitability of technical trading rules. For example, a technical trading rule similar to the one adopted in this section has been utilized by Kho (1996). This author has tested the profitability of a technical trading rule which combines a moving-average trading rule with a filter band symmetrically placed around the historical average of price realizations for trading signals to be executed.[53]

Complementary research strategies are employed to implement the alternative tests for implicit price barriers in FX markets. In a first step, the exchange rate data and the empirical model already utilized in Section 3.2 are adopted to estimate a GARCH model allowing to trace out a time-varying conditional exchange rate volatility. The variance equation of this model is enriched with a dummy variable capturing whether the deviation of the current spot rate from its uncentered historical moving average exceeds a critical threshold level. The significance and the sign of this dummy variable allow to draw conclusions regarding the impact of discretely spaced market entry and exit thresholds of technical FX noise traders on the volatility of freely floating exchange rates. This research strategy closely resembles the approach already utilized in Section 3.2. In a second step, the state-contingent noise trader dummy variables are utilized to set up a distribution-free nonparametric test and a kernel density regression model which allow the robustness of the GARCH-model-based inference on implicit trading regimes in FX markets to be assessed. I also estimate vector autoregressive systems of simultaneous equations which have the advantage that they do not depend upon the specific definition chosen for the trading regime dummies and, thus, render it possible to further explore the robustness and validity of the empirical results derived in this chapter.

The empirical analysis conducted in this section is structured as follows: Section 3.3.1 is utilized to introduce an alternative quantitative framework of implicit trading triggers and implicit trading regimes in FX markets. The results of the estimation of augmented GARCH models permitting one to control for the effect of implicit trading thresholds on conditional exchange rate volatility are documented and interpreted in Section 3.3.2. In Section 3.3.3, nonparametric testing routines and vector autoregressive systems are implemented to asses the

---

[53]   For more evidence on the profitability of technical FX trading strategies, see, e.g., Levich and Thomas (1993), Neely et al. (1997), Chang and Osler (1999), Szakmary and Mathur (1997) and the references to earlier studies cited therein. For recent empirical evidence challenging the results reported in some of the papers contributing to this strand of research, see, e.g., LeBaron (1999).

robustness of the GARCH-based evidence on implicit noise-trading-induced adjacent trading and volatility regimes in foreign exchange spot markets.

3.3.1 Mechanical Trading and Implicit Trading Regimes in FX Markets

A core feature of the empirical model constructed in Section 3.2 to quantitatively substantiate the impact of noise trading on the dynamics of the conditional volatility of exchange rates is the set of dummy variables introduced in equation (3.29). These dummy variables served to indicate whether or not the spot rate observed in period t has settled in the neighborhood of an implicit price barrier. Implicit price barriers were allowed to occur at exchange rate realizations ending in a round number. The volatility-based test for implicit trading thresholds to be developed in this section also relies on a set of dummy variables to identify implicit trading regimes in spot markets for foreign exchange and to recover their impact on the conditional variability of exchange rates. As compared to the traditional volatility-based test for implicit price barriers in FX markets, however, the dummy variables employed in the subsequent empirical analyses are defined in a very different way.

The economic reasoning underlying the definition of the regime dummies utilized in the alternative volatility-based test for implicit trading regimes in FX markets can best be elucidated by recalling the state-contingent investment mechanism employed by noise traders in the model of exchange rate determination outlined in Section 3.1. It was argued in the theoretical study that noise traders, who were assumed to be not aware of the actual stochastic process driving economic fundamentals, evaluate the relative strength of the domestic currency by comparing the prevailing spot rate with a medium- or longer-term target value, e_0. Following Frenkel (1997), fundamentalists or trend-chasing chartists were assumed to enter (to exit) the spot market for foreign exchange when the domestic currency has depreciated or appreciated by a sufficient amount. When the gap between the current exchange rate and this (subjective) target value becomes large enough, noise traders begin to trade foreign exchange and the economy passes into another trading regime. Rational agents anticipate the change in the structure of the spot FX market taking place at the market entry and exit thresholds of technical traders and this, in turn, implies that the instantaneous volatility of exchange rates tends to rise (to decline) as the exchange rate reaches the destabilizing (stabilizing) trigger rates at which noise traders start to submit buy or sell orders.

In order to translate these theoretical considerations into an empirically testable quantitative model, it is necessary to introduce a formal concept of medium- or longer-term reference levels of exchange rates employed by noise traders to evaluate the relative strength of the domestic currency. Several alternative models which could be used to accomplish this task have been discussed in the branch of the international finance literature examining technical trading rules commonly used by practitioners in FX markets (see footnote 53 for references). A simple class of asset allocation techniques described in this literature extracts trading signals by comparing the current spot rate to a moving average of past prices. As this type of trading strategies is in line with the investment rules assumed in the theoretical model of Section 3.1 to characterize the position taking of noise traders, the moving average representation is also used in this empirical study to figure out the medium-term target value of the exchange rate employed by noise traders to assess the relative strength of the domestic currency.

In the context of the noise trader model of exchange rate determination outlined above, this definition of a reference spot rate implies that in the case of a two-sided destabilizing noise trading strategy the instantaneous volatility of the exchange rate should tend to rise as the absolute deviation of the current spot rate from its moving average representation starts to increase. This line of argumentation suggests that an alternative strategy to discriminate between different volatility regimes is to enrich the variance equation of a standard GARCH (p,q) model with a dummy variable which assumes the value zero whenever the current exchange rate can be found in the neighborhood of its moving average and the value one otherwise:

$$(3.38) \quad h_t = \omega + \sum_{i=1}^{p} \alpha_{p,i}\, u_{t-i}^2 + \sum_{i=1}^{q} \beta_{q,i}\, h_{t-i} + \delta\, dummy_{i,t}.$$

The difference between equation (3.38) and the specification of the conditional variance equation (3.34) used in the GARCH model set up in Section 3.2 lies in the definition of the dummy variable $dummy_{i,t}$. The dummy variable added to the variance equation of the GARCH models estimated in the previous section assumed the value one if and only if the current exchange rate could be found in the neighborhood of an implicit price barrier identified by the last trailing digits of the observed spot rate. The dummy variable utilized in the augmented conditional variance equation (3.38), in contrast, assumes the value one whenever the current exchange rate, E_t, tends to leave the vicinity of its moving average $MA_{t,i}$ of length i at time t. To further operationalize this latter concept, it is assumed that the exchange rate has left the "neighborhood" of the moving average of past exchange rates whenever the absolute distance between the current exchange rate and its moving average $|E_t - MA_{t,i}|$ exceeds a certain critical threshold level obtained by multiplying the historical maximum of $|E_t - MA_{t,i}|$ with a scaling factor $0 < \vartheta < 1$. The dummy variable $dummy_{i,t}$ is thus defined as follows:

$$(3.39) \quad dummy_{i,t} = \begin{cases} 1 & \text{if } |E_t - MA_{t,i}| > \vartheta \times \max|E_t - MA_{t,i}| \\ 0 & \text{otherwise} \end{cases},$$

where the uncentered historical moving average $MA_{t,i}$ of length i at time t of the exchange rates under investigation is computed as

$$(3.40) \quad MA_{t,i} = \frac{1}{i} \sum_{n=0}^{i-1} E_{t-n}.$$

The robustness of the results of the following empirical study with respect to both the numerical value assigned to the arbitrary scaling factor ϑ and the arbitrary lag-length used to compute the moving averages of the exchange rate series is assessed by considering three alternative specifications for each of these parameters:

$$(3.41) \quad \vartheta \in \{0.15, 0.2, 0.25\}, \qquad i \in \{50, 100, 150\}$$

The set of lag lengths i employed to compute $MA_{t,i}$ series implies that historical moving averages of spot rates computed for rolling time-windows of approximately one, two, and three quarters of a trading year are utilized in the current empirical examination. The specific numerical values chosen for the scaling factor allow one to check whether the results of the volatility-based test for implicit trading regimes in FX markets depend upon the width of the exchange rate fluctuation range used to define the neighborhood of the moving average representation. The three alternative realizations of ϑ given in equation (3.41) define a narrow, a medium-sized, and a wide interval around the moving averages of the respective spot rates. The summary statistics given in Table 3.5 indicate that for all currencies in the sample approximately one-third (one-half) of the exchange rate realizations can be found in the narrow (broad) interval placed around the uncentered historical moving average of the spot rates.

Table 3.5: Alternative Moving Average Specifications and the Number of Realizations in the Trading Regimes under Different Threshold Assumptions

Currency pair	MA_{50} -target value			MA_{100} -target value			MA_{150} -target value		
	Interval 1	Interval 2	Interval 3	Interval 1	Interval 2	Interval 3	Interval 1	Interval 2	Interval 3
DM/US	1143	857	625	1240	1011	842	1301	1126	983
US/DM	1155	876	633	1293	1047	876	1329	1159	1028
DM/YEN	1223	1016	843	1125	944	809	1081	895	735
YEN/DM	1244	1044	885	1166	984	856	1143	976	844
YEN/US	1031	759	560	1106	823	578	1121	849	670
US/YEN	742	449	281	845	567	359	1002	693	546
CAN/US	1093	879	688	1098	892	745	1147	973	816
US/CAN	1041	797	611	1072	858	701	1129	907	751
BP/US	731	472	312	737	547	405	771	587	495
US/BP	690	479	332	700	530	420	732	584	501

Note: The columns headed Interval 1 (Interval 2, Interval 3) depict for each currency pair the number of exchange rate realizations falling into the respective fluctuation ranges around the uncentered historical moving average defined in equation (3.41).

3.3.2   Implicit Trading Regimes and the Dynamics of Conditional Exchange Rate Volatility

The volatility-based test for implicit trading regimes in FX markets developed in Section 3.3.1 was implemented by fitting parsimonious GARCH(1,1) models with error terms sampled from a generalized error distribution with mean zero and unit variance to the exchange rate time series already used to set up the test routine for implicit trading triggers in financial markets outlined in Section 3.2. The conditional variance equations of the estimated GARCH models were augmented by including the trading regime dummy variables formalized in equation (3.39). Before the GARCH models were estimated, day-of-the-week regressions were run for all spot rate returns series under investigation. As in Section 3.2, the conditional variance equations of the models specified for the US/BP and the BP/US spot rate returns were enriched with an additional dummy variable to account for the shift in the exchange rate regime which has taken place in the summer of 1992 due to the breakdown of the EMS. The marginal significance and the sign of the coefficient δ indicate whether implicit trading regimes can be detected in actual FX markets and, if so, whether the existence of such implicit trading ranges tends to dampen or to inflate conditional exchange rate volatility.

Tables 3.6 to 3.8 give the results of the alternative volatility-based test for implicit trading regimes in FX markets. The estimates depicted in Table 3.6 were obtained by setting the time window used to compute uncentered historical moving averages of the exchange rates under investigation to $i = 150$. Table 3.7 reports the corresponding results obtained for $i = 50$ and Table 3.8 documents the estimates computed by setting $i = 100$. In each table, estimates for three models differing in the scaling factor ϑ employed to place symmetric trading regime bands around the respective $MA_{t,i}$ representations are presented.[54] Figures in parentheses below the estimated coefficients give the ratio of the respective parameters and their standard errors.[55]

The test results reported in the tables reveal that the coefficient δ of the trading regime dummy is significant at conventionally utilized significance

---

[54] Since market participants trade on the exchange rate and not on the logarithm of this asset price, I did not take the logarithm of the respective exchange rates to compute the trading strategy dummies. The average correlation between the state-contingent dummy variables defined for a currency pair and the corresponding reversed currency pair assumes a numerical value of roughly 0.85–0.9. Therefore, the models estimated to trace out the impact of implicit trading regimes on the conditional volatility of an exchange rate and the respective exchange rate in reversed notation will be similar to each other. To retain the analogy to the analyses presented in Section 3.2 and to obtain a first impression of the robustness of the results with respect to perturbations to the trading regime dummies, however, both sides of the "medal" were considered so that the tables provide, for example, estimates obtained for both DM/US and US/DM.

[55] I also compared the nominal with the empirical size of the test of the null hypothesis $\delta = 0$. To this end, the following Monte Carlo simulation experiment was performed. In a first step, an easy-to-simulate simple ARCH(1) process consisting of 2100 data points and with conditional variance equation $h_t = \omega + \alpha u_{t-1}^2$ and with a normally distributed error term was simulated 5000 times. The parameter ω was set equal to 0.01 and the autoregressive coefficient was fixed at 0.9. In a second step, an ARCH(1) model with a variance equation also containing a noise trading regime dummy variable $(h_t = \omega + \alpha u_{t-1}^2 + \delta \, dummy_t)$ was estimated for each returns series generated in the first step. In a final step, the sampling distribution of δ was used to test the null hypothesis that this coefficient is not significantly different from zero. Focusing attention on the intermediate model with $\vartheta = 0.2$ and $MA_{t,100}$, it turned out that the coefficient δ was significantly different from zero in almost 4 percent of the simulations at the 1 percent and in roughly 12 percent of the simulations at the 5 percent marginal significance level. Though derived for a simple ARCH(1) model, these results suggest that, when interpreting the figures presented in the tables, one should keep in mind that, when using sampling distributions, it might be necessary to adjust the significance levels assigned to the coefficients δ of the various estimated models slightly downward. As indicated by the figures shown in the tables (and further corroborated by the results of the robustness checks outlined below), however, such an adjustment should not affect the main economic conclusions derived from the empirical work discussed in this section.

Table 3.6: Implicit Trading Triggers and Exchange Rate Volatility (MA_{150} representation)

	DM/US	US/DM	YEN/US	US/YEN	DM/YEN
	\multicolumn{5}{c}{Model I: $dummy_1 = 1$ if}				
	\multicolumn{5}{c}{$\left| E_t - MA_{t,150} \right| > 0.15 \times \max \left| E_t - MA_{t,150} \right|$ and zero otherwise}				
ω	0.0028	0.0024	0.0084	0.0088	0.0127
	(1.4660)	(1.1970)	(2.3362)	(2.3486)	(2.7892)
α	0.0320	0.0328	0.0318	0.0321	0.0595
	(4.1135)	(4.1922)	(3.4793)	(3.4127)	(4.4671)
β	0.9564	0.9570	0.9382	0.9402	0.8996
	(92.8583)	(95.5730)	(57.9131)	(57.3040)	(42.8306)
δ	*0.0045*	*0.0041*	*0.0081*	*0.0064*	*0.0112*
	(1.7389)*	*(1.7604)**	*(2.1542)***	*(1.7792)**	*(2.3712)***
$\bar{\kappa}$	1.1601	1.1601	1.1150	1.1157	1.3014
	(22.4218)	(22.4041)	(31.2433)	(30.9980)	(24.6552)
LL	−1914.91	−1915.10	−1809.75	−1810.75	−1867.79
	\multicolumn{5}{c}{Model II: $dummy_2 = 1$ if}				
	\multicolumn{5}{c}{$\left| E_t - MA_{t,150} \right| > 0.2 \times \max \left| E_t - MA_{t,150} \right|$ and zero otherwise}				
ω	0.0035	0.0031	0.0101	0.1638	0.0013
	(1.7311)	(1.5811)	(2.4736)	(2.884)	(2.9156)
α	0.0312	0.0317	0.0294	0.0525	0.0571
	(4.0267)	(4.0809)	(3.2741)	(1.5422)	(4.4754)
β	0.9555	0.9564	0.9381	0.4484	0.9040
	(89.8932)	(92.9249)	(54.1610)	(2.5052)	(43.6609)
δ	*0.0054*	*0.0048*	*0.0095*	*0.1617*	*0.0105*
	(1.8675)*	*(1.7957)**	*(2.1541)***	*(2.8086)***	*(2.0639)***
$\bar{\kappa}$	1.1603	1.1605	1.1186	1.1062	1.2945
	(22.4485)	(22.4024)	(30.9620)	(32.3067)	(25.5019)
LL	−1914.41	−1914.70	−1809.04	−1812.80	−1867.94
	\multicolumn{5}{c}{Model III: $dummy_3 = 1$ if}				
	\multicolumn{5}{c}{$\left| E_t - MA_{t,150} \right| > 0.25 \times \max \left| E_t - MA_{t,150} \right|$ and zero otherwise}				
ω	0.0037	0.0037	0.0107	0.0108	0.1212
	(1.8855)	(1.7862)	(2.4336)	(2.3930)	(2.8613)
α	0.0292	0.0315	0.0292	0.0306	0.0533
	(3.8900)	(4.0028)	(3.1980)	(3.2490)	(4.4700)
β	0.9572	0.9557	0.9389	0.9392	0.9127
	(94.7138)	(89.9015)	(52.2476)	(0.0180)	(48.0659)
δ	*0.0061*	*0.0051*	*0.0093*	*0.0084*	*0.0097*
	(2.0736)**	*(1.8407)**	*(1.9605)***	*(1.7012)**	*(1.8768)**
$\bar{\kappa}$	1.1619	1.1610	1.1196	1.1181	1.2908
	(22.4846)	(22.3778)	(30.6345)	(30.4376)	(26.3769)
LL	−1913.71	−1914.54	−1809.63	−1810.52	−18867.88

Table 3.6 continued

	YEN/DM	BP/US	US/BP	CAN/US	US/CAN
	Model I: $dummy_1 = 1$ if $\left|E_t - MA_{t,150}\right| > 0.15 \times \max\left|E_t - MA_{t,150}\right|$ and zero otherwise				
ω	0.0152	0.0013	0.0013	0.0007	0.0002
	(2.9841)	(1.3683)	(1.4305)	(1.1267)	(1.0076)
α	0.0636	0.0295	0.0270	0.0183	0.0241
	(4.3467)	(4.0109)	(3.8733)	(3.3861)	(3.9273)
β	0.8806	0.9598	0.9633	0.9683	0.9644
	(36.8083)	(114.1862)	(123.0489)	(149.8093)	(131.1657)
δ	*0.0180*	*0.0071*	*0.0077*	*0.0014*	*0.0012*
	(3.0724)***	*(2.8182)****	*(2.8597)****	*(4.2952)****	*(3.7978)****
$\bar{\kappa}$	1.3074	1.0553	1.0561	1.2314	1.2258
	(24.6182)	(23.2366)	(23.1831)	(24.9680)	(25.1486)
LL	−1865.97	−1663.71	−1663.79	−69.39	−72.03
	Model II: $dummy_2 = 1$ if $\left|E_t - MA_{t,150}\right| > 0.2 \times \max\left|E_t - MA_{t,150}\right|$ and zero otherwise				
ω	0.0154	0.0019	0.0022	0.0004	0.0004
	(3.1330)	(1.7918)	(2.0195)	(2.4180)	(2.0443)
α	0.0585	0.0306	0.0294	0.0222	0.0222
	(4.3397)	(3.9590)	(3.8608)	(3.5346)	(3.5885)
β	0.8907	0.9588	0.9593	0.9600	0.9633
	(38.9050)	(108.6527)	(108.7760)	(120.1887)	(130.4105)
δ	*0.0162*	*0.0079*	*0.0095*	*0.0018*	*0.0016*
	(2.6374)***	*(2.5334)***	*(2.6168)****	*(3.7633)****	*(3.7429)****
$\bar{\kappa}$	1.2994	1.0551	1.0570	1.2289	1.2285
	(25.8737)	(23.3028)	(23.2704)	(25.3548)	(25.0980)
LL	−1865.91	−1664.61	−1664.34	−67.94	−69.99
	Model III: $dummy_3 = 1$ if $\left|E_t - MA_{t,150}\right| > 0.25 \times \max\left|E_t - MA_{t,150}\right|$ and zero otherwise				
ω	0.0138	0.0024	0.0025	0.0006	0.0005
	(2.9876)	(2.1027)	(2.1524)	(2.6278)	(2.3594)
α	0.0530	0.0303	0.0307	0.0258	0.0269
	(4.3106)	(3.8505)	(3.8545)	(3.7209)	(3.8708)
β	0.9051	0.9579	0.9569	0.9554	0.9581
	(43.6770)	(104.2100)	(101.5585)	(110.1607)	(115.1439)
δ	*0.0131*	*0.0097*	*0.0110*	*0.0022*	*0.0018*
	(2.3389)**	*(2.4775)***	*(2.5714)***	*(3.7141)****	*(3.4522)****
$\bar{\kappa}$	1.2957	1.0568	1.0573	1.2281	1.2260
	(26.4159)	(23.2569)	(23.2649)	(25.4257)	(25.3448)
LL	−1866.32	−1664.62	−1664.18	−68.22	−70.39

Note: Figures in parentheses represent the ratio of the respective coefficient and its standard error. In the case of the coefficient δ, asterisks * (**, ***) are utilized to denote significance at the 10 (5, 1) percent level. The rows entitled *LL* give the maximized values of the log-likelihood function. The parameter δ captures the potential impact of implicit trading triggers on the conditional volatility of the exchange rate returns under investigation.

Table 3.7: Implicit Trading Triggers and Exchange Rate Volatility (MA_{50} representation)

	DM/US	US/DM	YEN/US	US/YEN	DM/YEN
	Model I: $dummy_1 = 1$ if $\left\| E_t - MA_{t,50} \right\| > 0.15 \times \max \left\| E_t - MA_{t,50} \right\|$ and zero otherwise				
ω	0.0012	0.0010	0.0077	0.0103	0.0134
	(0.8038)	(0.6307)	(2.5067)	(2.7660)	(2.6902)
α	0.0254	0.0264	0.0192	0.0165	0.0490
	(3.5307)	(3.5870)	(2.5734)	(2.0396)	(3.8548)
β	0.9633	0.9635	0.9391	0.9388	0.8764
	(102.2442)	(103.1325)	(64.0823)	(57.6647)	(33.9104)
δ	*0.0075*	*0.0068*	*0.0214*	*0.0257*	*0.0341*
	(2.1872)**	*(1.9360)**	*(3.9374)****	*(3.8317)****	*(3.7959)****
$\bar{\kappa}$	1.1580	1.1574	1.1283	1.1391	1.3247
	(22.6556)	(22.5995)	(31.1339)	(29.8199)	(24.0166)
LL	−1914.14	−1914.78	−1799.52	−1799.10	−1859.17
	Model II: $dummy_2 = 1$ if $\left\| E_t - MA_{t,50} \right\| > 0.2 \times \max \left\| E_t - MA_{t,50} \right\|$ and zero otherwise				
ω	0.0032	0.0022	0.0115	0.0145	0.0175
	(1.8441)	(1.2569)	(2.8800)	(3.3939)	(3.0832)
α	0.0213	0.0249	0.0220	0.0180	0.0467
	(2.9965)	(3.4008)	(2.6810)	(2.0737)	(3.7643)
β	0.9596	0.9625	0.9325	0.9291	0.8738
	(95.9089)	(100.7980)	(55.9807)	(54.6486)	(32.6874)
δ	*0.0143*	*0.0091*	*0.0246*	*0.0411*	*0.0382*
	(2.9462)***	*(2.3240)***	*(3.3101)****	*(3.9237)****	*(3.8736)****
$\bar{\kappa}$	1.1641	1.1609	1.1199	1.14502	1.3249
	(22.6894)	(22.4674)	(32.4735)	(28.6904)	(24.2029)
LL	−1910.47	−1913.69	−1802.25	−1797.83	−1856.57
	Model III: $dummy_3 = 1$ if $\left\| E_t - MA_{t,50} \right\| > 0.25 \times \max \left\| E_t - MA_{t,50} \right\|$ and zero otherwise				
ω	0.0050	0.0039	0.0108	0.0140	0.0218
	(2.6194)	(2.2285)	(2.9287)	(3.3393)	(3.3644)
α	0.0193	0.0192	0.0198	0.0197	0.4779
	(2.7791)	(2.7802)	(2.6027)	(2.3515)	(3.7970)
β	0.9580	0.9616	0.9419	0.9352	0.8663
	(97.2103)	(103.9773)	(64.9918)	(59.6634)	(30.4669)
δ	*0.0196*	*0.0171*	*0.0242*	*0.0433*	*0.8663*
	(3.3491)***	*(3.2536)****	*(3.1291)****	*(3.3797)****	*(3.7292)****
$\bar{\kappa}$	1.1694	1.1691	1.1194	1.1408	1.3240
	(22.8126)	(22.6100)	(32.5481)	(28.3533)	(24.1397)
LL	−1907.47	−1908.93	−1803.60	−1800.36	−1856.99

Table 3.7 continued

	YEN/DM	BP/US	US/BP	CAN/US	US/CAN
	Model I: $dummy_1 = 1$ if				
	$\left|E_t - MA_{t,50}\right| > 0.15 \times \max\left|E_t - MA_{t,50}\right|$ and zero otherwise				
ω	0.0134	0.0016	0.0019	0.0001	0.0003
	(2.8358)	(1.4923)	(1.8310)	(1.1499)	(0.3783)
α	0.0423	0.0307	0.0289	0.0199	0.0127
	(3.5621)	(3.7671)	(3.7077)	(3.4169)	(2.7076)
β	0.8743	0.9543	0.9577	0.9649	0.9759
	(33.3669)	(99.1903)	(104.3241)	(135.5871)	(181.3767)
δ	0.0405	0.0121	0.0122	0.0019	0.0018
	(4.0758)***	(3.0085)***	(2.8086)***	(3.9797)***	(5.0313)***
$\overline{\kappa}$	1.3357	1.0591	1.0607	1.2361	1.2403
	(24.2657)	(23.0540)	(23.0706)	(25.2053)	(25.3423)
LL	−1853.92	−1663.01	−1663.60	−67.82	−67.00
	Model II: $dummy_2 = 1$ if				
	$\left|E_t - MA_{t,50}\right| > 0.2 \times \max\left|E_t - MA_{t,50}\right|$ and zero otherwise				
ω	0.0178	0.0026	0.0021	0.0003	0.0001
	(3.2958)	(2.1849)	(2.1438)	(2.0368)	(1.1936)
α	0.0422	0.0294	0.0259	0.0164	0.0130
	(3.6154)	(3.7463)	(3.5955)	(3.0283)	(2.8713)
β	0.8722	0.9550	0.9611	0.9670	0.9760
	(33.5448)	(99.5187)	(113.8062)	(152.6446)	(198.3693)
δ	0.0428	0.0167	0.0169	0.0024	0.0019
	(4.0898)***	(2.7758)***	(2.9438)***	(4.3060)***	(4.6734)***
$\overline{\kappa}$	1.3330	1.0582	1.0597	1.2353	1.2299
	(24.3440)	(23.2677)	(23.3232)	(25.2492)	(25.7800)
LL	−1853.46	−1662.93	−1662.69	−66.14	−68.19
	Model III: $dummy_3 = 1$ if				
	$\left|E_t - MA_{t,50}\right| > 0.25 \times \max\left|E_t - MA_{t,50}\right|$ and zero otherwise				
ω	0.0228	0.0023	0.0022	0.0004	0.0003
	(3.6054)	(2.1789)	(2.2260)	(2.5882)	(2.1497)
α	0.0440	0.0264	0.0245	0.0197	0.0160
	(3.6433)	(3.6974)	(3.5684)	(3.3560)	(3.1254)
β	0.8620	0.9604	0.9629	0.9645	0.9715
	(30.5399)	(112.4355)	(119.7423)	(141.4003)	(176.9010)
δ	0.0482	0.0203	0.0234	0.0023	0.0025
	(3.9931)***	(2.7630)***	(3.1660)***	(3.4412)***	(4.3059)***
$\overline{\kappa}$	1.3303	1.0579	1.0617	1.2206	1.2207
	(24.3350)	(23.4664)	(23.3835)	(25.7375)	(26.1107)
LL	−1853.25	−1662.63	−1661.43	−69.49	−68.99

Note: Figures in parentheses represent the ratio of the respective coefficient and its standard error. In the case of the coefficient δ, asterisks * (**, ***) are utilized to denote significance at the 10 (5, 1) percent level. The rows entitled *LL* give the maximized values of the log-likelihood function. The parameter δ captures the potential impact of implicit trading triggers on the conditional volatility of the exchange rate returns under investigation.

Table 3.8: Implicit Trading Triggers and Exchange Rate Volatility (MA_{100} representation)

	DM/US	US/DM	YEN/US	US/YEN	DM/YEN
	Model I: $dummy_1 = 1$ if $\left|E_t - MA_{t,100}\right| > 0.15 \times \max\left|E_t - MA_{t,100}\right|$ and zero otherwise				
ω	0.0022	0.0016	0.0008	0.0099	0.0144
	(1.2110)	(0.8494)	(2.5116)	(2.5591)	(2.8321)
α	0.0304	0.0303	0.0267	0.0255	0.0601
	(4.1039)	(4.0781)	(3.2851)	(2.9028)	(4.3316)
β	0.9584	0.9598	0.9399	0.9366	0.8842
	(96.7000)	(98.9082)	(63.7224)	(53.6363)	(37.0598)
δ	0.0053	0.0051	0.0119	0.0154	0.0194
	(1.8241)*	(1.6902)*	(2.8376)***	(2.7212)***	(3.2232)***
$\bar{\kappa}$	1.1570	1.1579	1.1158	1.1255	1.3061
	(22.7139)	(22.6832)	(31.7121)	(30.1181)	(24.7702)
LL	−1914.62	1914.94	−1806.24	−1805.15	−1865.12
	Model II: $dummy_2 = 1$ if $\left|E_t - MA_{t,100}\right| > 0.2 \times \max\left|E_t - MA_{t,100}\right|$ and zero otherwise				
ω	0.0037	0.0030	0.0090	0.0110	0.0152
	(1.8551)	(1.5380)	(2.6726)	(2.7334)	(3.0926)
α	0.0280	0.0291	0.0231	0.0224	0.0559
	(3.7682)	(3.8957)	(3.0441)	(2.7772)	(4.2662)
β	0.9546	0.9568	0.9433	0.9416	0.8900
	(88.2515)	(92.9834)	(65.5219)	(59.4236)	(39.5293)
δ	0.0093	0.0074	0.0137	0.0165	0.0200
	(2.5541)**	(2.2749)**	(2.8322)**	(2.5724)**	(3.2069)***
$\bar{\kappa}$	1.1624	1.1599	1.1215	1.1260	1.3087
	(22.8057)	(22.7191)	(31.3794)	(30.4655)	(24.7376)
LL	−1911.87	−1913.38	−1805.63	−1806.29	−1864.21
	Model III: $dummy_3 = 1$ if $\left|E_t - MA_{t,100}\right| > 0.25 \times \max\left|E_t - MA_{t,100}\right|$ and zero otherwise				
ω	0.0042	0.0040	0.0106	0.0136	0.0178
	(2.1525)	(1.9241)	(2.6827)	(2.6208)	(3.2984)
α	0.0247	0.0305	0.0226	0.0261	0.0553
	(3.4383)	(3.5361)	(2.8910)	(2.8891)	(4.2195)
β	0.9565	0.9567	0.9425	0.9341	0.8853
	(93.8951)	(92.7895)	(60.4888)	(49.6610)	(36.7748)
δ	0.0118	0.0105	0.0166	0.0212	0.0233
	(2.9077)***	(2.7508)***	(2.5777)***	(2.1782)**	(3.0950)***
$\bar{\kappa}$	1.1663	1.1646	1.1216	1.1241	1.3080
	(22.7700)	(22.6641)	(31.8292)	(30.4913)	(24.8916)
LL	−1909.85	−1911.33	−1805.85	−1807.65	−1863.44

Table 3.8 continued

	YEN/DM	BP/US	US/BP	CAN/US	US/CAN
	Model I: $dummy_1 = 1$ if $\|E_t - MA_{t,100}\| > 0.15 \times \max\|E_t - MA_{t,100}\|$ and zero otherwise				
ω	0.0168	0.0017	0.0018	0.0003	0.0001
	(3.0295)	(1.6952)	(1.8466)	(1.5789)	(0.7471)
α	0.0600	0.0275	0.02728	0.0228	0.02265
	(4.0954)	(3.7719)	(3.7501)	(3.6431)	(3.7565)
β	0.8650	0.9598	0.9606	0.9615	0.9656
	(32.3316)	(111.3640)	(111.3791)	(115.9287)	(130.9716)
δ	0.0297	0.0095	0.0103	0.0016	0.0014
	(3.8685***)	(2.9937)***	(2.7845)***	(3.5862)***	(4.0813)***
$\bar{\kappa}$	1.3188	1.0593	1.0591	1.2303	1.2308
	(24.5105)	(23.2556)	(23.2325)	(24.9760)	(25.0980)
LL	−1861.71	−1662.58	−1663.51	−69.50	−70.39
	Model II: $dummy_2 = 1$ if $\|E_t - MA_{t,100}\| > 0.2 \times \max\|E_t - MA_{t,100}\|$ and zero otherwise				
ω	0.0234	0:0025	0.0022	0.0004	0.0003
	(3.3739)	(2.1829)	(2.1523)	(2.3977)	(1.9834)
α	0.0594	0.0279	0.0264	0.0186	0.0203
	(3.9925)	(3.7263)	(3.6858)	(3.3157)	(3.5907)
β	0.8492	0.9591	0.9630	0.9644	0.9664
	(27.1197)	(105.9914)	(117.3604)	(138.1622)	(146.7714)
δ	0.03741	0.0153	0.0136	0.0020	0.0017
	(3.3736)***	(2.8260)***	(2.7851)***	(4.1206)***	(3.8655)***
$\bar{\kappa}$	1.3157	1.0603	1.0593	1.2306	1.2234
	(24.7178)	(23.1937)	(23.2088)	(25.5561)	(25.6454)
LL	−1860.56	−1663.01	−1664.19	−66.38	−69.83
	Model III: $dummy_3 = 1$ if $\|E_t - MA_{t,100}\| > 0.25 \times \max\|E_t - MA_{t,100}\|$ and zero otherwise				
ω	0.0210	0.0025	0.0022	0.0004	0.0004
	(3.4373)	(2.1829)	(2.1523)	(2.6848)	(2.2443)
α	0.0551	0.0279	0.0264	0.0216	0.0229
	(4.0711)	(3.7263)	(3.6858)	(3.5435)	(3.7620)
β	0.8709	0.9591	0.9630	0.9608	0.9634
	(32.1655)	(105.9914)	(117.3603)	(129.9516)	(135.8881)
δ	0.0300	0.0153	0.0136	0.0023	0.0017
	(3.3603)***	(2.8260)***	(2.7851)***	(3.8580)***	(3.7532)***
$\bar{\kappa}$	1.3088	1.0604	1.0593	1.2225	1.2223
	(25.0579)	(23.1937)	(23.2088)	(25.8553)	(25.7506)
LL	−1861.74	−1663.01	−1664.19	−68.37	−69.84

Note: Figures in parentheses represent the ratio of the respective coefficient and its standard error. In the case of the coefficient δ, asterisks * (**, ***) are utilized to denote significance at the 10 (5, 1) percent level. The rows entitled *LL* give the maximized values of the log-likelihood function. The parameter δ captures the potential impact of implicit trading triggers on the conditional volatility of the exchange rate returns under investigation.

levels. Thus, the marginal significance of the trading regime dummy indicates that at least for the sample period under investigation the implicit trading regimes defined by the $dummy_{i,t}$ series has indeed played an important role in the determination of the conditional variability of these currencies. This impression is further confirmed by the fact that the significance of the respective trading regime coefficients is robust with respect to a variation in both the interval defining the neighborhood of noise traders' no-trade interval and the time window employed to generate rolling historical moving average reference spot rate series.

From the viewpoint of exchange rate and of options pricing theory, it is also interesting to note that those trading regime coefficients found to be significantly different from zero have a positive sign. This empirical result indicates that the detected trading-induced implicit shifts in the dynamics of the variance equation of exchange rate returns exert an increasing impact on the conditional exchange rate variability as the exchange rate reaches noise traders' trigger rates. In the context of the options pricing model laid out above, this finding implies that the volatility strike structures implicit in these currencies should exhibit an U-shaped functional form resembling either a smile or a smirk. This is consistent with the stylized fact that volatility strike structures inferred from real-world FX options often assume a convex shape.

A number of diagnostic tests were performed to investigate whether the estimated GED-based GARCH models capture the essential features of the processes driving the conditional volatilities of the returns of the currency pairs included in the sample. Following the research strategy adopted in Section 3.2, it has been examined whether the standardized residuals of the GARCH models are symmetrically distributed with a zero mean and a unit variance. It has also been checked whether any significant remaining autocorrelation can be detected in the standardized and the squared standardized residuals of the models. In addition, the KS statistic has been implemented to explore whether the estimated GED distribution functions provide an acceptable representation of the sample distribution function of the standardized residuals of the models.

The results of these tests are given in Table 3.9. To shorten the exposition, only the results obtained for the $MA_{t,100}$ model with a scaling factor of $\vartheta = 0.2$ are plotted in the table. As can be seen in the table, the diagnostic tests indicate that the estimated GARCH models offer a fairly acceptable representation of the underlying data-generating processes. As compared with Section 3.2, the KS test statistics for the GARCH models specified for the CAN/US and the US/CAN returns series now also turn out to scratch the 1.63 one percent critical value applying in the case that the parameters of the distribution function assumed under the null hypothesis are known. This indicates that the change of the

Table 3.9: Diagnostic Statistics for the Models of Implicit Trading Regimes and Exchange Rate Volatility (Model II, MA_{100} -target value)

Currency pair	M1	M2	M3	ARCH(4)	Q(4)	KS
DM/US	0.2740	1933.48	0.4038	5.3102	2.3655	0.6825
	(0.7841)	(0.4753)	(0.6864)	(0.2569)	(0.6689)	
US/DM	−0.2307	1934.02	−0.3507	4.4931	2.1963	0.6775
	(0.8175)	(0.4788)	(0.7259)	(0.3434)	(0.6997)	
YEN/US	−0.2364	1993.85	0.5558	0.3425	4.3327	1.0646
	(0.8131)	(0.1843)	(0.5784)	(0.9869)	(0.3629)	
US/YEN	0.3440	1990.05	−0.4710	0.4348	4.5886	1.0147
	(0.7309)	(0.2006)	(0.6377)	(0.9795)	(0.3322)	
DM/YEN	0.0897	1947.90	0.9616	8.9132	1.9477	1.2266
	(0.9285)	(0.4264)	(0.3364)	(0.0633)	(0.7454)	
YEN/DM	−0.0805	1944.92	−1.2658	8.0016	2.3314	1.1197
	(0.9359)	(0.4516)	(0.2057)	(0.0915)	(0.6751)	
BP/US	−0.1951	1923.43	0.5554	4.6461	4.6475	0.8365
	(0.8453)	(0.4114)	(0.5787)	(0.3256)	(0.3254)	
US/BP	0.2004	1923.69	−0.5702	4.4208	4.6407	0.8184
	(0.8412)	(0.4131)	(0.5686)	(0.3520)	(0.3262)	
CAN/US	−0.1546	1955.71	0.7615	4.9600	4.1165	1.6280
	(0.8771)	(0.3842)	(0.4464)	(0.2914)	(0.3905)	
US/CAN	0.1668	1955.89	−0.4292	5.3062	3.6251	1.6260
	(0.8675)	(0.3832)	(0.6678)	(0.2573)	(0.4591)	

Note: M1, M2, and M3 denote moments-based specification tests explained in the text (p. 94). ARCH(4) and LM(4) are Lagrange multiplier tests for remaining autocorrelation and ARCH effects in the standardized and the squared standardized residuals, respectively. Figures in parentheses represent marginal significance levels. In the column headed KS, the Kolmogorov–Smirnov statistic is presented. Benchmark critical values for the Kolmogorov–Smirnov test under the assumption that the parameters of the distribution function under the null hypothesis are known are 1.22, 1.36, and 1.63 at the 10 (5, 1) percent significance level (see, e.g., DeGroot 1989).

dummy variable has also helped to improve the capability of the GED-based GARCH model to account for the essential features of the returns and the conditional volatility of the Canadian dollar/US dollar spot rate series.

All in all, the outcomes of the various diagnostic tests support the estimated specification of the GARCH models and help to reinforce the impression that noise trading might be an important determinant of exchange rate volatility and, thus, of the shape and of the dynamics of the volatility smile implicit in foreign currency options premia.

To summarize, the results of the above volatility-based test for implicit trading regimes in real-world FX markets are much more encouraging than the findings obtained by applying the more traditional volatility-based test for implicit price barriers implemented in Section 3.2. The dummy variables capturing whether the realized spot rate has settled in the neighborhood of an implicit trading trigger are significant for the majority of currency pairs under investigation. This result is robust with respect to the model specification chosen to test for implicit trading regimes in FX markets. A further important point regards the fact that the significant trading regime dummies included in the equations depicting the dynamics of the conditional volatility of exchange rate returns have been found to be positive. This estimation outcome signals that the conditional variability of spot rate returns tends to rise as the absolute deviation of the exchange rate from its moving average representation increases. Recognizing the predictions of the options valuation model developed in Section 3.1, these results imply that implicit trading-induced regime shifts might be, at least to some extent, at the root of smiling volatility strike structures implicit in the FX options on these currencies. Thus, combining the results of the theoretical and the empirical analyses, financial institutions or economic agents participating in the trading of options on one or the other of the currencies analyzed in this section should take into account noise trading and implicit trading regimes when it comes either to the pricing or to the hedging of positions involving these contracts.

3.3.3   Robustness of the Results

To supplement the GARCH-based statistical inference, several alternative quantitative models were estimated to provide additional insights into the interplay between exchange rate volatility and implicit trading regimes in FX markets. Intending to study whether the findings reported in Section 3.3.2 are robust with respect to the estimator chosen to trace out the conditional volatility of exchange rate returns, I used alternative estimates of the respective conditional exchange rate volatilities obtained by resorting to a technique championed by Schwert (1989) to set up the sensitivity tests described in detail below. While GARCH models use squared residuals to obtain an estimate of the conditional volatility of a time series, this methodology relies on the absolute value of the residuals of the mean equation to accomplish this task. To implement the model suggested by Schwert (1989), a fourth-order autoregression was estimated in a first step for the various exchange rate returns series under investigation. The equations were enriched with five dummy variables to allow for potentially differing daily intercepts. The equations estimated for US/BP and BP/US returns also contained a dummy variable accounting for the shift in the exchange regime related to the breakdown of the EMS in 1992. The same procedure was applied in a second step to the absolute values of the estimated residuals of these equations. The fitted values of the equations estimated at the second stage provide an estimate of the conditional volatilities of the various exchange rate returns series included in the sample.

Equipped with these conditional volatility series, I first employed nonparametric statistical techniques to shed some light on the robustness of the GARCH-based empirical evidence on implicit trading regimes in real-world foreign exchange markets documented above. The first nonparametric method applied to the data set under investigation is the Wilcoxon–Mann–Whitney ranks statistic. This test was used to challenge the null hypothesis that conditional volatilities corresponding to exchange rate realizations belonging to the interval $\left|E_t - MA_{t,i}\right| > \vartheta \times \max\left|E_t - MA_{t,i}\right|$ are drawn from the same (continuous) distribution as conditional volatilities observed when the corresponding spot rate has settled in the part of the real line defined by $\left|E_t - MA_{t,i}\right| \leq \vartheta \times \max\left|E_t - MA_{t,i}\right|$. The alternative hypothesis is that both sets of conditional exchange rate returns volatilities are drawn from different distributions which, however, can be transformed into each other by adding to the one or the other set of estimated volatilities an arbitrary constant (DeGroot 1989: 580). To implement the test, the first step is to rearrange all time series of conditional exchange rate returns volatilities under investigation in increasing order. In the second step, a rank reflecting their position in this ordering was assigned to the conditional volatilities observed when $\left|E_t - MA_{t,i}\right| > \vartheta \times \max\left|E_t - MA_{t,i}\right|$. If the null hypothesis were true, the volatilities belonging to this group should not tend to cluster in the ordering formed in the first step. Thus, the sum of their ranks can be used to assess whether or not the null hypothesis is supported by the data. Summing up over all ranks, subtracting the mean of the sum of ranks calculated under the null, and dividing by the standard deviation of the latter gives a standard normally distributed test statistic (Schlittgen 1998: 350). A rather large Wilcoxon–Mann–Whitney ranks statistic might result in a rejection of the null hypothesis in favor of its (one-sided) alternative that the median of the distribution of conditional FX volatilities observed whenever the spot rate has left the vicinity of its moving average representation is larger than its counterpart characterizing the distribution of all those volatilities forming the group defined by the contemporaneous spot rate realizations falling into the interval $\left|E_t - MA_{t,i}\right| \leq \vartheta \times \max\left|E_t - MA_{t,i}\right|$.

Table 3.10 summarizes the results of this exercise.[56] The results of the nonparametric test strongly suggest that implicit trading regimes as discriminated by

---

[56] The results of implementing the Wilcoxon–Mann–Whitney ranks tests for the exchange rates in reversed notation closely resemble the test statistics presented in Table 3.11 and are, therefore, not presented.

Table 3.10: A Nonparametric Test for the Link between Conditional Exchange Rate Volatility Options and Implicit Trading Regimes

Currency pair	Wilcoxon–Mann–Whitney Ranks Tests		
	MA_{50}-target value	MA_{100}-target value	MA_{150}-target value
	Model I: $dummy_1 = 1$ if $\left\vert E_t - MA_{t,i}\right\vert > 0.15 \times \max\left\vert E_t - MA_{t,i}\right\vert$ and zero otherwise		
US/BP	11.5107	12.3989	14.0234
US/CAN	8.1825	7.7337	9.5729
US/DM	5.0401	5.3272	6.8237
US/YEN	9.1111	8.7172	5.4247
DM/YEN	10.1302	9.1503	8.2800
	Model II: $dummy_2 = 1$ if $\left\vert E_t - MA_{t,i}\right\vert > 0.2 \times \max\left\vert E_t - MA_{t,i}\right\vert$ and zero otherwise		
US/BP	11.8913	13.3644	14.9193
US/CAN	9.1145	8.9295	9.3551
US/DM	7.0376	6.2020	8.2441
US/YEN	9.5067	9.6002	8.0922
DM/YEN	11.7954	10.5968	10.6347
	Model III: $dummy_3 = 1$ if $\left\vert E_t - MA_{t,i}\right\vert > 0.25 \times \max\left\vert E_t - MA_{t,i}\right\vert$ and zero otherwise		
US/BP	11.4395	14.5585	14.4800
US/CAN	9.6557	8.6657	9.2093
US/DM	8.1785	7.5234	9.0463
US/YEN	10.3699	9.2338	7.6992
DM/YEN	12.2160	11.5087	8.7249

Note: The table gives the values of Wilcoxon–Mann–Whitney ranks tests. The test statistics is utilized to assess whether the median of the distribution of foreign exchange rate volatilities changes when the corresponding spot rates leave the vicinity of the respective moving average representations. The Wilcoxon–Mann–Whitney ranks test is asymptotically standard normally distributed. See DeGroot (1989: 580–584) for further details.

the state-contingent dummy variables formalized in equation (3.39) may exert a significant impact on the level of conditional exchange rate volatility. It can be seen in the table that the results of the Wilcoxon–Mann–Whitney ranks tests are significant at conventional marginal significance levels. It is also interesting to note that the outcomes of the nonparametric testing approach turn out to be robust with respect to the $MA_{t,i}$ target terms and the scaling factor, ϑ, utilized to trace out the neighborhood of noise traders reference exchange rates. Moreover,

in line with the impression obtained from the GARCH models, the magnitude of
the test statistics depicted in the table further indicates that conditional FX
market volatilities tend to rise as the current spot rate moves farther away from
its historical moving average representation.

The second nonparametric technique employed to further scrutinize the
potential link between the level of exchange rate volatility and the position of the
prevailing exchange rate relative to its medium-term floating target value is
kernel regressions. These regressions provide kernel density estimates of the distributions of the conditional exchange rate return volatility series in the sample.
A kernel density estimate can be interpreted as a smoothed relative frequency
histogram of a time series. A conventional step-wise linear histogram is computed by figuring out the relative frequencies of equally weighted observations
found within intervals of arbitrary width equidistantly spaced between the
minimum and the maximum of an analyzed time series. In a kernel regression, in
contrast, a so-called kernel or smoothing function is utilized to transform the
discontinuous histogram into a continuous real-valued function.

To describe the idea behind this estimation technique in more detail, let the
mapping $\hat{h} \mapsto G_{RF}$ relating estimated conditional volatilities of magnitude $\hat{h}$
with the corresponding relative frequencies G_{RF} with which these volatilities
are observed be given by the unknown nonlinear function $g_K(\hat{h})$. In a kernel
regression, an estimate $\hat{g}_K(\hat{h})$ of this function for any arbitrary realization $\hat{h}$ of
the respective volatility series under investigation is calculated as the weighted
arithmetic average of the local intensities of observations found in a small
neighborhood around $\hat{h}$ (see, e.g., Campbell et al. 1997: 499; Härdle 1990: 19):

$$(3.42) \quad \hat{g}_K(\hat{h}) = \frac{1}{T} \sum_{t=1}^{T} \varsigma(t,T,\hat{h}) G_t,$$

where the magnitude of the weighting factors $\varsigma(t,T,\hat{h}_t)$ declines as the distance
between $\hat{h}$ and the conditional volatilities found in a band of width, w, spaced
symmetrically around this reference value increases.

In a kernel regression, the concrete form of the function $\varsigma(t,T,\hat{h})$ is determined by specifying a continuous kernel density function $K_w(\hat{h})$ satisfying
$K_w(\hat{h}) \geq 0$ for all $\hat{h}$ and $\int_{\hat{h}} K_w(s)ds = 1$. To obtain the kernel volatility density
estimates used in the subsequent analyses, a Gaussian kernel was used (see, e.g.,
Campbell et al. 1997: 501):

$$(3.43) \quad K_w(\hat{h}) = \frac{1}{\sqrt{2\pi}w} \exp\left(-\frac{\hat{h}^2}{2w^2}\right)$$

With this kernel at hand, the weighting function can then be reexpressed as (see Campbell et al. 1997: 500):

$$(3.44) \quad \varsigma(t,T,\hat{h}) = \frac{K_w(\hat{h}-\hat{h}_t)}{\dfrac{1}{T}\sum_{t=1}^{T}K_w(\hat{h}-\hat{h}_t)},$$

where the term showing up in the denominator of this equation is divided by the number of observations to guarantee that the weights sum up to unity and $K_w(\hat{h}-\hat{h}_t)$ expresses that the weighting function captures the distance between $\hat{h}$ and the volatilities in the neighborhood of this value. When the kernel weights given in equation (3.44) are plugged into equation (3.42) the Nadayra–Watson kernel density estimator obtains (Härdle 1990: 25).

The smoothness of the estimated kernel density rises as the numerical value ascribed to the bandwidth parameter, w, is raised. Thus, choosing the parameter w too large can result in an excessively smooth kernel density estimate which overfits the data and washes out the inherent nonlinearity of the function $g_K(\hat{h})$. To tackle this problem, several approaches allowing an optimal bandwidth parameter to be selected for a given kernel function have been suggested in the literature. In this section, density estimates were generated based on the optimal bandwidth for a Gaussian kernel as discussed in Silverman (1986: 43–48).

This estimation technique is implemented separately for conditional FX volatilities observed when $|E_t - MA_{t,i}| \le \vartheta \times \max|E_t - MA_{t,i}|$ and for the complementary group of volatilities realized when the reverse inequality, $|E_t - MA_{t,i}| > \vartheta \times \max|E_t - MA_{t,i}|$, holds. A comparison of the resulting kernel density estimates then allows me to examine whether the distributions of the respective conditional volatilities in the sample differ across trading regimes. The results of this exercise are given in Figure 3.7. To preserve space, only estimates obtained for the intermediate model with a $MA_{t,100}$ moving-average representation and a scaling factor of $\vartheta = 0.2$ are graphed.

The kernel densities depicted in the figure have several interesting properties. Visual inspection of the figure reveals that the densities obtained for the US/BP and the US/YEN clearly exhibit a state-contingent component. While a similar proposition can also be made with respect to the US/CAN and YEN/DM densities, the effect of the shift in the implicit trading regime on conditional exchange rate returns volatility is less pronounced in the case of the US/DM exchange rate. No clear-cut pattern emerges when the kernel densities estimated for the US/DM volatilities for the $|E_t - MA_{t,100}| \le 0.2 \times \max|E_t - MA_{t,150}|$ and the $|E_t - MA_{t,100}| > 0.2 \times \max|E_t - MA_{t,150}|$ regimes are compared. While the density

Figure 3.7: Estimated State-Contingent Empirical Conditional Volatility Densities

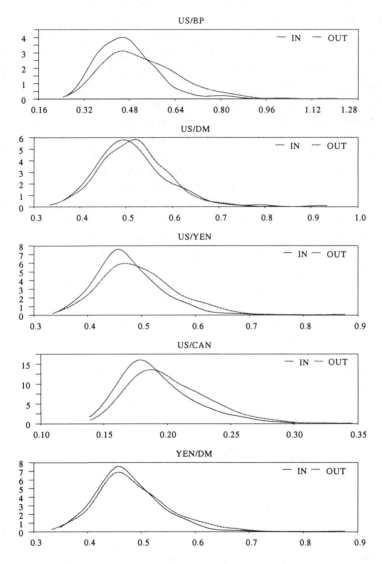

Note: The figure plots state-contingent densities of exchange rate volatilities for an intermediate model with $MA_{t,100}$ and $\vartheta = 0.2$ on the vertical axis as a function of the level of spot rate returns volatilities on the horizontal axis. The density functions labeled "out" ("in") give the estimated density applying whenever the current spot rate has settled within (outside) the no-trade band placed by technical traders around the uncentered historical moving average of the spot rate.

describing the distribution of the conditional exchange rate volatilities observed when this exchange rate has settled inside its implicit fluctuation band exhibits a fatter right tail, the complementary distribution tends to allocate more probability mass to volatility realizations found in an intermediate range slightly above the median of the distribution. All in all, however, the results of the kernel densities confirm the findings of the Wilcoxon–Mann–Whitney ranks tests for implicit trading regimes in FX markets.

The tests presented so far rely on a set of dummy variables utilized to define the neighborhood of the medium-term reference exchange rate level employed by noise traders to evaluate the relative strength of a currency. As the definition of the vicinity of noise traders' target exchange rate is always to some extent arbitrary, the final test used to challenge the noise trader hypothesis of the volatility strike structure does not rely on the specific definition adopted to create the selection dummies, $dummy_{i,t}$. To shed some light on the dynamic interplay between the absolute deviation of the current spot rate from its historical un-centered moving-average representation and the conditional volatility of exchange rate returns, bivariate vector autoregressive models including these two series were estimated.[57]

Conceptually, my research strategy is akin to the one adopted by Whitelaw (1994) to assess the link between expected returns of stock prices and the corresponding conditional volatilities. The vector of the endogenous variables of the vector autoregressive models (VAR) estimated in this section is defined by $Y_t \equiv (absdif_t \quad \hat{h}_t)'$, where $absdif_t \equiv |E_t - MA_{t,i}|$ and $\hat{h}_t$ denotes the respective conditional exchange rate returns volatilities as obtained by implementing the estimation technique suggested by Schwert (1989). For the sake of brevity, only results for the model based on an $MA_{t,i}$ term with $i = 100$ are presented. The reduced form representation of the bivariate systems to be estimated are then given as below:

$$(3.45) \quad Y_t = A_0 + \sum_{i=1}^{p} A_i Y_{t-i} + e_t,$$

where A_0 is a (2×1) vector of constants, A_i are (2×2) matrices of coefficients, and e_t represents a (2×1) disturbance vector. Note, that the vector autoregressions do not include the $dummy_{i,t}$ series and, thus, do not depend upon the scaling factors ϑ utilized to trace out these series. Using ordinary least squares

---

[57] See, e.g., Enders (1995: 294–316) and Hansen (1993: 236–239) for textbook expositions of issues related to the estimation and interpretation of vector autoregressive models.

(OLS), consistent and asymptotically efficient estimates of the coefficients of the reduced-form representation of the bivariate system obtain. The lag length p of this system was determined by minimizing the Schwartz–Bayesian Criterion (Enders 1995: 315). According to this criterion, the selected lag lengths comprise 15, 24, 25, 16, 20 trading days for the US/CAN, US/DM, US/BP, US/YEN, and DM/YEN models, respectively. Thus, lagged daily realizations of the endogenous variables covering approximately one month of trading time were included in the VAR. Given these lag lengths, a Portmanteau test indicated that the null hypothesis of no remaining joint residual autocorrelation could not be rejected at conventional significance levels.

As long as the roots of the characteristic equation of the system of simultaneous equations formalized in equation (3.45) can be found inside the unit circle, the unrestricted bivariate vector autoregression can be represented in its infinite vector moving-average representation as

$$(3.46) \quad Y_t = \overline{A}_0 + \sum_{i=0}^{\infty} L^i U_i\, e_t,$$

where $\overline{A}_0$ is a (2×1) vector of coefficients, U_i denotes a (2×2) matrix comprising the coefficients of the reduced system, and L symbolizes the lag operator. The moving-average representation of the underlying structural model is given by:

$$(3.47) \quad Y_t = \overline{A}_0 + \sum_{i=0}^{\infty} L^i R_i\, \varepsilon_i,$$

where R_i is a (2×2) matrix and $\varepsilon_t \equiv (\varepsilon_{absdif,t} \quad \varepsilon_{\hat{h},t})$ is the vector of orthogonal serially uncorrelated structural shocks. These structural shocks can be identified from the sequence of the residuals e_t upon imposing an identifying restriction on the system. Several alternative identification strategies for vector autoregressive systems have been discussed in the literature. Here, I employ an identification scheme proposed by Sims (1980), who has suggested obtaining a unique Choleski decomposition of the residuals by imposing a specific ordering of the endogenous variables included in the system. The ordering of a set of time series in a VAR implies that a shock to a variable placed in a lower position of this ordering scheme exerts no impact effect on the variables placed in a relatively higher position of the ordering. For the bivariate system given in equation (3.47), conditional exchange rate volatility was placed in the second position of the ordering. It should, however, be mentioned that obtaining a recursive system by reversing the ordering did not result in a substantial qualitative change of the estimation results.

Having recovered the components of the vector of orthogonal structural shocks, the moving average representation (3.47) of the vector autoregressive system given in equation (3.45) can be used to trace out the shape of impulse response functions. These functions summarize the impact of a one-time shock to one of the structural disturbance terms, ε_t, on the dynamics of the variables included in the model. Figure 3.8 summarizes the results of this exercise. The dynamic response of *absdif$_t$* ($\hat{h}_t$) to a one-standard deviation shock to $\varepsilon_{\hat{h},t}$ ($\varepsilon_{absdif,t}$) is depicted in the graphs collected in the left (right) column of the figure. To save space, only the impulse response functions for the model using a $MA_{t,100}$ reference rate to compute noise traders' medium-term target exchange rate are presented. Visual inspection of Figure 3.8 suggests that the impulse response functions harmonize with economic prejudices. As suggested by the theoretical model of exchange rate determination outlined in the first section of this chapter, a positive structural shock caused by $\varepsilon_{absdif,t}$ exerts an amplifying effect on conditional exchange rate volatility. For all currency pairs, the volatility magnifying effect of this shock tends to reach a maximum after approximately one or two weeks of trading days.

This observation might indicate that, as time goes by, more and more trend-extrapolative noise traders try to jump on the bandwagon as it becomes apparent that the deviation of the spot rate from its moving target has increased. Such an interpretation is in line with the shape of the impulse response functions shown on the left-hand-side of the figure. These functions depict the dynamic response of the absolute deviation of the spot rate from its target level in the aftermath of a one-standard deviation disturbance to $\varepsilon_{\hat{h},t}$. Though the effect of such a shock on *absdif$_t$* is relatively small in magnitude and for two currency pairs hardly significant, the respective impulse functions show a pronounced hump-shaped functional form in three out of five cases. Harmonizing with the line of argumentation put forward above, the delayed response of the absolute deviation of the exchange rate from its moving average following a $\varepsilon_{\hat{h},t}$ shock might be interpreted to indicate that it takes some days before this innovation has diffused and the bandwagon travels at full speed. Finally, it should also be noted that the impulse response functions, reveal that shocks caused by an innovation either in $\varepsilon_{absdif,t}$ or in $\varepsilon_{\hat{h},t}$ die out in the long run. Interpreted in terms of the theoretical model laid out above, this dynamic property of the vector autoregressive systems reflects that in the longer run every shock hitting the system results in an adjustment of the moving average of the spot rate which, in turn, implies that the economy switches back into a no-noise trading regime.

Figure 3.8: Selected Impulse Response Functions for the Estimated Bivariate Systems

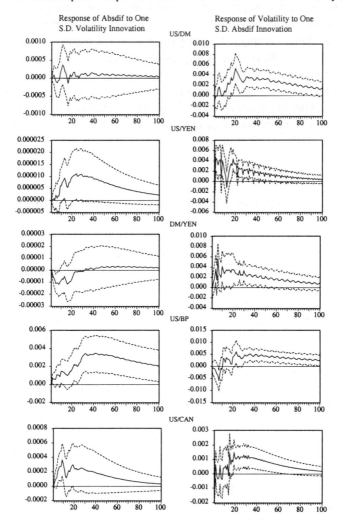

Note: The impulse response functions are obtained from a bivariate model containing the absolute deviation of the current spot rate from its $MA_{t,100}$ reference value (abbreviated as "absdif") and the respective conditional exchange rate returns volatilities obtained by implementing the estimation procedure developed by Schwert (1989). The impulse response functions depict the time path of a series to a one-standard deviation (S.D.) shock to the other series included in the system. Dashed lines represent +/–2 standard error bounds obtained from a Monte Carlo experiment with 1 000 simulation runs. The ordering of the variables used to obtain a unique Choleski decomposition is: absdif, conditional exchange rate volatility.

To summarize, the supplementary evidence obtained by implementing non-parametric testing techniques and by estimating vector autoregressive systems helps to further build up confidence in the robustness and the validity of the empirical evidence on implicit trading regimes in FX markets obtained by implementing the GARCH models suggested in Section 3.3.2. Even more important, the fact that it is possible to detect systematic links between the relative strength of a currency and conditional exchange rate volatility suggests that taking in account these effects might help options traders and financial institutions to improve the performance of strategies constructed to value or to insure long or short positions taken in options on these currencies.

3.4   Noise Trader in a Heston-Style Model: A Primer

The preceding empirical analysis has underscored that noise trading in spot markets for foreign currencies might be an important determinant of the shape of volatility strike structures implicit in real-world FX options premia. The model introduced in Section 3.2 lends itself to the incorporation of these trading effects into a contingent claim valuation model. Its practical applicability, however, is hampered by the fact that the incorporation of state-contingent noise trading into the underlying structural model of exchange rate determination results in a non-linear spot rate, instantaneous volatility, and interest rate differential function. This feature of the model makes it impossible to derive explicit analytical formulas for foreign currency option premia and hampers the applicability of the model to price and to hedge contingent claims in real-time in actual FX markets.

This motivates the discussion of the watered-down noise trader FX option valuation model contained in this section. Retaining the core feature of the model introduced in Section 3.2, the valuation model outlined below emphasizes the importance of the trading behavior of fundamentalists and chartists in the spot market for the dynamics of the exchange rate and for the valuation of FX contingent claims. Rather than presupposing an exogenously given exchange rate process, a stylized continuous-time stochastic noise trader exchange rate model inspired by Frankel (1996) is employed to represent the dynamics of this asset price. The model renders it possible to trace out the implications of the trading elasticities and market shares of heterogeneous groups of technical traders implementing different trading strategies for the exchange rate path. To focus on the *economic* implications of the model and to keep the formal analysis as simple as possible, the model is constructed to resemble the stochastic volatility option pricing models of Heston (1993), Scott (1997), and Bakshi and Chen (1997) structurally. As suggested by these authors, the model features both a stochastic exchange rate volatility and stochastic domestic and foreign interest rates. The trading behavior of technical traders in the spot market not only affects the volatility structure of the exchange rate process but enters also into the stochastic dynamics of the domestic and foreign locally risk-free interest rates.

The analysis proceeds as follows. Section 3.4.1 is used to outline a stylized stochastic exchange rate model with noise traders. The basic equation employed for the determination of the exchange rate is discussed and the stochastic environment is outlined. The influence of the microstructure of the spot market on the volatility of the exchange rate is examined and the dynamics of the domestic and the foreign term structure of interest rates are derived. In Section 3.4.2, a numerical example is coded up to discuss the implications of technical trading in the spot market for the valuation of foreign currency options.

3.4.1 The Structure of the Economy

In order to derive closed-form analytical expressions for the valuation of FX contingent claims, the basic model is intentionally kept as streamlined as possible. The stylized noise trader exchange rate model underlying the FX option pricing model is inspired by a model developed by Frankel (1996). To describe the model, let the logarithm of the relative supply of domestic and foreign assets and the logarithm of the relative demand for domestic assets be denoted by s_a and d_a, respectively. In the tradition of the monetary model of exchange rate determination used in Section 3.1, the logarithm of the spot exchange rate e can then be expressed as $e = s_a - d_a$. The foreign exchange market is populated by a continuum of speculating portfolio managers. It is assumed that market participants can be subdivided into two main classes of traders. The first group of portfolio managers named fundamentalists is assumed to expect the exchange rate to revert toward an expected long-run equilibrium value e_0 at a constant rate φ_f. The second group of traders active in the spot market are extrapolating chartists. A current deviation of the exchange rate from an expected long-run equilibrium level induces these chartists to believe that this wedge will become even larger in the next instant of time at rate φ_c. In order to reduce the number of state variables needed in the subsequent analyses, it is further assumed that fundamentalists and chartists agree upon the numerical value of the medium-run exchange rate, e_0.

Let the respective elasticities of fundamentalists' and chartists' demand for foreign-currency-denominated assets with respect to their exchange rate expectations be denoted by ς_f and ς_c. Assume further that the fraction of market participants belonging to the first group of FX traders is given by ψ. Given this notational assumptions, the aggregate demand for domestic assets can be written as $d_a = \psi \varsigma_f \varphi_f (e - e_0) - (1 - \psi) \varsigma_c \varphi_c (e - e_0)$. Substituting this expression into the equation derived for e and collecting terms yields the following exchange rate equation (see Frankel 1996):

$$(3.48) \quad e = \frac{1}{\gamma_1} s_a + \frac{\gamma_2}{\gamma_1} e_0,$$

where it has been defined for notational convenience that $\gamma_1 \equiv 1 + \psi \varsigma_f \varphi - (1 - \psi) \varsigma_c \varphi_c$ and $\gamma_2 \equiv \psi \varsigma_f \varphi_f - (1 - \psi) \varsigma_c \varphi_c = \gamma_1 - 1$ and the implicit assumption is that $\gamma_1 \neq 0$. Equation (3.48) demonstrates that the terms γ_1 and γ_2 determine the sign and the magnitude of the impact of changes in the relative supply of domestic assets and of the long-run exchange rate expected by FX traders on the level of the logarithm of the exchange rate. The coefficients γ_1 and γ_2 are functions of the elasticities ς_f and ς_c, of the speed of adjustment parameters φ_f and φ_c, and of the relative strength of trader groups ψ. Depending upon the relative magnitude of these structural parameters, the coefficients γ_1 and γ_2 can assume positive or negative numerical values and can be absolutely greater or smaller than one.

It remains to describe the stochastic structure — interpreted under an equivalent martingale measure — of the economy in more detail. Consider first the logarithm of the ratio of the relative supply of foreign and domestic assets s_a. It is presumed that this variable is affected by a state variable $y(t)$ according to the following stochastic differential equation:

$$(3.49) \quad ds_a = (\mu_s + g_s y)dt + \sigma_s \sqrt{y} dW_1,$$

where $\{W_1(t), t \geq 0\}$ denotes a standard Gauss–Wiener process. Equation (3.49) states that the drift of s_a can be decomposed into a deterministic $\mu_s dt$ and a stochastic growth component $g_s y dt$ with μ_s and g_s representing some constants. The impact exerted by the state variable $y(t)$ on the diffusion term of the logarithm of the relative supply of foreign and domestic assets is scaled by the constant parameter σ_s. I follow Heston (1993) and specify the dynamics of $y(t)$ as a mean reverting square root process:

$$(3.50) \quad dy = \kappa_y (\theta_y - y) dt + \xi_y \sqrt{y} dW_2.$$

The parameter κ_y reflects the speed of mean reversion, θ_y symbolizes the mean reversion level, and the coefficient ξ_y denotes the volatility parameter.[58]

Taking into consideration that real-world foreign exchange markets are typically characterized by alternating phases of tranquility and turbulence, it is assumed that the volatility of the expectations formation process is itself stochastic. The expected long-run equilibrium exchange rate estimated by fundamentalists and chartists evolves — under the equivalent martingale measure — according to the following equation:

$$(3.51) \quad de_0 = (\mu_s + g_{e_0} y)dt + \sigma_{e_0}\sqrt{q}dW_3,$$

with g_{e_0} and σ_{e_0} denoting constants. Note that it is assumed that the drift of the expected equilibrium exchange rate calculated by foreign exchange market participants contains the deterministic component $\mu_s dt$ of the process which describes the drift of the relative supply of domestic and foreign assets and is also affected by the state variable $y(t)$ driving that process. This assumption can be thought of to reflect a type of "error correction" relation between the relative supply of and relative demand for domestic and foreign assets; i.e., noise traders take the expected component of supply side shocks into consideration when computing the long-run equilibrium exchange rate. The stochastic noise term $q(t)$ entering into equation (3.51) represents the influence, for example, of rumors and of other market-inherent speculative dynamics on the expectation formation of portfolio managers. This stochastic disturbance term is modeled as follows:

$$(3.52) \quad dq = \kappa_q(\theta_q - \sqrt{q})dt + \xi_q\sqrt{q}dW_4,$$

with κ_q, θ_q, and e_q denoting constants.

To summarize the correlation structure between the Brownian motions entering into the model, define $dW = (dW_1 \quad dW_3)'$ and $d\tilde{W} = (dW_2 \quad dW_4)'$ and write $dWdW' = Idt$, $d\tilde{W}d\tilde{W}' = Idt$, $dW d\tilde{W}' = Pdt$, where I is a (2×2) identity matrix and P is a (2×2) diagonal matrix with correlation coefficients ρ_{12} and ρ_{34} as components P_{11} and P_{22}, respectively.

---

[58] The construction formalized in equation (3.49) and (3.50) is similar to the specification employed in Bakshi and Chen (1997) to model the dynamics of two state variables affecting the supply of domestic and foreign outside money, respectively. Intending to parsimoniously capture the essential characteristics of the stochastic structure of the international economy under investigation, the impact of such factors on the exchange rate process is represented by means of a single state variable.

Given this structure of the economy, I am now in a position to derive the dynamics of the antilog $E(t)$ of the exchange rate. Applying the rules of stochastic calculus, the following stochastic differential equation obtains:

$$(3.53) \quad dE = \overline{\mu} E dt + \frac{\sigma_s}{\gamma_1} E \sqrt{y} dW_1 + \frac{\gamma_2 \sigma_{e0}}{\gamma_1} E \sqrt{q} dW_3,$$

where $\quad \overline{\mu} \equiv \left[\frac{1}{\gamma_1} (\mu_s + g_s y) + \frac{\gamma_2}{\gamma_1} (\mu_s + g_{e0} y) \right] + \frac{1}{2} \left[\left(\frac{\sigma_s}{\gamma_1} \right)^2 y + \left(\frac{\gamma_2 \sigma_{e0}}{\gamma_1} \right)^2 q \right].$

The economic feature which distinguishes the formula provided in equation (3.53) from the asset price processes utilized, for example, by Heston (1993), Bakshi and Chen (1997), and Nielson and Saá-Requejo (1993) is that the structural parameters of the above exchange rate process capture the assumptions made with respect to the investment behavior of foreign exchange traders in the spot market. Equation (3.53) shows that the presence and the interaction of fundamentalists and chartists affects both the drift and the diffusion term of the exchange rate process. In order to further investigate the implications of the trading behavior of economic agents for the latter, note that the variance of exchange rate returns is given by

$$(3.54) \quad V(t) = \left(\frac{\sigma_s}{\gamma_1} \right)^2 y(t) + \left(\frac{\gamma_2 \sigma_{e0}}{\gamma_1} \right)^2 q(t).$$

Though the specific shape of this function depends upon the magnitude of the parameters chosen to simulate the model, it is useful to resort to the concrete numerical example for this function illustrated in Figure 3.9 to discuss the channels through which noise trading affects exchange rate volatility in the present model. The figure plots the volatility of the exchange rate as a function of the fraction of fundamentalists trading in the spot market and the exchange rate elasticity of chartists' demand for foreign assets. While the former variable reflects the allocation of economic agents among trader groups, the latter coefficient captures the aggressiveness of chartists position taking. Taken together, both factors summarize the intensity with which the trend-chasing trader group participates in spot FX trading. The depicted surface reveals that in the present model it neither necessarily holds that exchange rate volatility is always a decreasing function of the relative market share of fundamentalists in the spot market nor that a higher trading elasticity of chartists unambiguously amplifies the variability of exchange rates. Rather, the impact of the different forms of noise trading in the spot market on the instantaneous exchange rate volatility depends crucially upon the magnitude of the terms γ_1 and γ_2 and, thus, upon the numerical values assigned to the various parameters capturing the technical position taking of agents acting in the spot market for foreign exchange.

To discuss the economic factors shaping the exchange rate volatility function plotted in Figure 3.9, consider the response of the exchange rate to a positive exogenous one-time shock to the Brownian motion $\{W_1(t), t \geq 0\}$ affecting the relative supply of domestic to foreign assets. Assume that the initial position of the economy is characterized by a very low ψ and a relatively high ς_c and then successively increase the market share of fundamentalists. Starting in such a situation, Figure 3.9 indicates that, for the given parameter constellation, exchange rate volatility rather tends to increase rather than to decline upon enhancing the fraction of fundamentalists populating the spot market. If the rise in ψ is sufficiently large, the depicted volatility function rapidly increases as the singular point $\gamma_1 \to 0$ is reached.

Figure 3.9: Noise Trading and Exchange Rate Volatility

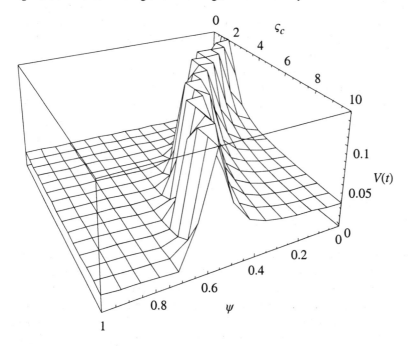

Note: The plotted surface is based on the following set of numerical parameter values: $\varsigma_f = 5$, $\varphi_f = 0.5$, $\varphi_c = 0.5$, $y(t) = q(t) = 0.15$.

Any rise in the relative supply of domestic assets must be compensated by an exchange rate movement which induces the members of the two trader groups active in the spot market to enlarge the fraction of financial wealth invested in domestic assets. By assumption, the economy starts in a situation in which the price formation process in the spot market is mainly driven by the trading behavior of chartists. Speculators adhering to the chartist investment philosophy, in turn, will enlarge the share of domestic assets in their portfolios if and only if the domestic currency appreciates. If the elasticity ς_c is sufficiently large a relatively small appreciation of the exchange rate suffices to induce a significant rise in chartists' demand for domestic assets. Consequently, the initial exogenous shock to the relative supply of domestic assets will result in a rather moderate exchange rate movement.

Now assume that the fraction of fundamentalists trading in the spot market is successively raised. As long as the coefficient ψ can be found below a certain threshold, the sign of exchange rate returns in response to $dW_1 > 0$ remains negative. Nevertheless, the more traders follow a fundamentalist investment strategy the more important the impact of the behavior of this trader group on the exchange rate process is. For a given expected equilibrium exchange rate, fundamentalists interpret a current appreciation of the exchange rate as a signal of a long-run depreciation of the domestic currency. In order to be sheltered from depreciation losses, these traders instantaneously sell domestic assets. This, in turn, implies that the current movement of the exchange rate must be sufficiently large to stimulate chartists to compensate both the rise in the relative supply variable, s_a, *and* the decline in the demand for domestic assets due to fundamentalists' trading behavior. For this reason, the successive rise in the fraction of fundamentalists in the spot market eventually increases the responsiveness of the exchange rate to innovations of the state variables driving the economic system. As this magnification effect amplifies exchange rate volatility, we have the result graphed in Figure 3.9 that for certain numerical parameter combinations the variability of the spot rate is raised as the market share of fundamentalists increases.

I now analyze the implications of the above noise trader exchange rate model for the dynamics of the domestic, r, and the foreign, r^*, locally risk-free instantaneous interest rates. The international differential in instantaneous interest rates obtains by recognizing that the model has been interpreted under an equivalent martingale measure. This implies that $\mathbb{E}_t^{\tilde{g}}(dE) = (r - r^*)Edt$, where the operator $\mathbb{E}_t$ denotes conditional expectation taken under the equivalent martingale measure $\tilde{g}$.[59] To fix not only the differential between instantaneous interest rates but also the level of the domestic and the foreign instantaneous interest rates, I follow Dumas et al. (1993, 1995b) and assume that the international instantaneous interest rate differential can be decomposed as $r_D = \bar{r} + k(r - r^*)$ and $r_F = \bar{r} + (1-k)(r - r^*)$, where r_D and r_F represent the respective levels of the domestic and foreign instantaneous interest rates, $\bar{r}$ denotes a central interest rate level, and $0 < k < 1$ is a weighting factor. Using this set of assumptions, the domestic and foreign instantaneous interest rates can be expressed as

$$(3.55) \quad r_l = \alpha_{1,l} + \alpha_{2,l}\, y + \alpha_{3,l}\, q, \qquad l = D, F,$$

where $\quad \alpha_{1,D} \equiv \bar{r} + \left(\dfrac{1+\gamma_2}{\gamma_1}\right)\mu_s k, \qquad \alpha_{2,D} \equiv k\left(\dfrac{g_s + \gamma_2 g_{e0}}{\gamma_1} + \dfrac{1}{2}\left(\dfrac{\sigma_s}{\gamma_1}\right)^2\right),$

$$\alpha_{3,D} \equiv \frac{1}{2}k\left(\frac{\gamma_2 \theta_{e0}}{\gamma_1}\right)^2, \quad \alpha_{1,F} \equiv \bar{r}\left(1 - \frac{1-k}{k}\right) + \alpha_{1,D}\frac{1-k}{k}, \quad \alpha_{j,F} \equiv \frac{1-k}{k}\alpha_j,$$

$j = 2,3.$

Equation (3.55) shows that domestic and foreign locally risk-free instantaneous interest rates are driven by two factors: the state variable $y(t)$ affecting the relative supply of domestic assets and the volatility of the rumors component driving the long-run equilibrium exchange rate expected by FX traders. Disturbances affecting the expected long-run equilibrium exchange rate unambiguously increase interest rates. Because the state variable $y(t)$ directly enters into the drift of the exchange rate process, the sign of the impact exerted by $y(t)$ on the domestic and foreign instantaneous interest rates depends upon the sign and magnitude of γ_1 and γ_2 as well as on the drift coefficients g_s and g_{e0}.

By definition, the current price, $P^l(t,T)$, of a default-free discount bond with time-to-maturity $\tau = T - t \geq 0$ can be expressed as (see, e.g., Vasicek 1977: 183; Ingersoll 1987: 395):

$$(3.56) \quad P^l(t,T) = \mathbb{E}_t^{\tilde{g}}\left[\exp\left(-\int_t^T r_l(u)du\right)\right], \qquad l = D, F,$$

where conditional expectations are taken under the equivalent martingale measure. The bond price equation (3.56) states that the current value of a default-

---

[59] Note that this equation only states that the condition of uncovered interest rate parity holds under the equivalent martingale measure. This proposition does *not* include the assertion that this condition holds in general.

free discount bond embodies information about the entire integral of expected future short rates over the remaining time to expiry of the bond. As both state variables driving domestic and foreign instantaneous risk-free interest rates evolve according to square root processes, the structure of the pricing formula applicable to value default-free discount bonds is the same as in Cox et al. (1985b) and in Chen and Scott (1995) so that it is not necessary to reproduce it here. The discount bond solutions can be utilized to compute the domestic and foreign yield curves which are defined as $\eta(t,T) \equiv -\log P^l(t,T)/(T-t)$.

3.4.2   Noise Trader and Foreign Currency Options

With the expressions derived for the exchange rate process and for the domestic and the foreign term structure of interest rates at hand, it is now possible to set up a valuation framework applicable to the pricing of European-style options on foreign currency. Under the equivalent martingale measure $\tilde{g}$, the current value of a European FX call with strike price X and time to expiry $\tau = T - t \geq 0$ can be expressed as:

$$(3.57) \quad C(t,T) = \mathbb{E}_t^{\tilde{g}}\left[\exp\left(-\int_t^T r_D(u)du\right)\left(E(T)-X\right)\mathbf{1}_{\{E(T)>X\}}\right] \equiv C(E(t),y(t),q(t),t,T),$$

where the valuation function $C(E(t),y(t),q(t),t,T)$ is twice differentiable in $E(t)$, $y(t)$, and $q(t)$ and once differentiable in t, and $\mathbf{1}$ denotes an indicator function. Following the same steps as described in the review of the model originated by Heston (1993) contained in Section 2.3.2.2, these notational conventions can be used to reexpress the FX call pricing formula as

$$(3.58) \quad C(E(t),y(t),q(t),t,T) = E(t)P^F(t,T)Q^1 - XP^D(t,T)Q^2,$$

where, as in Section 2.3.2.2, the Q^j with $j = 1,2$ denote the risk-neutral probabilities that the option expires in-the-money. Upon substituting equation (3.58) into the fundamental option valuation equation and upon using the arguments made in Bakshi and Chen (1997), closed-form expressions for the characteristic functions of the probabilities Q^j can be derived. An alternative strategy to express these functions in terms of elementary mathematical functions is to resort to a solution algorithm recently advanced by Scott (1997). As demonstrated in Chen and Scott (1995), this method is particularly suited to solve for the prices of contingent claims in the type of models used in the present analysis featuring various state variables. It was, therefore, adopted to perform the numerical simulations outlined below. The difference between the approach of Heston (1993) and this technique is that the former is based on the idea to solve partial differential equations for the probabilities that the option ends up in the money while the latter draws on concepts and results derived in stochastic calculus to evaluate the involved expectations more directly.[60] Whichever method is used, the characteristic functions applying in the present model are structurally the same as those given in Scott (1997) and in Bakshi and Chen (1997). The difference between their expressions and the valuation model formalized in equation (3.58) lies in the economic interpretation of the formulas used to calculate premia of FX options. The distinguishing feature of the model used in this section is that the structural parameters entering into the formulas for the discount bonds $P^l(t,T)$ and the characteristic functions of the probabilities Q^j also depend on the trading behavior of technical investors in the spot market.

Equipped with closed-form analytical expressions for the characteristic functions of the probabilities Q^j, the model can be set up numerically to illustrate qualitatively the impact of noisy spot trading for the pricing of foreign currency options. The results of these simulations are summarized in Figure 3.10. The figure plots at-the-money and in-the-money foreign currency option premia as a function of the fraction ψ of noise traders following a fundamentalist investment strategy. Premia for at-the-money options were calculated for a large $(k = 0.1)$ and a small $(k = 0.9)$ open economy. This allows me to discuss the fact that in the model formalized above noise trading not only affects option prices directly through its impact on the diffusion coefficients of the exchange rate process but also indirectly through its impact on domestic and foreign interest rates. The parameters summarizing the trading behavior of noise traders in the underlying spot market were chosen as in Figure 3.9, implying that, for a given ς_c, the function $V(t)$ introduced in equation (3.54) to denote the volatility of the exchange rate exhibits a hump-shaped form. To focus attention on the implications of technical spot trading for option premia, the coefficients of correlation between the innovation terms of the stochastic processes driving the economy were set equal to zero.

Figure 3.10 provides three interesting insights into the link between technical trading in the spot market and foreign currency option premia:

---

[60] Scott (1997) has utilized his approach to compute closed-form expressions for European-style equity option premia in a stochastic interest rate jump-diffusion economy featuring a stochastic volatility which follows a mean-reverting square root process. Because of the last assumption, the model is very much in the spirit of the Heston (1993) model. Another recent application of this technique can be found in Schöbel and Zhu (1999).

Figure 3.10: The Impact of Noise Trading on Option Prices

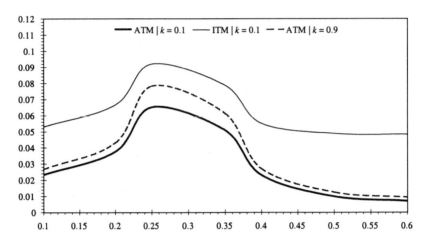

Note: The figure plots premia of foreign currency options with a time-to-maturity of three months on the vertical axis as a function of the market share of fundamentalists in the spot market on the horizontal axis. The numerical parameter values used to compute option values are $\varphi_f = \varphi_c = 0.5$, $\varsigma_c = \varsigma_f = 5$, $\mu_s = g_s = g_{e_0} = 0.01$, $\sigma_s = \sigma_{e_0} = 0.15$, $\kappa_y = \kappa_q = 5$, $\theta_y = \theta_q = 0.15$, $\xi_y = \xi_q = 0.15$, $\bar{r} = 0.15$.

• The first insight is that the hump-shaped functional form of the exchange rate volatility function given in equation (3.54) transmits onto the premia of the corresponding foreign currency options. As argued in Section 3.1, under the given set of trading elasticities the trend-chasing trader group dominates the spot market if the proportion ψ of agents following a contrarian investment strategy is rather low. As the market share of fundamentalists is raised, movements of the exchange rate must be of a magnitude guaranteeing that the aggregate sign and size of positions taken by trend-extrapolating dealers serve not only to balance the impact of exogenous stochastic shocks on the relative demand for domestic assets. Instead, the orders submitted by chartists must also help to compensate the influence of the quantitatively important orders submitted by contrarian investors. Figure 3.10 reveals that the resulting rise in exchange rate volatility exerts a quantitatively substantial impact on the prices of foreign currency options. The graphed functions also indicate that the premia of FX options begin to decrease once the relative importance of fundamentalists as captured by the parameter ψ has reached a certain critical threshold level and exchange rate volatility tends to decline again.

• The second insight provided by Figure 3.10 is that the premia of options which are in-the-money are higher than those obtained for options with a strike price equal to the prevailing spot rate. As in the stochastic volatility models reviewed in Chapter 2 of this study, this result is not entirely due to the impact of the moneyness on the price of the contract. Rather, it also reflects that in this model in-the-money options tend to have a higher implied volatility than their at-the-money counterparts. This is a standard finding in the literature on stochastic volatility option pricing and is thus not interesting in itself. The important point is that the function showing the dependence of in-the-money premia upon the share of contrarians in the underlying spot market parallels the corresponding function summarizing the impact of variations in this parameter on the prices of at-the-money options. From this observation, it can be concluded that in the present economy fluctuations of agents acting in the spot market for foreign currency between the trend-chasing and contrarian investor groups result in an upward or downward shift of the volatility strike structure. Given the structure of the demand function for domestic-currency-denominated assets, a similar proposition can be made to characterize the link between the volatility smile implicit in FX options and the trading elasticities of chartists and fundamentalists in the spot market. This is in sharp contrast to the comparative static results obtained for the more complex noise trader foreign currency option pricing model introduced in Section 3.1. In the present watered-down option pricing model a variation of the parameters summarizing the behavior of technical traders only alters the level of the volatility smile but leaves its shape more or less unchanged. In the model developed in Section 3.1, in contrast, varying the aggressiveness of trend-chasing spot traders resulted in a change of the convexity of the smile. Thus, while in the present setting the level of the volatility strike structure gives an impression of the influence of noise trading on exchange rate volatility, in the option valuation model discussed earlier in this chapter it was the shape of the smile that served to trace out the impact of technical market analysis on the dynamics of the spot rate.

• Finally, the noise trader foreign currency option valuation model can also be utilized to analyze the link between technical spot trading, interest rate dynamics, and the valuation of FX contingent claims. Under the set of numerical parameter values used to compute the figure, the domestic currency shows a tendency to depreciate. This positive drift implies that the level of domestic locally risk-free interest rates is higher than the level of the yield on holding foreign discount bonds whenever $k > 0.5$. Because a higher domestic interest rate increases the opportunity costs of selling an option, Figure 3.10 shows that in the scenario under investigation foreign currency option premia tend to be higher in a large $(k = 0.1)$ than in a small $(k = 0.9)$ open economy. Moreover, because the structural parameters characterizing the investment strategies of economic agents in the underlying spot market enter into the discount bond formulas, the graph indicates that a change in the characteristics of technical exchange rate trading also affects foreign currency options through this interest rate channel.

To summarize, the simplified noise trader FX option valuation model discussed in this section provides an analytically tractable framework of analysis which allows some interesting facets of the interplay between noise trading in the spot market, exchange rate dynamics, and the prices of foreign exchange contingent claims to be discussed. The advantage of the model is that it draws on ideas formulated in the literature on more standard stochastic volatility option pricing models and, therefore, provides closed-form analytical solutions for option premia. This feature of the model implies that it can be employed to shed light on the link between noise trading and FX options for purposes of, for example, real-time trading. The cost of framing the discussion in terms of a more standard valuation setting is that the model helps to explain theoretically the impact of technical trading on the level rather than on the shape of the volatility smile implicit in foreign currency options. If it is the primary goal of the analysis to trace out the determinants of the convexity of the smile, the preferred model of analysis should be the more elaborated FX option valuation model suggested in Section 3.1. Notwithstanding, as the empirical analysis has led to the conclusion that noisy spot trading is an important factor driving exchange rate volatility, it is also worthwhile to have a relatively simple contingent claim valuation model at hand which facilitates the discussion of some of the channels through which technical FX trading might influence foreign currency option premia.

3.5   Summary

Main Results

The first section of this chapter has been devoted to the construction and the simulation of a continuous-time noise trader foreign currency option valuation model. Based on an extension of a model of exchange rate determination originated by Krugman and Miller (1993), it has been highlighted how the impact of the state-dependent market entry and exit of technical spot traders on both the volatility of the current spot rate and the international interest rate differential transmits onto the arbitrage-free prices of European-style plain vanilla FX options. Building on earlier contributions of Platen and Schweizer (1998) and Grossman and Zhou (1996), it has been demonstrated that the noise trader foreign currency option pricing model provides a rich and flexible setting which allows the smile and smirk effects most often characterizing real-world implied volatility strike structures to be interpreted in economic rather than in purely technical terms. A Monte Carlo simulation study revealed that in the theoretical model the shape of the endogenously derived volatility smiles and smirks implicit in FX option premia depends, for example, upon the width of the interval of inaction of technical traders and on the trading elasticity of these agents. Emphasizing the link between the trading behavior of economic agents in the spot market and the convexity of the volatility strike structure, the framework of analysis offers an economically attractive explanation for the pricing errors resulting when the first-generation FX option valuation approaches are applied to price and to hedge real-world foreign currency options.

An important result of the theoretical study is that both the instantaneous exchange rate volatility and volatilities implicit in foreign currency option premia embed valuable information regarding implicit support or resistance levels in FX spot markets. The volatility of the underlying exchange rate and foreign-currency-options-implied volatilities tend to increase (to decrease) as the spot rate reaches a destabilizing (stabilizing) trigger threshold, inducing technical traders to enter or to exit the market for foreign exchange. In the empirical analysis contained in Sections 3.2 and 3.3, this result was exploited to perform volatility-based tests for implicit trading regimes in actual FX spot markets. In Section 3.2, it was examined whether or not volatility-based tests point to the presence of implicit trading-induced price barriers at exchange rate realizations ending in zero at the second and third digit after the decimal point. Focusing on a sample period beginning in January 1990 and ending in December 1997, only rather weak evidence supporting this traditional interpretation of the barriers hypothesis was found in the case of the DM/YEN, the US/BP, the CAN/US, and the US/CAN returns series.

To obtain further interesting insights into the microstructure of FX markets, alternative volatility-based tests for implicit trading regimes were employed in Section 3.3. Combining elements of popular technical-filter-based and moving-average-based trading rules, the structure of the competing volatility-based test allows one to examine whether exchange rate volatility tends to rise when the absolute deviation of the spot rate from a medium-term target level exceeds a critical threshold level. This test design is intended to capture the state-contingent nature of the investment strategies adopted by noise traders in the theoretical model of exchange rate determination outlined in Section 3.1. The results of this version of the volatility-based test for implicit trading regimes in FX markets are very promising. The level of the conditional volatilities of exchange rate returns obtained by estimating GARCH models were found to contain a significant state-contingent component. To be more precise, the test detected for the majority of currency pairs included in the empirical analysis that exchange rate volatility tends to increase as the spot rate moves farther away from its moving average representation. Nonparametric tests and vector autoregressions were employed to document the robustness of this result. Against the background of the theoretical analysis laid out in Section 3.1, these findings indicate that generally not immediately observable implicit trigger thresholds and implicit trading regimes might help to explain the occurrence of smiles in the volatility strike structures implicit in FX options contracts on these exchange rates.

Moreover, the significance of the results of the alternative test for implicit trading regimes in FX markets contrasts remarkably with the borderline significance of the trading trigger dummies plugged into the variance equations of the GARCH models utilized to implement the traditional test for implicit price barriers in financial markets. The relative performance of the test routines might indicate that technical traders in real-world FX markets follow the type of state-dependent moving-average investment strategies modeled in this chapter rather than one of the convex portfolio insurance strategies discussed in Krugman and Miller (1993). In the baseline model advocated by Krugman and Miller, the instantaneous volatility of the spot rate increases as the exchange rate reaches one of those critical trading thresholds at which standing orders of a nonnegligible number of stop-loss traders are executed. Once the spot rate has crossed the trading trigger at which noise traders swap into domestic (foreign) assets and shows a tendency to further appreciate (depreciate), the instantaneous volatility of the exchange rate drops to a lower level which also applies in the homogenous trader scenario. In contrast, in the version of this framework of analysis outlined in the theoretical part of this chapter, instantaneous exchange rate volatility does not fall to its GK baseline level once chartists' trading triggers have been passed. Instead, the presence of this group of technical traders in the spot market implies $e_f > 1$ also for $e(t) > \bar{e}$ and for $e(t) < \underline{e}$. Thus, noise trading alters the intrinsic relation between economic fundamentals and the spot rate and this implies that the base level of exchange rate volatility rises when chartists participate in FX trading. Therefore, the behavior of exchange rate volatility as implied by the model discussed in Section 3.1 above harmonizes with the outcomes of the second tests for implicit trading regimes in FX markets, whereas the dynamics of spot rate volatility derived in the basic Krugman and Miller (1993) model do not. The type of state-contingent trend-chasing technical trading in spot FX markets modeled in Chapter 3 might thus be a more important determinant of the shape of real-world volatility strike structures implicit in foreign currency options than the type of convex program trading strategies analyzed by Krugman and Miller (1993). This line of argumentation suggests that a promising direction for future research might be to develop even more refined volatility-based testing procedures which render it possible to discriminate even more neatly between alternative noise trading mechanisms.

In a final step, the empirical evidence stimulated the discussion of a simplified noise trader foreign currency option valuation model. For this purpose, a two-factor contingent claim valuation model in the tradition of the models originated by Heston (1993), Scott (1997), and Bakshi and Chen (1997) was used to study the influence of technical trading in the spot market on the arbitrage-free prices of options on foreign currency. The framework of analysis was a stochastic version of a simple and tractable noise trader setup of exchange rate determination suggested by Frankel (1996). An interesting feature of this model is that exchange rate volatility does not necessarily increase as the influence of trend-chasing noise traders in the spot market is raised. The overall impression obtained by numerically simulating the model confirmed the notion that noise trading in spot FX markets can exert a significant impact on the premia of foreign currency options. An implication of the simplified FX option valuation is that a variation of the parameters which characterize the position taking of noise traders mainly affects the level of individual FX options prices and generates shifts of the volatility smile. In contrast, in the model utilized in Section 3.1, the aggressiveness of technical investors helped to explain the relative pricing of options on foreign currency with different strike prices as visualized by plotting the volatility strike structure.

What Lies Ahead?

Both the theoretical and the empirical work presented in Chapter 3 could be extended in several directions in future research. From the viewpoint of economic theory, it might be particularly interesting to use volatilities implicit in actual foreign currency options instead of estimated conditional returns volatilities to perform either the traditional or the alternative volatility-based test for implicit trading regimes in financial markets.[61] A very interesting topic for future research would also be to examine how the skewness implied by the empirically observed relative pricing of in-the-money and out-of-the-money foreign currency options and the overall shape of the entire volatility smile evolve as the underlying spot or forward rate changes its relative position with respect to its medium-term target level. This would also allow further insights to be gained

---

[61] An example of such a research approach can be found in a recent contribution by Campa and Chang (1998). These authors utilize volatilities implicit in real-world FX option quotes to analyze the impact of the perforate price barriers which defined the EMS target zone regime on the variability of major European currencies as anticipated by foreign currency option traders.

into the factors influencing the performance of both vega hedging strategies and derivative trading rules which are based on a combination of several different option contracts.

It should also be noted that the framework of analysis suggested in Chapter 3 cannot only be employed to model the relation between noisy spot trading and the shape of the volatility strike structure implicit in FX options prices but might also serve as a useful starting point for analyses of markets for options on other financial securities as well. For example, the empirical evidence reported in, for example, Rubinstein (1994) suggests that the skewed implied volatility smirk which could be inferred from stock options in the aftermath of the tremendous market crash of October 19, 1987, might embody options traders' anticipation of the existence of implicit trigger prices in the market for the underlying shares at which a nonnegligible number of trend-chasing noise traders are expected to enter the spot market. Such a line of argumentation could constitute an alternative theory of the volatility strike structure implicit in options on stocks and stock indices and could complement the portfolio insurance and dynamic hedging theories of the smile discussed in Grossman and Zhou (1996) and in Platen and Schweizer (1998). Recent empirical results documented in Bakshi and Madan (1999) indicate that a closer examination of the link between the dynamics of options prices and potential stock market rallies might be a promising area for future research. The theoretical and empirical framework of analysis developed in Chapter 3 could provide a flexible alternative point of departure for taking some further steps in this direction.

With a sufficiently large number of empirically observed options data at hand, it would also be interesting to use the watered-down noise trader FX option pricing model discussed in Section 3.4 as a technical tool in an empirical analysis aiming at inverting real-world option prices numerically to determine the structural parameters characterizing the trading behavior of technical investors in spot markets. Such a research strategy is routinely used in the options pricing literature. For example, Bates (1996b) utilizes a broad set of actual FX options with different strike prices to estimate the structural parameters of a stochastic volatility jump-diffusion model. As compared to the computer time required to determine the numerical values of the set of structural parameters of such relatively complex option pricing models, the costs of estimating the simplified noise trader model outlined in Section 3.4 should only be slightly higher. The returns of numerically inverting observed option prices to determine the structural coefficients of this model, in contrast, can be substantial. For example, a prominent structural parameter of the noise trader FX option pricing model discussed in Section 3.4 is the proportion of fundamentalists/chartists trading in the spot market. The model could thus be utilized to make inferences regarding the allocation of spot traders among this different investment groups from real-world FX option premia. The noise trader FX option valuation model approach, thus, provides empirical researchers and economic policymakers with a platform to develop alternative testing strategies to determine the quantitative importance of chartism and fundamentalism in actual FX markets.

3.5.1 Policy Implications

The theoretical and empirical analyses contained in this chapter indicate that the poor empirical performance of the first-generation FX option pricing models might reflect that these overly simplistic approaches to the valuation of price-contingent claims do not take account of the impact of noisy spot trading on the dynamics of exchange rates and their volatilities. The framework used in the present chapter, in contrast, offers economic policymakers the technical background and the terminology required to interpret the pricing errors of the baseline reference FX option valuation approach in an economically meaningful way. The model allows one to relate empirically observed option prices and, thus, the shape of the volatility strike structure to the trading behavior of economic agents participating in FX spot trading. As regards economic policy, the relevance of this facet of the model stems from the fact that in the recent empirical literature FX options prices have frequently been advocated as instruments which allow policymakers to extract valuable and otherwise unavailable information regarding market participants exchange rate expectations and to evaluate the effectiveness of policy measures efficiently.

For example, Campa and Chang (1996) have suggested FX options-based indicators of the credibility of exchange rate target zones. A similar approach has been taken by Campa et al. (1997), Malz (1996), and Mizrach (1996), who use the cross section of option prices to extract implicit (risk-neutral) future spot rate distributions from which credibility measures of exchange rate systems can be constructed. Galati and Melick (1999) utilize such an approach to elaborate on the effectiveness of central bank interventions. Leahy and Thomas (1996) have used options prices to study the impact of the sovereignty referendum which took place in the Canadian province Quebec in 1995 on the moments of exchange rate distributions implicit in foreign currency options.[62]

---

[62] For a survey of approaches which can be used to extract the informational content of derivative securities, see Söderlind and Svensson (1997). Further applications of these approaches to the discussion of monetary and exchange rate policy issues, see,

While these studies employ FX options premia to analyze heavily discussed and extremely relevant monetary policy issues, they are "nonparametric" insofar as they describe empirical regularities but do not relate these stylized facts to a structural explanation founded in economic theory. The analyses outlined in the preceding sections point to such an explanation. For example, while nonstructural approaches allow policymakers to use descriptive statements to discuss changes in the shape of the volatility smile, the structural economic models discussed in this chapter render it additionally possible to relate, for example, an increase in the convexity of the smile to the influence of extrapolative technical trading in the underlying spot market.

Hence, the insights into the microstructure of FX markets offered by the analysis contained in Chapter 3 are not only interesting from the viewpoint of a financial market participant or a financial institution involved in the trading of derivative securities. But the theoretical and empirical results derived in the preceding sections may also provide an important additional piece of information which could be exploited by economic policymakers and central banks discussing issues related to the evolution, the variability, and the management of exchange rates. Thus, the analysis contained in this chapter might contribute to the debate on the usefulness of the informational content embedded in option prices to time the implementation and to evaluate the success of various policy measures. The noise trader hypothesis of the volatility smile embedded in foreign currency options discussed theoretically and validated empirically above not only allows policymakers merely to describe changes in the shape of the smile but also offers arguments needed to provide an economically reasonable structural interpretation of these phenomena.

Of course, competing explanations for convex volatility strike structures have been put forward in the area of research investigating the link between agents' trading behavior and the shape of the smile. Therefore, the model suggested in this chapter only provides one possible economic explanation for the pricing errors produced by the first-generation FX option pricing approach. However, given both the quantitative importance of technical trading in FX markets reported in the empirical literature and the estimation results outlined above, I believe that, from an empirical point of view, this explanation is a relevant one.

A related issue relevant for monetary and exchange rate policy is whether central banks should intervene when either the conditional volatility of the spot

<hr>

e.g., in Bank of Japan (1995), Butler and Cooper (1997), Europäische Zentralbank (2000), Neuhaus (1995), and Söderlind (1998). For an application of these approaches to the evaluation of the effectiveness of foreign exchange market interventions of central banks, see Chapter 4 of this study.

rate or its volatility as implied in foreign currency option quotes shows a tendency to rise as the spot rate moves farther away from a medium-term target value. The analyses contained in Chapter 3 suggest that such an increase in estimated or implied exchange rate volatility might be due to the implementation of destabilizing noise trading strategies in the spot market. The relevant policy issue is then whether monetary authorities should enter FX markets to calm "disorderly" markets as the wedge between the prevailing exchange rate and its longer-term target value and/or at-the-money volatilities implicit in observed FX option quotes increase. In this respect, central banks could interpret an increase in the volatility of the exchange rate as anticipated by FX option traders as a signal that market turbulences are gathering steam. Before reacting to spot market jitters, however, the central question to be answered is whether interventions in the foreign exchange market are indeed an effective instrument allowing central banks to narrow the wedge between the exchange rate and its target value and/or to bring down exchange rate volatility. This issue will be taken up in Chapter 4.

4   Exchange Rate Policy and FX Options

The FX option pricing models outlined in the previous chapters of this study are built on the assumption that exchange rate dynamics can be described either by means of an exogenously given stochastic differential equation or are determined entirely by the speculative position taking of private economic agents. In this chapter, I enrich this theoretical setting by taking into consideration that even since the breakdown of the Bretton Woods system in 1973, real-world exchange rates have often been subject to central banks' foreign exchange market interventions. During prolonged periods of time, exchange rates were thus not driven by the trading behavior of private agents alone but also by the actual or anticipated policy actions of monetary authorities.

In Section 4.1, a continuous-time model of exchange rate determination developed by Lewis (1995) is employed to examine how the impact of an effective central bank intervention policy on the dynamics of the exchange rate transmits onto the arbitrage-free premia of foreign currency options. The model to be laid out complements earlier work on FX option pricing under explicitly regulated asset price processes and examines the influence of a nonzero probability of occasional central bank foreign exchange interventions on the valuation of foreign currency options.

The theoretical discussion has clear-cut empirically testable implications. The model predicts that, if compared to a free float, an effective central bank intervention policy has the potential to reduce both the wedge between the current exchange rate and its central parity and the volatility of this important financial market variable. However, while the model utilized in the analysis simply assumes that the actions taken by central banks affect the level and the volatility of spot rates, it remains a heavily discussed empirical question whether central bank interventions do indeed tend to stabilize the level of exchange rates around a central parity defined by economic policy and/or to dampen the volatility of this asset price. This important issue will be addressed in Section 4.2.

To perform the empirical analysis outlined in Section 4.2, the success of central bank intervention policy is measured in terms of a multifactor success criterion which allows two dimensions of the effectiveness of central bank foreign exchange market operations to be taken into consideration simultaneously: (1) their impact on the level and (2) on the volatility of the spot exchange rate.

This multifactor success criterion is then used to estimate an ordered qualitative response model to assess the success of the interventions of the Deutsche Bundesbank in the US/DM spot market. The empirical analysis utilizes daily official German intervention data for the period of time following the Louvre Accord, ranging from 2/1/1987 to 12/3/1990, which was characterized by frequent (and often coordinated) interventions. The so-called Louvre Accord was the main outcome of a G-7 meeting held at the Louvre in Paris on February 22, 1987 and was launched to stabilize exchange rates at or around the then prevailing levels (Funabashi 1988).

One of the main results of the theoretical study performed in Section 4.1 is that foreign currency option premia reflect the impact of monetary authorities' FX market operations on the level and the volatility of exchange rates. In the empirical study contained in Section 4.2, I use this finding and resort to volatilities implicit in FX options to test for the effectiveness of central bank interventions with respect to expected exchange rate volatility (see also Bonser-Neal and Tanner 1996; Madura and Tucker 1991). This chapter, therefore, also contributes to the literature examining how market participants and central banks can exploit the informational content implicit in foreign currency options to gain deeper insights into the functioning of FX markets and into the impact of monetary policy actions on the time path of spot exchange rates.

4.1 Central Bank Interventions and FX Option Pricing

The arbitrage-free valuation of FX options in stochastic continuous-time economies is frequently based on the first-generation valuation models discussed in Chapter 1 of this study. A characteristic feature of these models is that in the derivation of the pricing formula it is assumed that the underlying exchange rate on which the option is written follows an exogenously given unconstrained geometric Brownian diffusion process. The implicit convention behind this assumption is that real-world exchange rates are allowed to float freely and can, in principle, assume any numerical value on the positive real line. The experience of the post Bretton Woods era, however, suggests that this assumption might be overly simplistic and might in certain historical situations provide only a poor description of the numerous variants of empirically observed exchange rate systems allowing for varying degrees of exchange rate flexibility. In reality, governments often try to manage exchange rates in an attempt to cope with the "open-economy trilemma" (Obstfeld and Taylor 1998) expressing the impossibility to establish free cross-border capital flows, exchange rate flexibility, and monetary autonomy simultaneously. Active exchange rate policy is frequently implemented by conducting occasional FX market interventions or by constraining spot exchange rates so that they evolve within explicit fluctuation intervals. The so-called Plaza Communiqué agreed upon by G-5 central banks' governors and finance ministers on September 22, 1985, and the Louvre Accord proclaimed at a G-7 summit held in Paris on February 22, 1987, are examples of political events marking attempts to implement exchange rate systems characterized by occasional interventions. An example of a policy regime aiming at invoking an explicit exchange rate target zone is given by the former European Monetary System. Clearly, the ad hoc specification of exchange rate dynamics underlying the first generation FX option pricing models neglects the potential influence of such economic policy strategies on the time path of the exchange rate and thus on the premia of currency options.

Recently, modeling strategies which take some of the implications of limited exchange rate flexibility into consideration have been proposed in the literature on currency option pricing in explicit exchange rate target zones. Ingersoll (1997) models the impact of credible and irrevocable exchange rate thresholds on the pricing of currency options by introducing a reflected Brownian exchange rate process. Sorensen (1997) and Ekvall et al. (1993) suggest capturing the impact of bounds on exchange rates on the pricing of currency options by assuming that the state variable of the economy follows an exogenously specified unbounded Ornstein–Uhlenbeck process. While these approaches allow closed-form solutions for European-style FX options to be derived, they do not take into account the nonlinearities of the exchange rate path described in the literature on exchange rate target zones.[63] In exchange rate target zone models, the nonlinearity of the exchange rate function arises due to economic agents' expectations regarding the state-contingent monetary policy intervention mechanism activated as the exchange rate reaches either the upper or the lower reflecting boundary of its explicit fluctuation interval.[64] Based on the first-generation target zone model developed by Krugman (1991) for describing exchange rate dynamics within explicit and credible exchange rate bands, Dumas et al. (1993) demonstrate how to integrate this nonlinearity of the exchange rate function into a currency option valuation model. Since the integration of the nonlinearity of the

---

[63] For a survey of the literature on exchange rate determination in exchange rate target zones, see Svensson (1992).

[64] The nonlinearity of the exchange rate path might be caused either by stabilizing or by destabilizing exchange rate expectations. For the latter case, see, e.g., Bertola and Caballero (1992).

exchange rate path into the option pricing model makes it impossible to derive closed-form solutions for the premium of the derivative security, they implement the model numerically and show that the nonlinearity of the exchange rate path translates onto the function describing premia of European-style FX options as a function of regulated economic fundamentals. This baseline model has been extended by Dumas et al. (1995b) by modeling exchange rate dynamics as a composite process consisting of a Gauss–Wiener component of economic fundamentals and a Possion jump process reflecting occasional realignments of central parities. Kempa et al. (1998) have further modified this model in two respects. They have introduced stochastic realignment risk, as suggested in Bertola and Svensson (1993), to account for the limited credibility problem often beleaguering real-world currency bands and mean reversion in fundamentals, along the lines of Lindberg and Söderlind (1994), to reflect intramarginal interventions of central banks. A contingent claim valuation model featuring endogenous realignment risk has been proposed by Christensen et al. (1998). They analyze the properties of FX option prices in a two-factor target zone model with the current and hypothetical free-float or shadow exchange rates being the state variables of the system. In their model, the realignment risk increases as the current exchange rate approaches the boundaries of its fluctuation range and as the wedge between the current and the shadow spot rate widens.

The contingent claim valuation models mentioned so far have primarily been designed as theoretical tools to price European-style FX options in explicit exchange rate target zones. The empirical analysis contained in Section 4.2, however, examines the impact of intervention policy on the level and on the volatility of the US/DM exchange rate during the Louvre period, which was characterized by *occasional* interventions rather than by the imposition of an explicit exchange rate fluctuation range. To derive empirically testable hypotheses regarding the impact of such an intervention regime on the level and the *expected* volatility of the exchange rate as implied in foreign currency options, Section 4.1 draws on work by Lewis (1995) to develop an FX option pricing model featuring infrequent central bank FX market operations. Harmonizing with the available data on the empirically observed intervention policy of major central banks during the Louvre regime, the exchange rate model of Lewis (1995) implies that the timing of occasional interventions is itself a stochastic variable. This is in contrast to FX option pricing models built on Krugman's (1991) model, in which central bank FX market interventions occur if and only if the exchange rate reaches the boundaries of its fluctuation interval. This also implies that the model departs from the assumption made in valuation models in which intramarginal interventions take place continuously and are an increasing deterministic function of the deviation of the exchange rate from its central parity. A further point particularly important as regards option pricing theory is that in the exchange rate model championed by Lewis (1995), central bank interventions affect both the drift and the volatility of the fundamentals used to price foreign exchange. In models resorting to an Ornstein–Uhlenbeck process to depict interventions continuously affecting the spot rate, central banks' foreign exchange market operations only affect the drift component of the stochastic process driving economic fundamentals.

Using this model of exchange rate determination in the presence of infrequent central bank foreign exchange market interventions, a simple valuation formula applicable to European-style foreign currency option contracts is discussed in Section 4.1.1. This formula is a modified version of the closed-form pricing expression developed by Garman and Kohlhagen (1983) with appropriately adjusted domestic and foreign interest rates and a modified exchange rate volatility accounting for a nonzero probability of central bank interventions assumed to be constant over the domain of the exchange rate. This is in contrast to the FX option pricing models based upon Krugman's (1991) target zone model mentioned above which converge in the limit case of an infinite band width to the baseline version of the unadjusted GK model. In this respect, the framework of analysis used below also departs from models of intra-marginal interventions featuring an Ornstein–Uhlenbeck process for economic fundamentals which, depending upon whether the condition of uncovered interest rate parity is assumed to hold, degenerate in the limit case either to the Ekvall et al. (1993) or to the Lo and Whang (1995) option pricing models. While these latter models are also special cases of the original GK model, they assume that the unbounded exchange rate follows a stationary mean-reverting stochastic process. In the model discussed in Section 4.1.1, the unbounded exchange rate is driven by a geometric Gauss–Wiener process with drift and diffusion coefficients modified to account for the probability of infrequent central bank foreign exchange market operations.

The second part of the theoretical analyses contained in Section 4.1.2 is devoted to a close examination of the impact of infrequent central bank interventions on the premia of foreign currency options. Numerical simulations of the model are used to argue that the sign of the effect of an increase in the probability that a central bank will enter the spot market for foreign currency in the next instant of time is ambiguous in the valuation model used in this chapter. As will be discussed extensively in Section 4.1.2, the sign of the impact of an effective intervention policy on foreign currency option premia can only be figured out when the implications of central bank operations for both exchange rate volatility and the international interest rate differential are taken into consideration. In Section 4.1.2, the implications of this result for the subsequent empirical analysis will also be discussed.

4.1.1   The FX Option Pricing Model

The basic assumption behind the version of the stochastic continuous-time flex-price monetary model of exchange rate determination introduced into the literature by Lewis (1995) stipulates that the logarithm of the value of foreign currency can be expressed as the sum of a set of economic fundamentals, f, and the expected rate of change of the nominal exchange rate over the time span dt conditioned on the information set available in the current period t:

(4.1) $e = f + \upsilon \, \mathbb{E}_t(de)/dt$,

where υ denotes the interest elasticity of money demand. The implicit assumptions underlying equation (4.1) are that capital is perfectly mobile internationally, that economic agents are risk neutral, and that the condition of uncovered interest rate parity holds in its logarithmic form. Economic fundamentals f^* net of changes in the monetary base due to central bank FX market interventions are assumed to follow the stochastic differential equation given below:

(4.2) $\mathrm{d}f^* = \mu \mathrm{d}t + \sigma \mathrm{d}W$.

In equation (4.2), μ reflects a drift parameter, the constant σ denotes the diffusion coefficient of the process, and $\mathrm{d}W$ is the differential of a standard Gauss–Wiener process with expected value zero and unit variance.

To move from equation (4.2) to the process driving fundamentals in the presence of infrequent central bank interventions, it is assumed that monetary authorities intervene in the FX market occasionally and that the intervention probability is an exogenously specified constant $0 \le \tilde{\pi} < 1$ for all realizations of the fundamentals. The central bank chooses the size of interventions so as to exactly compensate the change in the fundamentals which would have occurred had the drift and diffusion component given in equation (4.2) unfolded their impact on the fundamentals. This implies that monetary authorities might either purchase or sell foreign currency when the exchange rate is above (below) its central parity. In line with the empirical facts documented in Section 4.2 below, the direction of the intervention is thus itself stochastic in the model advocated by Lewis (1995).[65]

In order to derive the stochastic process reflecting the dynamics of the intervention-augmented economic fundamentals, f, Lewis (1995) starts with a discrete-time version of the model and computes then the continuous-time limit of the conditional mean and of the conditional variance of the discrete-time process by forcing the size of time steps to converge to zero.[66] Upon carrying out these manipulations and taking account of the assumption that the probability of an intervention is constant for all realizations of f, one obtains the following process for the intervention-augmented fundamentals:

$$(4.3) \quad df = \mu(1-\pi)dt + \sigma\sqrt{1-\pi}\,dW.$$

Applying the rules of stochastic calculus, equation (4.3) results in the following stochastic differential equation describing exchange rate dynamics in the presence of infrequent central bank foreign exchange interventions:

$$(4.4) \quad de = \left\{ e_f\mu(1-\pi) + \frac{1}{2}\sigma^2 e_{ff}(1-\pi) \right\}dt + e_f\sigma\sqrt{1-\pi}\,dW,$$

so that the differential of the antilog of the spot exchange rate can be expressed as

$$(4.5) \quad dE = \left\{ e_f\mu(1-\pi) + \frac{1}{2}\sigma^2 e_{ff}(1-\pi) + \frac{1}{2}e_f{}^2\sigma^2(1-\pi) \right\}E\,dt + e_f\sigma\sqrt{1-\pi}\,E\,dW.$$

Taking conditional expectations of the process in equation (4.4), substituting the resulting expression into equation (4.1), and rearranging terms gives the following second-order inhomogeneous ordinary differential exchange rate equation with constant coefficients:

$$(4.6) \quad e = f + \upsilon\mu(1-\pi)e_f + \frac{1}{2}\upsilon\sigma^2(1-\pi)e_{ff}.$$

---

[65] The FX option model could also be extended to a situation in which the probability of central bank interventions depends upon economic fundamentals and exchange rates are restricted to fluctuate within implicit bands. See Lewis (1995) for a discussion of such an exchange rate model and Pierdzioch (2000) for an analysis of the implications of such extensions of the model for the pricing of foreign currency options.

[66] For a detailed description of this procedure, see Lewis (1995: 709, Technical Appendix).

Ruling out extrinsic bubbles by imposing appropriate transversality conditions, it follows that the particular and the general solution to this equation coincide and the exchange rate function can be written as

(4.7) $e(t) = f(t) + \upsilon\mu(1 - \tilde{\pi})$ so that $de = df$.

Equation (4.7) shows that the distortion of the process driving economic fundamentals caused by infrequent central bank foreign exchange market interventions serves to lower the drift of the spot rate process.

With the stochastic process driving the exchange rate in the presence of occasional central bank foreign exchange market interventions at hand, it is now possible to set up a foreign currency option pricing model. To integrate infrequent central bank interventions into a foreign currency option valuation model is necessary to fix not only the differential between but also the level of the domestic, r_D, and the foreign, r_F, riskless interest rates. To accomplish this task, I follow Dumas et al. (1993, 1995b) and assume that the international interest rate differential can be decomposed in the following manner:

(4.8a) $r_D = \bar{r} + k(r - r^*),$

(4.8b) $r_F = \bar{r} + (1 - k)(r - r^*).$

The next step is to define a valuation function, $C(E,t)$, twice differentiable in E and once in t. Upon applying the standard no-arbitrage argument, the fundamental parabolic partial differential contingent claim valuation equation applying in this economy can be specified as

(4.9) $\dfrac{1}{2}C_{EE}E^2\sigma^2(1 - \tilde{\pi}) + \mu(1 - \tilde{\pi})C_E E - (\bar{r} + k\mu(1 - \tilde{\pi}))C - C_\tau = 0,$

where the definition $\tau \equiv T - t$, which implies $C_\tau = -C_t$, has been applied. In the case of European-style FX options, this equation must be solved subject to

(4.10) $C(E,0) = [E - X]^+,$

(4.11) $\lim\limits_{E \to 0} C(E,\tau) = 0,$

(4.12) $C(E,\tau) \leq E.$

The valuation problem stated in equations (4.9)–(4.12) consists of an appropriately modified version of the fundamental contingent claim valuation equation and the corresponding set of boundary and terminal conditions also applying in the case of the first-generation FX option pricing model of Garman and Kohlhagen. The solution to this boundary value problem giving the premium of European-style FX options in the presence of a constant probability of infrequent central bank foreign exchange interventions can thus be pinned down as

$$(4.13) \quad C^{MF}\left(E,X,r_D,r_F,\sigma\sqrt{1-\tilde{\pi}},\tau\right)=C^{GK}\left(E,X,r_D,r_F,\tilde{\sigma},\tau\right),$$

with $\tilde{\sigma}=\sigma\sqrt{(1-\tilde{\pi})}$, so that the diffusion coefficient utilized to price the option is a decreasing function of the intervention probability. The valuation formula provided in equation (4.13) can be stated more explicitly as

$$(4.14) \quad C^{MF}\left(E,X,r,r^*,\tilde{\sigma},\tau\right)=E\exp[(-\bar{r}-(1-k)\mu(1-\tilde{\pi}))\tau]\Phi\left(\tilde{d}_1\right)$$
$$-X\exp[(-\bar{r}-k\mu(1-\tilde{\pi}))\tau]\Phi\left(\tilde{d}_2\right),$$

with $\quad \tilde{d}_1 \equiv \dfrac{\ln\left(\dfrac{E}{X}\right)+\left(\mu(1-\tilde{\pi})-0.5\tilde{\sigma}^2\right)\tau}{\tilde{\sigma}\sqrt{\tau}} \quad$ and $\quad \tilde{d}_2 \equiv \tilde{d}_1 - \tilde{\sigma}\sqrt{\tau}.$

Structurally, this valuation formula is similar to the one derived in Ingersoll (1997). Ingersoll's option pricing model applies in the case of explicit bands with no intramarginal interventions. In contrast, the modified GK pricing formula given in equation (4.14) can be used to price European-style FX options in a policy regime featuring neither explicit nor implicit bands but occasional interventions.

4.1.2   The Impact of Infrequent Central Bank Interventions on FX Option Prices

To examine the impact of a variation in the probability of no interventions on the premium of the FX option contract, take the partial derivative of the augmented GK valuation formula provided in equation (4.14) with respect to $1-\tilde{\pi}$ to obtain

$$(4.15) \quad \frac{\partial C^{MF}\left(E,X,r_D,r_F,\tilde{\sigma},\tau\right)}{\partial(1-\tilde{\pi})}=-(1-k)\mu\tau E\exp[(-\bar{r}-(1-k)\mu(1-\tilde{\pi}))\tau]\Phi\left(\tilde{d}_1\right)$$
$$+k\mu\tau X\exp[(-\bar{r}-k\mu(1-\tilde{\pi}))\tau]\Phi\left(\tilde{d}_2\right)$$

$$+ E \exp[(-\bar{r} - (1-k)\mu(1-\tilde{\pi}))\tau]\Phi'(\tilde{d}_1)\frac{\partial \tilde{d}_1}{\partial(1-\tilde{\pi})}$$

$$- X \exp[(-\bar{r} - k\mu(1-\tilde{\pi}))\tau]\Phi'(\tilde{d}_2)\frac{\partial \tilde{d}_2}{\partial(1-\tilde{\pi})},$$

which can be rearranged to give

$$(4.16) \quad \frac{\partial C^{MF}(E,X,r_D,r_F,\bar{\sigma},\tau)}{\partial(1-\tilde{\pi})} = -\mu\tau X \exp[(-\bar{r} - k\mu(1-\tilde{\pi}))\tau]\Phi(\tilde{d}_2)$$

$$+ k\mu\tau \left(E \exp[(-\bar{r} - (1-k)\mu(1-\tilde{\pi}))\tau]\Phi(\tilde{d}_1) + X \exp(-\bar{r} - k\mu(1-\tilde{\pi}))\Phi(\tilde{d}_2) \right)$$

$$- \mu\tau C(E,X,r,r^*,\bar{\sigma},\tau) + \frac{1}{2}\Phi'(\tilde{d}_2)X\sigma \exp[(-\bar{r} - k\mu(1-\tilde{\pi}))\tau]\sqrt{\frac{\tau}{1-\tilde{\pi}}}.$$

From equation (4.16), it follows that the effect of an increase in the probability that the central bank will not intervene in the foreign exchange market unambiguously inflates the option premium if the drift term of the fundamentals process is zero and/or if the effect of occasional interventions on the foreign interest rate can be neglected. In all other cases, the impact of a variation in the intervention probability on option premia is ambiguous.

This ambiguity arises due to the fact that in the above model the probability that a central bank foreign exchange market intervention will take place simultaneously affects three variables important for the pricing of FX options:

- Equation (4.8a) states that for a positive μ raising the parameter $\tilde{\pi}$ sets the domestic interest rate on the decrease. A higher intervention probability lowers the foregone interest earnings accruing from investing in domestic risk-free assets and, thus, dampens the opportunity costs of writing the option. For this reason, investors tend to require a lower compensation for selling options and this, in turn, implies that the option premium decreases. Converse propositions apply for the case of $\mu < 0$.
- A variation in the parameter $\tilde{\pi}$ affects the foreign interest rate. Equation (4.8b) stipulates that for $\mu > 0$ $(\mu < 0)$ raising the intervention probability sets the foreign risk-free interest rate on the decrease (increase). This effect exerts an amplifying (depressing) impact upon the option premium because the interest accrued by holding foreign risk-free assets plays a similar part in the valuation of FX options as the continuous leakage of value from holding the underlying in valuation models for European options on stocks yielding a dividend rate proportional to the level of the stock price.

– Increasing the parameter $\bar{\pi}$ lowers the volatility parameter utilized to price options. Raising the intervention probability, thus, also affects the option price through the vega of the contract. As the GK valuation formula states that the option price is an increasing function of the volatility parameter, this effect results in a decline of the premium of the contract.

To summarize, the effect of a rise in the probability that a central bank FX market intervention will take place on the volatility of the spot rate and on the domestic interest rate tends to decrease the value of the option when the domestic currency exerts a tendency to depreciate. In such a scenario, the effect exerted on the foreign riskless interest rate increases the premium of the contract. Appropriately modified corresponding propositions hold for a currency which shows a tendency to appreciate. In any case, whether a higher intervention probability results in a lower option premium depends on the specific numerical parameter values plugged into the modified GK option pricing formula, $C^{MF}(E,X,r_D,r_F,\bar{\sigma},\tau)$, outlined in equation (4.14).

The sign of the effect of a variation of the intervention probability on the premium of the FX option depends critically upon the parameter k reflecting how the international interest rate *differential* is decomposed to compute the *level* of the domestic and of the foreign riskless interest rates. Figure 4.1 serves to highlight the influence of this parameter on FX option premia in the present model. The figure plots at-the-money option prices computed by resorting to the modified GK formula presented in equation (4.14) as a function of the intervention probability, $\bar{\pi}$, and the drift, μ, of the process driving economic fundamentals. Figure (4.1, Panel A) assumes that the parameter k is relatively small, so that the international interest rate differential corresponding to a given probability of central bank interventions is mainly opened by an appropriate adjustment of the foreign risk-free interest rate. Figure (4.1, Panel B), in contrast, is derived by assuming that the parameter k is relatively large, so that the bulk of variations in the interest rate differential can be attributed to changes in the riskless domestic rate of interest. Both figures plot at-the-money option values under the assumption that the drift parameter, μ, is of a moderate size.

The depicted surfaces show that the sign of the effect of an increase in the drift of economic fundamentals on the premia of the at-the-money FX option depends upon the magnitude of the parameter k. For a relatively small k the option price turns out to decline as the drift of the fundamentals becomes larger, whereas for an interest rate differential allocation parameter k close to unity the option price is increasing in μ.

Figure 4.1: The Impact of the Intervention Probability on At-the-Money FX Options in the Managed Float: Part I

Panel A

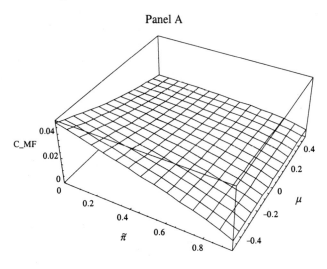

Panel B

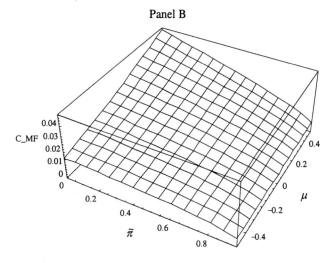

Note: The numerical parameter values selected to compute the option price surfaces are $\bar{r} = 0.1$, $\sigma = 0.25$, and $E = X = 1$. The time-to-maturity was fixed at one month. Figure 4.1 (Panel A) obtains by setting $k = 0.1$ and Figure 4.1 (Panel B) results by setting $k = 0.9$. The above graph and all following figures presented in this section plot option prices for intervention probabilities up to 0.95.

A small k might capture the fact that the domestic economy is relatively large compared to the rest of the world capital market, so that the risk-free interest rate r can almost be viewed as an exogenous parameter. As the drift of the fundamentals μ becomes smaller and even negative in such an environment, the resulting appreciation expectations for the domestic currency tend to exert a relatively stronger impact on the foreign risk-free interest rate than on the domestic rate of interest. Figure 4.1 (Panel A) reveals that for a relatively small k, the decline in the level of the domestic interest rate requiring a decrease in the option premium tends to be dominated by the effect of the lower proportional "dividend" rate on holding foreign assets requiring a rise in the price of the FX option.

Figure 4.1 (Panel B) reveals that for a relatively large k, the situation is reversed. In this situation, the domestic economy is relatively small compared to the size of the world capital market. Therefore, expectations regarding changes in the level of the exchange rate must be accommodated mainly by adjusting the domestic risk-free interest rate. For example, the depreciation expectations fostered by a relatively large positive drift parameter, μ, result in a positive international interest rate differential. If the numerical value assumed by the parameter k is relatively large, this requires a strong rise in r_D and a comparatively moderate increase in r_F. This, in turn, implies that the rise in the opportunity costs of writing the option caused by the higher domestic interest rate dominates the increase in the opportunity costs of holding the contract attributable to the higher foreign interest rate.

Figure 4.1 also suggests that at least for a drift parameter, μ, of a relatively small absolute size at-the-money FX option premia are strictly decreasing in the intervention probability, $\tilde{\pi}$. This finding indicates that for an absolutely small μ the effect of a raise in $\tilde{\pi}$ on the volatility of the stochastic process driving the intervention-augmented fundamentals is stronger in terms of at-the-money option premia than its impact on the drift rate of this process. This result harmonizes with economic intuition because the vega of the option attains a global maximum for contracts which are at-the-money.

Figure 4.2 demonstrates that the ordering of these effects might be reversed if at-the-money options are priced in an economic environment displaying a relatively large positive drift of fundamentals. The figure reveals that for a sufficiently large μ, a relatively small k, and for small and medium-sized intervention probabilities the premium of the at-the-money FX option might be an increasing function of $\tilde{\pi}$. The economic reasoning behind this finding is that for a large positive drift of fundamentals and a rather small probability that the central bank will enter the market, the volatility effect is dominated by the impact of the

Figure 4.2: The Impact of the Intervention Probability on At-the-Money FX Options in the Managed Float: Part II

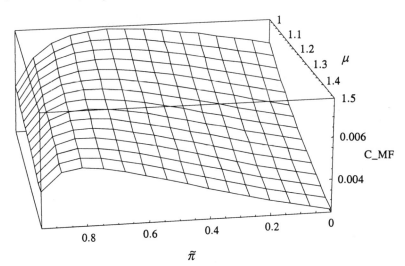

Note: For the numerical parameter values utilized to compute the figure, see Figure 4.1 (Panel A).

intervention probability on the foreign interest rate. Under these conditions, only rather high intervention probabilities ensure that the volatility effect dominates and the option premium begins to decline as $\tilde{\pi}$ increases.

The previous results demonstrate that for at-the-money options with a base currency issued by a relatively large domestic economy (which is characterized by a relatively small k) the volatility effect tends to dominate the interest rate effect as long as the drift of the process driving economic fundamentals is of a moderate size. Figure 4.3 highlights that a corresponding proposition does not hold in the case of in-the-money options. For such contracts, assigning even small positive numerical values to the parameter μ can change the relative magnitude of the effects. The economic reason behind this finding is that the interest rate sensitivity of the option is an increasing function of the moneyness of the contract (see, e.g., Kolb 1997: 170), so that for in-the-money FX options the effect of a variation in the intervention probability $\tilde{\pi}$ on vega tends to be more easily outperformed by the simultaneous impact on the rho of the option.[67]

---

[67] Note that the rho of the FX option with respect to both the domestic and the foreign interest rate must be considered.

Figure 4.3: The Impact of a Variation in the Intervention Probability on In-the-Money Options in the Managed Float: Part III

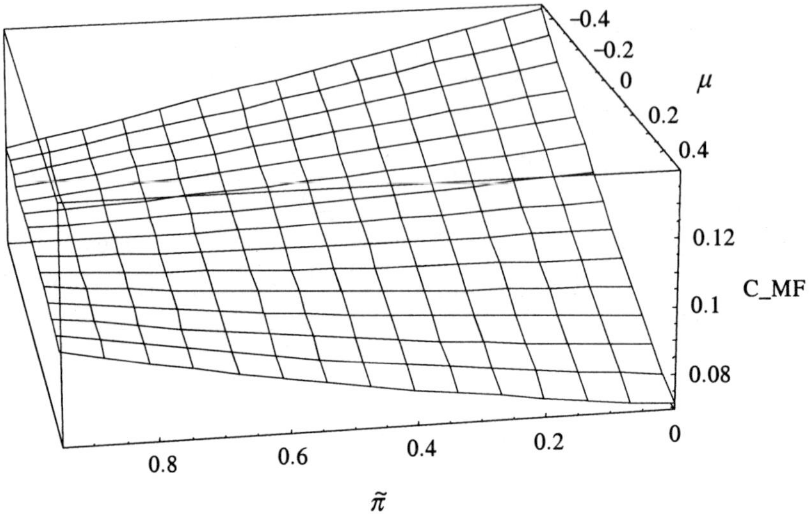

Note: The figure is based on the following set of numerical parameter values: $E = 1.1$, $X = 1$. The other parameters are as given in Figure 4.1 (Panel A).

The conclusion to be drawn from the results reported in this section is that in empirical analyses the sign of the effect of central bank interventions on the premia of foreign currency options depends upon the characteristics of the economic environment. This feature of the model suggests that in studies using option premia to disentangle effective from ineffective central bank FX market operations, one should carefully take into account the impact of central bank interventions on both international interest rates and exchange rate volatility.

To underscore this point, suppose economic agents resort to the historical record of central bank foreign exchange market interventions to conjecture a probability, $\tilde{\pi}$, that such an intervention will also take place during the next instant of time. Suppose further that interventions effectively alter the drift and lower the volatility of the exchange rate process. If the interest rate effect of this policy dominates its volatility effect, the model developed above predicts that FX options prices might show a tendency to increase. If a researcher did not know the exact numerical value of $\tilde{\pi}$ and were not able to capture exactly the interest rate effect of such a policy, he or she might even spuriously find that implied volatilities inferred from these options contracts also tend to increase. Of course, it would then be tempting to erroneously interpret the recovered rise in the volatility implicit in foreign currency options as an indication that the central banks' exchange rate policy is ineffective in the sense that it does not contribute to calming disorderly markets.

This problem can only be resolved by taking a closer look at the international economic environment in which central banks' foreign exchange market interventions take place. In the empirical section below, I examine the effectiveness of interventions conducted by the Deutsche Bundesbank in the US$/DM spot market during a period ranging from 2/1/1987 to 12/3/1990. Using daily observations, the mean and the median of the differential between the (domestic) US and the (foreign) German one-month eurodollar rates can be calculated as amounting to 2.7780 percent per annum and 3.1920 percent per annum, respectively. During the time period under investigation the Bundesbank intervened at 167 days in the US$/DM spot market. According to Dominguez and Frankel (1993b), only 87 of these FX market operations were reported in the financial press. These figures can be utilized to compute an objective (a proxy for a subjective) unconditional probability of a Bundesbank intervention as $167/803 \approx 0.21$ $(87/803 \approx 0.11)$. The above model can now be employed to define a virtual drift of economic fundamentals as $\mu_{virtual} \equiv (r - r^*)/(1 - \tilde{\pi})$. A back-of-the-envelope calculation based on the objective unconditional probability of an intervention yields $\mu_{virtual} \approx 0.0352$ if the mean of the interest rate differential is utilized and $\mu_{virtual} \approx 0.0404$ if the median is utilized. Carrying out the same computations with the proxy for the subjective probability of an intervention, the virtual drift rate of fundamentals is $\mu_{virtual} \approx 0.0312$ when the mean of the interest rate differential is utilized and $\mu_{virtual} \approx 0.0359$ when the median is plugged into the above formula. These figures (and visual inspections of the exchange rate series plotted in Figure 4.6 below) indicate that during the sample period the volatility effect can safely be expected to dominate at least for the at-the-money options employed in the empirical analysis presented in Section 4.2.

4.2 Implied Volatilities and the Effectiveness of Central Bank Interventions

In this section, daily official data are utilized to shed light on the effectiveness of the interventions of the Deutsche Bundesbank in the US/DM spot market during the three years following the Louvre Accord ranging from 2/1/1987 to

12/3/1990.[68] The interest in this period was due to the fact that the Bundesbank and other major central banks frequently participated in foreign exchange trading during this period. The effectiveness of interventions is examined by constructing a multifactor success criterion which allows the impact of this type of FX market operations on the level and on the expected volatility of the US/DM spot rate to be modeled within a unified framework. The success criterion is derived from the insights provided by the theoretical analyses performed in the preceding section. The criterion forms the dependent variable in an ordered qualitative response model estimated to gauge the significance of the potential relation between the spot market interventions conducted by the Bundesbank and the following change in the level and in the volatility of the exchange rate. As suggested by Bonser-Neal and Tanner (1996) and Madura and Tucker (1991), daily implied volatility quotes inferred from Philadelphia Stock Exchange American-style options are employed to capture anticipated exchange rate volatility.

To construct a success criterion, I use the two main results of the theoretical analyses contained in the preceding section. Based on the intervention model of Lewis (1995), which was discussed in Section 4.1.1, it can be concluded that an effective intervention policy has the potential to narrow the wedge between the prevailing spot rate and its central parity as defined by monetary authorities. Furthermore, the study of the option pricing model in Section 4.1.2 has revealed that, for the sample period and exchange rate under investigation, volatilities inferred from foreign currency options should tend to decrease as the intervention probability increases. Using this intervention probability as a measure of the intensity of central banks' FX market operations, the effectiveness of this policy strategy can thus be measured by analyzing its impact on the volatility implicit in foreign currency options.

The success criterion applied to analyze the effectiveness of the intervention policy of the Bundesbank during the Louvre period summarizes these results. According to the criterion used in the empirical analysis presented below, an intervention is classified as effective if it tends to close the wedge between the current exchange rate and an implicit target level and, at the same time, serves to lower the expected volatility of the US/DM spot price as implied in foreign currency options premia. If one of these conditions is not satisfied, the inter-

---

[68] The purpose of the empirical analyses is to evaluate the effectiveness of the intervention policy of the Bundesbank insofar as it affected the level and the volatility of the spot rate. It is beyond the scope of this study to discuss other important macroeconomic and monetary policy issues and problems which come into play when the effectiveness of central banks' intervention policy is evaluated in a broader context. For a discussion of these issues, see Lehment (1980) and Scheide (1986).

vention is rated as partially effective. If both conditions do not hold, the intervention is identified as completely ineffective.

The research methodology utilized in this section draws on an idea recently formulated by Humpage (1999), who suggests using a dichotomous success criterion to study the effectiveness of central banks' FX market interventions. According to his two-state rule, an intervention is classified as successful if a sale (a purchase) of foreign currency is followed by an appreciation (a depreciation) of the domestic currency or if this policy action contributes to lower the rate of appreciation (depreciation) of the home currency. Focusing on the Louvre period, Humpage finds that the amount and the international coordination of interventions affected the probability of success of the FX market operations conducted by the Federal Reserve Bank of New York positively.

The work contained in this section extends Humpage's (1999) study in two respects. Firstly, I use an alternative success criterion which allows the impact of central bank FX market interventions on the level of the spot rate and on the expected volatility of this asset price to be modeled simultaneously. Secondly, to fully exploit the advantages of the success criterion used in the empirical analysis, I employ an alternative and potentially richer econometric methodology. While the success criterion constructed by Humpage allows the effectiveness of FX market interventions to be examined by using binary dependent variable models, the success criterion developed in this study makes a qualitative response model with ordered categories the natural candidate to be used in the empirical analysis.

The analysis is organized as follows. Section 4.2.1 is devoted to a discussion of the results reported in the related literature. In Section 4.2.2, the multivariate success criterion utilized to assess the effectiveness of central bank foreign exchange market interventions is developed and the applied econometric research strategy is discussed in detail. The data utilized in the empirical analyses are described in Section 4.2.3. The results of the estimations are presented and interpreted in the final section.

4.2.1   Results Reported in the Literature

In the literature concerned with the effectiveness of central banks' foreign exchange market interventions, the debate on the issue whether such operations tend to stabilize or to destabilize, or whether they affect market prices at all, has not been settled. Most contributions to this area of research analyze the effectiveness of interventions either in terms of their effect on the level of the spot rate or in terms of their impact on the volatility of exchange rates.

A study by Dominguez und Frankel (1993a) was one of the first empirical investigations in which daily official intervention data were used to assess the effectiveness of central banks' foreign exchange market interventions.[69] These authors resort to a univariate regression approach to trace out the impact of the foreign exchange market interventions conducted by the US Federal Open Market Committee and by the Deutsche Bundesbank.[70] Their study is concerned with testing the so-called portfolio balance channel through which sterilized interventions might affect exchange rates. This approach relies on the assumption that domestic and foreign assets are imperfect substitutes and that investors form globally diversified portfolios on the basis of expected market returns. An interesting feature of their empirical study is that survey data are used to extract a series approximating market participants' exchange rate expectations. In a portfolio balance model, sterilized intervention affects the spot rate by altering the relative supply of assets and, thus, the risk premia required to stimulate optimizing agents to hold the given asset stocks. The empirical results outlined in the study suggest that Federal Reserve and Deutsche Bundesbank interventions which took place during the mid-1980s might have influenced exchange rates.[71]

Additional evidence on the effectiveness of the interventions of the Federal Reserve and the Bundesbank is provided by Eijffinger and Gruijters (1992). In their empirical study, daily data covering the period from February 1985 to August 1988 are employed to assess the impact of central banks' FX market interventions on the level of the exchange rate. The overall impression which emerges from the results documented in their study is that during the sample period investigated, central bank interventions were rather ineffective. Furthermore, the authors report some evidence that the coordination of interventions tended to influence the effectiveness of this policy instrument positively. As interventions frequently occurred over a string of days, the authors also analyze

---

[69]   The results reported in recent studies are reviewed in this section. A description of earlier research on the effectiveness of foreign exchange market interventions of central banks as well as an elucidating survey of this strand of the literature is provided by Edison (1993). See also Almekinders (1995: 78 and Chapter 6). For a study focusing on the effectiveness of the foreign exchange market interventions carried out by the Bundesbank in the 1970s, see in particular Lehment (1980: 220).

[70]   In addition, the interventions of the Swiss National Bank as an example of a central bank of a small open economy are analyzed in order to examine the sensitivity of the obtained results.

[71]   Additional evidence on the effectiveness of interventions can be found in a study by Dominguez und Frankel (1993b).

whether the first intervention in a string is more effective than subsequent FX market interventions. While some evidence for this hypothesis is found with respect to German interventions, a similar evidence cannot be found with respect to US interventions.

Catte et al. (1992) argue decisively in favor of the effectiveness of G-3 central banks' foreign exchange market interventions. According to their success criterion, an intervention is ranked as effective whenever (i) the FX market intervention reversed the trend of the spot rate, and, (ii) the following intervention took place with an opposite sign. Given this success criterion, they report that interventions were successful in breaking and reversing dollar trends. They document that episodes during which interventions took place are also often periods during which turning points in the US$/DM exchange rate can be observed. Though it is tempting to interpret this latter result as an indication of the effectiveness of interventions in breaking trends in the US$/DM rate, Weber (1996: 258) emphasizes that it is also possible to identify a substantial number of turning points in the spot exchange rate series which do not fall into periods characterized by central bank foreign exchange interventions. Regarding the impact of interventions on the level of exchange rates, Weber estimates a vector autoregression and finds that the FX market interventions of the G-3 observed during the period 1985–1992 were ineffective in that this policy did not help to stabilize exchange rates in the long run.

Recent evidence presented in Humpage (1999) suggests that interventions conducted by the US central bank during the Louvre period effectively smoothed the US$/DM and the US$/yen spot rates. Using a binary dependent variable model, he reports that the probability that a US intervention would be successful was higher whenever the Federal Open Market Committee coordinated FX market interventions with other major central banks. According to the binary success criterion he uses in this study, central banks' FX market interventions are identified as effective if a sale (a purchase) of foreign currency is either followed by an appreciation (a depreciation) of the domestic currency or by a slowdown of the rate of appreciation (depreciation) of the home currency.

An event study technique to analyze the effectiveness of the foreign exchange market interventions of the US central bank and the German central bank has been used in a recent study by Fatum (2000). In his study, intervention data for a period ranging from September 1985 to December 1995 are utilized. An intervention is rated as effective if the central bank either succeeds moving the exchange rate in the direction intended by the FX market intervention or an exchange rate trend prevailing before the intervention is weakened.[72] The results reported in his study suggest that the interventions conducted by the US central bank and by the German central bank in the DM/US market during the sample period he analyzes were effective. In particular, Fatum finds that a coordination of the FX market interventions of the central banks tended to influence the effectiveness of interventions positively.[73]

Kaminsky and Lewis (1996) also report that interventions affected exchange rates. The empirical approach adopted by these authors is particularly suited to test the hypotheses that sterilized central bank FX market interventions mainly affect the exchange rate through the so-called signaling channel. The signaling channel stipulates that interventions allow economic agents to extract information regarding the future stance of monetary policy. Kaminsky and Lewis study the effectiveness of the interventions conducted by the US central bank in the US$/DM and the US$/yen market during a period beginning in 1985 and ending in 1990. In contrast to the predictions of the theoretical framework, the authors emphasize that US interventions convey information that future monetary policy moves in the opposite direction of the direction suggested by the sign of the intervention. Consequently, interventions are also found to induce an exchange rate change in the opposite direction of the direction indicated by the sign of the intervention.[74]

Concerning the impact of central banks' foreign exchange market interventions on exchange rate volatility, Bonser-Neal and Tanner (1996) use volatilities implicit in foreign currency options to analyze the impact of interventions on market participants' sentiment regarding the future volatility of the spot market. Controlling for the influence of macroeconomic announcements, they find that both Federal Reserve and Bundesbank interventions conducted during a period ranging from 1985 to 1991 in the US$/DM and US$/yen market either did not affect implied volatility significantly or even contributed to inflating the expected variability of the spot rate. Volatilities implicit in foreign currency options have also been used by Madura and Tucker (1991) to study the impact of inter-

---

[72]   Using an exchange rate trend to trace out the effectiveness of central bank interventions, it is also necessary to discriminate further between "blowing-with-the-wind" und "leaning-against-the-wind" interventions in order to avoid biased results (Fatum 2000: 9–10).

[73]   As regards this latter finding, it should be taken into account that "About half of the studies find that coordinated intervention is more effective than noncoordinated intervention; the other half find no special significance to the difference between regimes" (Edison 1993: 35).

[74]   For additional evidence on the signaling theory of central bank interventions, see, e.g., Ghosh (1992) and Fatum and Hutchison (1999) and the references cited therein.

ventions on exchange rate volatilities during the years following the Louvre Agreement. They find that the central bank foreign exchange market interventions conducted during this period of time did not dampen exchange rate volatility. Their findings thus corroborate the results documented in Bonser-Neal and Tanner (1996).

Baillie and Osterberg (1997b) resort to a consumption-based intertemporal asset pricing framework to argue that central banks' foreign exchange market interventions might affect the risk premium on foreign exchange. In their model, a cash-in-advance constraint implies that central banks' holdings of a foreign currency reduce the amount of that currency available for purchases in the goods markets. In the empirical part of the paper, they use daily data on interventions conducted by the Federal Reserve, the Bundesbank and the Bank of Japan during the Plaza and the Louvre period. Estimating a GARCH model to depict the evolution of risk premia over time, they report that, in particular, dollar purchases of the Federal Reserve Bank had a significant positive impact on the size of the DM/US\$ and the yen/US\$ risk premium. The empirical evidence they present also suggests that risk premia did not react significantly to the coordination of interventions. All in all, the authors conclude that their empirical evidence supports the notion that interventions tended to increase rather than decrease the variability of exchange rates.

Taking a noise trader approach, Hung (1997) points out that the impact of interventions on exchange rate volatility might change over time. Using data on US interventions in the US\$/DM and in the US\$/yen market covering the period from April 1985 to December 1986 as well as the Louvre period ranging from March 1987 to December 1989, Hung finds that interventions during the mid-1980s, intended to bring the strong dollar down, tended to decrease volatility. In contrast, interventions mainly intended to stabilize rates around prevailing levels in the aftermath of the Louvre Accord raised exchange rate volatility. These results are interpreted economically by resorting to arguments put forward in the noise trader literature. According to Hung's line of argumentation, volatility-decreasing interventions serve to foster chartists' trend-line-based demand for foreign currency. In contrast, volatility-increasing interventions enhance trading uncertainty and contribute to making momentum-based trading strategies less appealing to FX traders. These arguments imply that even interventions which raise exchange rate volatility can be viewed as effective as long as (i) these interventions are intended to stabilize exchange rates around a prevailing fundamental level, and (ii) chartists are suspected to drive a wedge between the spot rate and this target level.[75]

The literature mentioned so far examines the impact of interventions either on the level *or* on the variability of exchange rates. The analyses performed in this section differ from these approaches in that my research strategy renders it possible to model the effect of central bank FX interventions on the level and on the expected volatility of the exchange rate simultaneously within a unified framework. In the literature concerned with the study of the effectiveness of interventions, a comparable approach has been chosen, for example, by Dominguez (1998). However, Dominguez uses a GARCH model to examine the impact of central banks intervention on the level and the volatility of the spot exchange rate empirically.[76] Thus, the econometric approach chosen by Dominguez to perform empirical analyses differs substantially from the research strategy I adopt in this section.

Dominguez's study covers the period 1987–1994. Using a GARCH model, she finds that the FX market interventions of the German central bank reduced the volatility of the US\$/DM exchange rate. This contrasts with the results obtained for US interventions, which she finds to decrease (to increase) the conditional variability of the US\$/DM spot rate during 1985–1987 (1987–1994). Interestingly, secret interventions tended to exert a particularly strong increasing impact on exchange rate volatility. Additional results provide some evidence that the interventions conducted by the Bank of Japan exerted an increasing effect on the volatility of the US\$/yen spot rate. Using an implied-volatility-based least squares regression approach, Dominguez (1998) further finds that the results of the GARCH model are not robust insofar as German interventions are found to decrease exchange rate variability only during the mid-1980s but tended to in-

---

[75]   Hung's (1997) line of reasoning can be criticized for at least two theoretical reasons. *Firstly*, following De Long et al. (1990), it is possible to argue that volatility-increasing interventions could discourage risk-averse fundamentalists to counter the speculative demand of noise traders. Depending on the net effect on the demand for foreign currency, volatility-enhancing intervention therefore need not necessarily serve to bring the spot rate back to its fundamental value and would, therefore, be ineffective. *Secondly*, work by Krugman and Miller (1993) suggests that interventions which drive noise traders adhering to a trend-enforcing stop-loss strategy out of the market should result in a stabilization of exchange rates. This implies that FX market interventions which effectively alter the speculative position taking of noise traders should result not in an increase but in a decrease in exchange rate volatility.

[76]   Fatum and Hutchison (1999) employ a similar model to assess the informational role of US foreign exchange market interventions as a signal of future monetary policy. In doing so, they estimate the effect of interventions on federal funds futures price changes. In their model, only the coefficients in the conditional variance equation are significant and positive.

duce an increase in expected spot rate volatility during the Louvre and post–
Louvre period. Thus, although the results might differ across subperiods, the
general impression which emerges from her study is that interventions tended to
increase exchange rate volatility. In addition, redefining the intervention series in
terms of dummy variables further reveals that the positive impact of central
banks' FX market interventions on exchange rate volatility can be attributed to
the presence of a central bank rather than to the volume of an intervention.

In a recent study, Aguilar and Nydahl (2000) extended Dominguez's framework of analysis to study the impact of the interventions of the Swedish central
bank on the level and on the volatility of the SKr/US$ and the SKr/DM exchange
rates. The sample period analyzed in their study covers a period beginning 1993
and ending in 1996. Aguilar and Nydahl set up a multivariate GARCH model
which allows the impact of interventions on the level and the conditional volatility SKr/US$ and the SKr/DM exchange rate to be modeled within a unified
model. The results obtained from estimating this multivariate GARCH model, as
well as the findings of supplementary analyses which rely on options-implied
volatilities to trace out the effect of central bank interventions on anticipated exchange rate volatility, can be summarized by stating that the authors find only
rather weak evidence that interventions influence exchange rate volatility. When
the model is reestimated for certain subperiods, they find that interventions
tended to dampen (to increase) the volatility of the the the SKr/US$ in 1995 (in
1993). In addition, they find weak empirical evidence for a destabilizing impact
of interventions on SKr/DM spot rate volatility for the year 1994.

4.2.2   Discussion of the Research Strategy

The effectiveness of a central bank intervention is measured by analyzing its
impact on the absolute deviation of the exchange rate from a central parity
defined by monetary authorities and on the volatility of this asset price as
implied in the prices of foreign currency options. Both variables are typically
considered in empirical studies elaborating on the factors influencing the propensity of central banks to step into the foreign exchange market.[77] It is therefore
only consequent to evaluate the effectiveness of such policy actions in terms of
this set of variables. Over and above, both criteria are selected as they serve to
reflect the convention documented in the fourth article of the Articles of Agreement of the International Monetary Fund that central banks should seek to

---

[77] See also the references presented in Section 4.2.3.2 on the construction of an
instrument for interventions.

counter "disorderly market conditions."[78] Examining the absolute deviation of the exchange rate from an implicit central parity to measure the impact of intervention policy on the level of the exchange rate is motivated by the goal agreed upon by G-7 authorities at the Louvre Summit, which took place on February 2, 1987, to stabilize spot rates around the then prevailing levels. In specifying an implicit central parity, $\overline{E}$, established under the Louvre Agreement, I follow Funabashi (1988: 183), who reports a more or less official baseline rate of approximately 0.55 US\$/DM. The absolute deviation of the actual exchange rate from this target level is computed as

$$(4.17) \quad dev_t = \left| E_t - \overline{E} \right|.$$

In a next step, I introduce a latent continuous variable, S_t^*, to designate joint movements of the change in the deviation of the exchange rate from its central parity and the change in the expected volatility of the exchange rate as implied by foreign currency option prices. The continuous variable, S_t^*, is defined on the real line and is assumed to depend linearly on a $(m \times 1)$ dimensional vector, $\mathbf{x}_t$, of explanatory variables determining the conditional mean of S_t^* as formalized below:

$$(4.18) \quad S_t^* = \mathbf{x}_t' \mathbf{b} + \varepsilon_t,$$

where $\mathbf{b}$ denotes a $(m \times 1)$ vector of coefficients to be estimated and ε_t is a normally distributed error term with mean zero and variance σ_ε.

The motivation to employ the ordered probit model pioneered by Aitchison and Silvey (1957) to analyze the effectiveness of central bank interventions stems from the fact that S_t^* has a continuous state space and is, therefore, in general not observable.[79] To develop an empirically meaningful model, I follow the line of argumentation suggested, for example, by Hausman et al. (1992) and assume that it is only possible to observe a discrete variable S_t which assumes a known numerical value if the unobservable index variable, S_t^*, falls into a

---

[78] For a description of important aspects of the institutional framework defining the official objectives of central bank interventions, see Almekinders and Eijffinger (1994: 112).

[79] In the present analysis, the ordered probit model is utilized to assess the effectiveness of central bank interventions. In a related strand of the empirical literature, models belonging to this type of quantitative model have also been adopted to discuss the objectives of central bank policy. For reaction function models based on the ordered probit model allowing to discuss bank discount rate policy, see, e.g., Eichengreen et al. (1985) and Davutyan and Parke (1995).

certain interval of its state space. The ordered probit model can then be used to relate the observable realizations of S_t and the unobservable continuous variable, S_t^*, via the following assignment rule (Campbell et al. 1997: 123):

$$(4.19) \quad S_t = j \text{ if } S_t^* \in s_j, \quad j = 0,1,...,N,$$

where the sets s_j form an ordered partition of the state space of S_t^* into j nonoverlapping intervals. In the following analysis, it suffices to set $N = 2$, as this implies that the state space is subdivided into three disjunct intervals which allow discrimination between effective, partially effective, and ineffective central bank interventions.

I restrict my attention to days on which the absolute intervention amount I_t assumes a strictly positive numerical value and assume that the unobservable continuous latent variable, S_t^*, is in interval j whenever the following inequalilities hold:

$$(4.20) \quad S_t = \begin{cases} 2 \text{ if } I_t > 0 \quad \text{and} \quad \sigma_{t+1}/\sigma_t < 1 \wedge dev_{t+1}(1-L) < 0 \\ \\ 1 \begin{cases} \text{if } I_t > 0 \quad \text{and} \quad \sigma_{t+1}/\sigma_t < 1 \wedge dev_{t+1}(1-L) > 0 \ \vee \\ \text{if } I_t > 0 \quad \text{and} \quad \sigma_{t+1}/\sigma_t > 1 \wedge dev_{t+1}(1-L) < 0 \end{cases} \\ \\ 0 \text{ if } I_t > 0 \quad \text{and} \quad \sigma_{t+1}/\sigma_t > 1 \wedge dev_{t+1}(1-L) > 0, \end{cases}$$

where L denotes the lag operator. Equation (4.20) states that S_t^* is in state 2 whenever a decrease in both the expected volatility of the exchange rate inferred from FX option prices and in the deviation of the exchange rate from the target level $\overline{E}$ can be observed. The latent variable, S_t^*, can be found in state 1 whenever the change in the implied volatility and in dev_t move in opposite directions. Similarly, the unobservable continuous process assumes a realization belonging to state 0 if implied volatility increases and the exchange rate moves farther away from its central parity.

Equation (4.20) is a convenient tool to separate perfectly and partially effective interventions from ineffective central bank FX market interventions. An intervention is classified as fully effective if it tends to lower implied exchange rate volatility and serves to close the wedge between the current exchange rate and its central parity. Thus, if the intervention series is included in the vector x_t and it is found that this explanatory variable tends to increase the probability that S_t^* assumes a realization belonging to state 2, the exchange rate policy of the central bank can be claimed to be effective. If, in turn, foreign exchange market interventions primarily tend to raise the probability that S_t^* falls into the interior state space, a trade-off between the impact on expected exchange rate volatility and the deviation from the target level exists and the intervention policy can be claimed to be partially effective. Finally, a completely ineffective intervention policy can be identified by analyzing whether this policy instrument inflates the probability that S_t^* falls into the partition of its state space indicated by $S_t = 0$.

For estimation purposes, equation (4.20) can be reformulated in terms of the latent variable as follows:

$$(4.21) \quad S_t = \begin{cases} 0 \text{ if } S_t^* \leq S_1 \\ 1 \text{ if } S_1 < S_t^* \leq S_2 \\ 2 \text{ if } S_2 < S_t^*, \end{cases}$$

with S_1 and S_2 being threshold parameters separating the nonoverlapping states, S_j. Given that ε_t has been assumed to be normally distributed, the probability that S_t^* can be found in state j can be written as (see, e.g., Greene 1997: Chapter 19):

$$(4.22) \quad \text{Prob}(S_t = 0) = \Phi(S_1 - x_t'b),$$

$$\text{Prob}(S_t = 1) = \Phi(S_2 - x_t'b) - \Phi(S_1 - x_t'b),$$

$$\text{Prob}(S_t = 2) = 1 - \Phi(S_2 - x_t'b),$$

where $\Phi(\cdot)$ denotes the standard normal distribution function. The unknown parameters of the ordered probit model can be estimated efficiently by maximizing the following log-likelihood function (see Aitchison and Silvey 1957; Campbell et al. 1997):

$$(4.23) \quad LL = \sum_{t=1}^{n} \sum_{j=0}^{2} N_j \ln \text{Prob}(S_t = j),$$

where N_j denotes the number of realizations in category j.

4.2.3   The Data

4.2.3.1   The Time Series Used in the Empirical Analysis

The time period under investigation in this section ranges from January 1987 to March 1990 and covers the period following the G-7 summit which took place at the Louvre in Paris on February 22, 1987. I use official intervention data provided by the Deutsche Bundesbank to assess the effectiveness of the interventions of the German Central Bank in the US$/DM spot market during this period of time. Figure 4.4(a) plots the daily intervention data series. Positive interventions (+) denote a purchase of US dollars and negative interventions (−) denote sales of US dollars by the Bundesbank. The intervention amount is measured in millions of deutsche mark. During the sample period the Bundesbank carried out 167 interventions in the US$/DM spot market. The fluctuation of the daily exchange rate series employed in the empirical analysis around the implicit target level of 0.55 US$/DM reported in Funabashi (1988) are shown in Figure 4.4(b). The expected volatility of the spot exchange rate is measured in terms of volatility quotes implicit in at-the-money DM/US Philadelphia Stock Exchange (PHLX) American-style foreign currency options. Implicit volatilities measure market participants' sentiment regarding the average variability of the underlying exchange rate over the remaining time to maturity of the option. The US$/DM implied volatilities employed in this study are plotted in Figure 4.4(c). The series is identical to the time series utilized by Bonser-Neal and Tanner (1996).[80]

When modeling the impact of central banks' foreign exchange market interventions on the level and on the volatility of the spot exchange rate, it is important to account for the potential influence of other variables. The control variables considered in this study can be subsumed under three broad categories.

---

[80] I thank Catherine Bonser-Neal and Glenn Tanner for sharing their implied-volatility data with me. They employed the Barone-Adesi and Whaley (1987) quadratic approximation technique to infer volatilities from observed option prices. In their data set, implied volatilities are missing for the period August 26, 1988–October 3, 1998. To close this gap, I utilized daily closing prices for PHLX options with a moneyness between 0.98 and 1.02 and with a time to expiry of at least one week and at most three months. To be consistent with the research strategy adopted by Bonser-Neal and Tanner (1996), the missing implied volatilities were also computed by implementing the Barone-Adesi and Whaley (1987) technique. I also thank the Deutsche Bundesbank for generously providing me with the daily data on its foreign exchange market interventions.

Figure 4.4: Time Series Used in the Empirical Analyses

(a)

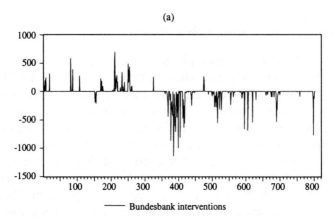

Bundesbank interventions

(b)

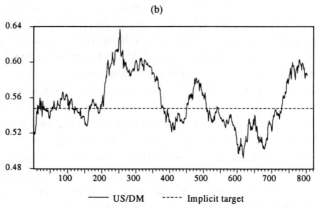

US/DM ----- Implicit target

(c)

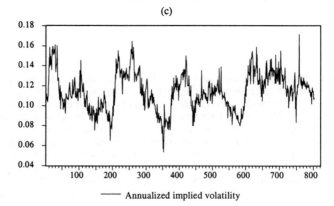

Annualized implied volatility

(1) The first category contains variables which capture the *characteristics of the intervention.*

Dominguez and Frankel (1993b) and Humpage (1999) report that the effectiveness of US interventions tended to be higher whenever major central banks coordinated their FX market interventions. To test whether a similar effect can also be observed in the case of German interventions, a dummy variable is constructed which assumes the value one whenever interventions were coordinated. Upon confronting the German data with the corresponding US intervention data, it was verified that 88 of the 167 German FX market interventions were coordinated.

A further possibly informative characteristic of an intervention is its sign. Because Figure 4.4(a) indicates that the direction of German interventions changed several times during the sample period, I defined a dummy variable which is 1 for positive and −1 for negative interventions and zero otherwise.

In the literature elaborating on the effectiveness of central bank interventions, it is often argued that it is important to distinguish between secret and publicly known interventions (see, e.g., Dominguez 1998). Taking this argument into account, I computed a dummy variable which takes on the value one whenever FX market participants might have known that a central bank intervention was going on. Publicly known interventions are identified by comparing the Bundesbank data with the time schedule reported in Dominguez and Frankel (1993b). In this time schedule they document reports in the financial press that an intervention had taken place.

As can be seen by scrutinizing Figure 4.4(a), the Bundesbank frequently intervened on successive days. Humpage (1999) argues that the intervention marking the beginning of such an intervention cluster might be more informative for market participants and might, therefore, be more effective than the preceding interventions. To account for this aspect, I define a dummy variable which assumes the value zero whenever an intervention is immediately preceded by another FX market intervention and one otherwise.

(2) The second category considered contains two variables summarizing other aspects of German *monetary policy.*

It has been argued by Lastrapes (1989) that exchange rate volatility might depend upon the prevailing monetary policy regime. Taking this argument into account, I selected the level of the discount rate to control for the overall stance of monetary policy. The second variable in this category was labeled *news* and assumes the value one whenever an event which is reported in Dominguez and Frankel (1993b) is not an intervention but nevertheless might be informative with respect to evaluating the overall stance of monetary or of exchange rate policy.

(3) Finally, a third category of variables was designed to account for the potential influence of other *financial market variables* on the evolution of S_t^*.

To account for possible weekend and day-of-the-week effects documented for exchange rates in, for example, Baillie and Bollerslev (1989), I also constructed two dummy variables which assume the value one on every Monday and Friday.

Using a regression approach, Bonser-Neal and Tanner (1996) report that movements in expected exchange rate volatility are significantly related to contemporaneous changes in stock market volatility, which is interpreted as a measure of overall financial market volatility. Motivated by this result, I computed an annualized time-varying conditional stock market volatility series by estimating a GARCH(1,1) model for the returns of the German stock market index published by the *Frankfurter Allgemeine Zeitung*. This model includes a constant as the regressor in the mean equation.

The system of equations forming the GARCH model can be efficiently estimated simultaneously using a nonlinear maximum likelihood routine. The results of implementing this routine as well as several important diagnostic tests performed to check for the adequacy of the model are summarized in Table 4.1. The figures reported in the table indicate that the coefficients of the GARCH model are all significant at the one percent level. Moreover, the result of the Wald test (WALD) presented in the first column of the table reveals that the sum of the ARCH and the GARCH terms entering into the conditional volatility equation is significantly different from one. This result suggests that the conditional stock market volatility is a stationary process and that the unconditional variance exists. The Lagrange multiplier (LM) tests championed by Breusch (1978) and Godfrey (1978) indicate that it is not possible to reject the null hypothesis of no remaining autocorrelation in the standardized residuals. The LM test (ARCH) introduced by Engle (1982) indicates that the null hypothesis of no further GARCH effects in the squared standardized residuals of the GARCH(1,1) model cannot be rejected. A few influential outliers mainly attributable to the stock market crashes of 1987 and 1990 are responsible for the striking significance of the test statistic suggested by Bera and Jarque (abbreviated as JB) (1982). The significance of this test indicates that it is not possible to retain the assumption that the standardized residuals of the GARCH model are standard normally distributed. To account for this departure from normality, robust standard errors were computed by using the quasi-maximum likelihood method developed by Bollerslev and Woolridge (1992) to reestimate the model.

Table 4.1: Modeling Conditional Stock Market Volatility

Mean equation	Variance equation			TARCH
Intercept[a]	constant	ARCH–coef.[b]	GARCH–coef.	coefficient
0.001534***	0.00001***	0.27528***	0.68480***	0.35049
(2.95)[c]	(2.66)	(2.26)	(10.06)	(1.13)
Diagnostic tests	LM(5)	WALD	ARCH(5)	JB
	8.30	0.37	0.28	22403.87***

[a]Figures in parentheses are standard normally distributed z-statistics computed as the ratio of the respective coefficients and the corresponding standard deviations. Robust standard errors were obtained by implementing the technique of Bollerslev and Woolridge (1992). — [b]Abbreviation for coefficient. — [c]*** indicate that the test statistic is significant at the 1 percent level.

As a final exercise, I tested for significant leverage effects in conditional stock market volatility by estimating the asymmetric Threshold ARCH model suggested by Glosten et al. (1993) and by Rabenmananjara and Zakoian (1993). However, the corresponding TARCH coefficient presented in the fifth column of Table 4.1 turned out to be insignificant.

The evidence summarized in Table 4.1 indicates that the baseline GARCH(1,1) model captures the dynamics of conditional stock market volatility well. This suggests that it is reasonable to employ the conditional stock market volatility series obtained from this model in the empirical analysis outlined below.

4.2.3.2 Constructing an Instrument for Interventions

Authors contributing to the strand of the literature examining the objectives of central bank foreign exchange market interventions often report that both swings in the level of the exchange rate and a rise in its volatility might play a prominent role in explaining the propensity of central banks to enter FX markets.[81] These results suggest that a potential simultaneity problem resulting in spurious parameter estimates might arise if the original Bundesbank intervention series is utilized to estimate the ordered probit model outlined in Section 4.2.2. To resolve this problem, the model should only be estimated after the original intervention series has been replaced by an appropriate instrumental variable. Humpage

---

[81] See, e.g., Eijffinger and Gruijters (1991), Almekinders and Eijffinger (1994, 1996), Baillie and Osterberg (1997a, 1997b), and Döpke and Pierdzioch (1999).

(1999) suggests constructing such an instrumental variable by specifying a full-fledged reaction function to model the intervention policy of central banks.[82]

The first step in estimating a reaction function is to identify an appropriate set of variables which serves to explain central banks' interventions policies.[83] I employ the lagged change of the absolute deviation of the exchange rate from its central parity (denoted as *factor*$_1$) to capture the impact of swings in the level of the US$/DM spot rate on the intervention propensity of the Bundesbank. The second factor (*factor*$_2$) assumed to affect the intervention probability reflects the overall tendency of exchange rate volatility to rise or fall and is formed by a five-day moving average of lagged implied volatility changes. Defining the central banks' propensity to intervene by I_t^*, these assumptions allow the following model to be formalized:

(4.24) $I_t^* = \beta_0 + \beta_1 factor_1 + \beta_2 factor_2 + \varepsilon_t^*$,

where ε_t^* is an independently and identically distributed error term with standard deviation σ^*.

The next step is to formulate a quantitative model which allows light to be shed on the relation between these factors and the amount of interventions. In this respect, I utilize the reaction function model suggested by Almekinders and Eijffinger (1994). In line with the intervention series plotted in Figure 4.6, these authors point out that it is not reasonable to assume that every arbitrarily small deviation of the explanatory variables of the model from their target levels implicitly defined by central banks triggers an intervention. Rather, it can be expected that central banks only decide to enter the foreign exchange market when the momentum of the movement of the exchange rate away from its central parity and/or in options implied volatilities exceed a certain critical level.

Assuming that the absolute intervention amount I_t is proportional to the central banks' propensity to intervene, I_t^*, one can conclude:

(4.25) $I_t = \begin{cases} I_t^* & \text{if} \quad I_t^* > 0 \\ 0 & \text{otherwise,} \end{cases}$

---

[82] Humpage (1999) departs from the research strategy adopted in this section in that he uses the sample selection model developed by Heckman (1979) to construct an instrument.

[83] A comprehensive survey of the numerous contributions to this area of research can be found in Almekinders (1995: Chapters 4 and 5). See also the references presented in footnote 81.

where, for ease of exposition, the critical propensity to intervene has been set equal to zero.

Equation (4.25) implies that interventions are truncated from below and that the reaction function should not be estimated using least squares. Rather, the truncated regression (Tobit) model developed by Tobin (1958) offers an appropriate econometric technique to reveal the link between the intervention propensity of the Bundesbank and the set of explanatory factors introduced above.

Table 4.2 provides maximum likelihood estimates of the Tobit model as well as some diagnostic statistics. All coefficients can be seen to be significant at the one percent level. To assess the overall explanatory power of the model, a likelihood ratio (LR) test was computed. To compute the LR test, both the unrestricted model in equation (4.24) and a model only containing an intercept were estimated. Taking the difference between the respective log-likelihood functions to compute (Greene 1997: 886)

$$(4.26) \quad \text{LR} = -2\left(LL_{restricted} - LL_{unrestricted}\right) \sim \chi^2_{number\,of\,restrictions}$$

yields a test statistic which is χ^2-distributed with degrees of freedom equal to the number of imposed restrictions. Table 4.2 shows that the LR test is highly significant with a marginal probability smaller than 0.0001.

Given that the Tobit model turns out to exhibit significant explanatory power, I am now in a position to follow Humpage (1999) in utilizing the predicted values obtained from the reaction function model as an instrumental variable in

Table 4.2: Reaction Function Derived by Estimating a Tobit Model

	Coefficient	Standard deviation	z-statistic
Constant	−0.3260***	0.0317	−10.2935
Factor $_1$	9.9453**	4.7329	2.1013
Factor $_2$	31.5777***	7.4882	4.2170
σ^*	0.3775***	0.0242	15.6174
Adjusted R^2	0.0254	standard error	0.1259
Log likelihood	−300.6904	uncensored observations	633
Restricted log likelihood	−312.6064	censored observations	164
LR test	23.8320***	marginal probability	<0.0001

Note: The significance of a regressor is analyzed by using the standard normally distributed ratio of the coefficient and its respective standard deviation (z-statistic). — ** (***) denote significance at the 5 (1) percent level.

the model constructed to analyze the effectiveness of central bank foreign exchange market interventions.

4.2.4   The Effectiveness of Bundesbank Foreign Exchange Market Interventions

This section presents maximum likelihood estimates of the parameters of the ordered probit model discussed in Section 4.2.2. The model is estimated over the 167 intervention days contained in the sample period under investigation.

Table 4.3 reports results for models constructed by including the various explanatory variables separately into the vector x_t. The table allows one to examine the individual effects of the explanatory variables on the probability that $S_t = j$ and $S_t^* \in s_j$ and to identify potential candidates for building a more complex model. The information needed to evaluate the various models is contained in the columns of the table. The first column depicts the respective explanatory variables. While the variable *buba* is defined as the absolute amount of actual Bundesbank interventions, the series *bubaexpected* contains the predicted absolute intervention amounts obtained from the Tobit model outlined in the previous section. The second, fourth, and sixth columns report the element β_1 of the coefficient vector **b** and the threshold parameters S_1 and S_2, respectively. The corresponding z-statistics indicating the individual significance of the estimated parameters are depicted in the third, fifth, and seventh columns of the table. A likelihood ratio test statistic used to evaluate the overall explanatory power of the respective models is contained in the left column of the table.

The results reported in Table 4.3 resemble those obtained by Humpage (1999) for US data. Only the variable *bubaexpected* shows a statistically significant power to influence the probability that the dependent variable S_t^* settles in state j. Though the arguments outlined below indicate that the coefficients of the ordered probit model must be interpreted with care, the positive sign of β_1 shows that the probability of a simultaneous decline in both the expected exchange rate volatility and in the wedge between the current level of the spot exchange rate and its target level increases with the absolute amount of Bundesbank interventions. Also, the probability that $S_t = 0$, which indicates that a FX market intervention of the central bank induces options-implied volatilities to rise and the exchange rate to move farther away from the central parity, turns out to be a decreasing function of *bubaexpected*. Also note that the coefficient of the variable *buba* is insignificant and has the "wrong" sign. This outcome under-

Table 4.3: Ordered Probit Model for Individual Effects of Explanatory Variables

Variable	β_1	z-statistic	S_1	z-statistic	S_2	z-statistic	LR test
			Interventions				
Bubaexpected	6.1784	1.9616	−0.3439	−1.8299	0.9981	5.0191	3.8687
Buba	−0.2282	−0.5665	−0.6970	−5.2593	0.6255	4.7693	0.3212
			Characteristics of interventions				
Coordination	−0.0926	−0.5371	−0.0926	−5.0100	0.6216	4.4924	0.2886
Sign	0.0810	0.8142	−0.6932	−5.9226	0.6309	5.4538	0.6634
Reported	−0.2434	−1.4085	−0.7827	−5.5541	0.5480	4.0235	1.9869
First	0.1324	0.7530	−0.5995	−4.7874	0.7242	5.6612	0.5673
			Monetary policy				
Discount	0.0354	0.3666	−0.5270	−1.4877	0.7946	2.2300	0.1345
News	0.3333	1.1369	−0.6223	−5.7634	0.7052	6.4081	0.1345
			Financial market variables				
Fazvola	0.8689	1.2062	−0.4625	−2.4607	0.8659	4.4608	1.4617
Monday	0.3157	1.4336	−0.5960	−5.3329	0.7350	6.3831	2.0623
Friday	−0.2601	−1.2495	−0.7124	−6.1378	0.6162	5.4164	1.5649

Note: The critical values for the LR test with one degree of freedom are 3.84146 and 2.70554 at the 5 (10) percent significance level (see Judge et al. 1988: 987).

scores the severity of the simultaneity problem and highlights the importance of constructing an instrumental variable for the original intervention series.

Other variables than *bubaexpected* do not contribute to explaining movements in the dependent variable. Significant in a broader sense are the financial market variables and the variable *reported*, which indicates whether an intervention was secret or publicly known. Notice that the coefficient capturing the influence of the latter variable shows a negative sign, a result which confirms the findings of Dominguez and Frankel (1993b: 114). This result signals that the interventions conducted by the Bundesbank tended to be less effective whenever market participants were aware that the central bank participated in the trading of foreign exchange. This finding might indicate that known Bundesbank interventions provoked speculative position taking against the central bank. Also note that in contrast to the findings of Dominguez and Frankel (1993b: 116) and Humpage (1999), but in line with the results reported in Baillie and Osterberg (1997b) for US interventions, the *coordination* dummy turns out to be insignificant.

In a next step, the vector of explanatory variables, x_t, was enlarged by estimating the joint effects of *bubaexpected* and an additional series on the depen-

Table 4.4: Estimates of Joint Effects in the Ordered Probit Model

Variable	Characteristics of interventions				Monetary policy		Financial market variables		
	coordination	sign	reported	first	discount	news	fazvola	Monday	Friday
Bubaexpected									
β_1	6.3048	6.0390	6.0912	5.9916	6.3864	5.9689	5.5301	6.3012	6.2754
z-statistic	1.9966	1.7900	1.9294	1.8902	2.0152	1.8864	1.6517	1.9963	1.9890
Added variable									
β_2	−0.1135	0.0123	−0.2362	0.0953	0.0576	0.2952	0.4401	0.3271	−0.2698
z-statistic	−0.6551	0.1153	−1.3630	0.5376	0.5902	1.0012	0.5734	1.4812	−1.2926
Thresholds									
s_1	−0.3986	−0.3573	−0.4762	−0.3162	−0.1321	−0.3288	−0.2808	−0.2810	−0.4023
z-statistic	−1.9378	−1.6169	−2.2479	−1.6223	−0.3260	−1.7405	−1.2892	−1.4565	−2.0770
s_2	0.9457	0.9848	0.8752.	1.0275	1.2118	1.0182	1.0630	1.0726	0.9473
z-statistic	4.4122	4.2843	4.0073	4.9768	2.9313	5.0841	4.6387	5.2096	4.6729
LR test									
H_0: $\beta_1 = \beta_2 = 0$	4.2980	3.8820	4.1577	5.7292	4.2173	4.8749	4.1979	6.0704	5.5441
H_0: $\beta_2 = 0$	0.4294	0.0133	0.2891	1.8606	0.3486	1.0062	0.3293	2.2018	1.6754
H_0: $\beta_1 = 0$	4.0095	3.2185	3.7423	5.1620	4.0828	3.5765	2.7362	4.0081	3.9792

Note: The critical values for the LR test with one degree of freedom are 3.84146 and 2.70554 at the 5 (10) percent significance level. The critical values for the LR test with two degrees of freedom are 5.99146 and 4.60517 at the 5 (10) percent significance level (Judge et al. 1988: 987).

dent variable. Table 4.4 reports the results of this exercise. The most striking finding is that the effect of the instrumental variable *bubaexpected* on S_t^* remains significant in all estimated models at least at the 10 percent significance level. Thus, enriching the set of independent variables with one of the other series considered to be potentially important in explaining the variation in S_t does not affect the explanatory power of the absolute intervention amount very much.

Table 4.4 further provides weak evidence that the effectiveness of the intervention policy of the Bundesbank might have depended on whether the FX market intervention was secret or publicly known. The negative sign of the corresponding coefficient shows that the effectiveness of an intervention tended to be higher whenever the Bundesbank succeeded in keeping the FX market intervention secret. Focusing attention on the model including the *reported* variable shows that the z-statistic of the coefficient reflecting the influence of the *reported* series assumes a numerical value of −1.36, so that the null hypothesis that the coefficient is not significantly different from zero can be rejected at a marginal significance level of 17 percent.

Table 4.5: Estimates of Joint Effects in the Ordered Probit Model Including a Dummy for Reported Interventions

Variable	Characteristics of interventions			Monetary policy		Financial market variables		
	coordination	sign	first	discount	news	fazvola	Monday	Friday
Bubaexpected								
β_1	6.1173	6.0173	6.0779	6.3571	5.9440	5.4099	6.2128	6.1922
z-statistic	1.9319	1.7795	1.9138	2.0016	1.8760	1.6126	1.9635	1.9580
Reported								
β_2	–0.2279	–0.2358	–0.2336	–0.2531	–0.2093	–0.2386	–0.2418	–0.2354
z-statistic	–1.2003	–1.3595	–1.2534	–1.4482	–1.1818	–1.3761	–1.3923	–1.3567
Added variable								
β_3	–0.0205	0.0065	0.0074	0.0755	0.2222	0.4632	0.3338	–0.2691
z-statistic	–0.1078	0.0610	0.0385	0.7670	0.7364	0.6038	1.5080	–1.2858
Thresholds								
s_1	–0.4814	–0.4831	–0.4726	–0.2078	–0.4497	–0.4108	–0.4151	–0.5333
z-statistic	–2.2165	–2.0135	–2.0394	–0.5083	–2.0911	–1.7266	–1.9225	–2.4611
s_2	0.8701	0.8683	0.8788	1.1466	0.9042	0.9424	0.9479	0.8250
z-statistic	3.8932	3.5370	3.6901	2.7552	4.0691	3.8391	4.2226	3.7186
LR test								
H$_0$: $\beta_1 = \beta_2 = \beta_3 = 0$	5.7409	5.7330	5.7307	6.3182	6.2729	6.0943	8.0119	7.3873
H$_0$: $\beta_1 = 0$	3.7524	3.1807	3.6815	4.0277	3.5369	2.6075	3.8771	3.8553

Note: The critical values for the LR test with one degree of freedom are 3.84146 and 2.70554 at the 5 (10) percent significance level. The critical values for the LR test with three degrees of freedom are 6.25139 and 4.60517 at the 5 (10) percent significance level (Judge et al. 1988: 987).

To further corroborate these results, models featuring a vector $\mathbf{x}_t$ containing *bubaexpected* and *reported* and a third series taken from the remaining subset of explanatory variables were estimated. The overall impression which arises when the results of these estimations which are documented in Table 4.5 are analyzed is that the findings obtained from the more parsimonious ordered probit models by and large turn out to be robust. As already detected when analyzing the figures presented in Table 4.4, the significance of the intervention instrument is somewhat hampered only in the equation containing the stock market variability *fazvola*. The other variables do not contribute to improve the understanding of the link between Bundesbank interventions and S_t^*.

It remains to quantitatively substantiate the impact of Bundesbank interventions on the probability that S_t^* settles in state j. To accomplish this task, I compared the effects attributable to a small intervention with the effects induced by a large-scale FX market intervention. A small (large) intervention is identified by fixing the absolute value of the intervention amount one standard deviation below (above) the mean absolute intervention amount computed over all Bundesbank FX market interventions in the sample. Table 4.6 reports the respective probabilities that $\text{Prob}(S_t = j)$, the corresponding marginal effects $\partial \text{Prob}(S_t = j)/\partial \mathbf{x}$, and elasticities computed as $[\partial \text{Prob}(S_t = j)/\partial \mathbf{x}][\mathbf{x}/\text{Prob}(S_t = j)]$ for both the model with the intervention amount as the only explanatory variable and the ordered probit model with *bubaexpected* and *reported* included in the vector $\mathbf{x}_t$.[84] The marginal effects allow one to identify the sign of an infinitesimal variation in the absolute intervention amount on the probability that S_t^* falls into category j. The elasticities give the percentage response of the respective probabilities, $\text{Prob}(S_t = j)$, to a one percent change in the intervention amount.

Table 4.6 provides several interesting insights. As already indicated by the discussion of the estimation results, the figures offered in the table demonstrate that the probability of an effective intervention is an increasing function of the absolute intervention amount. During the Louvre period, the foreign exchange

Table 4.6: Probabilities, Marginal Effects, and Elasticities in the Ordered Probit Model

Variable		Probability		Marginal effect		Elasticity	
		$\mu_b - \sigma_b$	$\mu_b + \sigma_b$	$\mu_b - \sigma_b$	$\mu_b + \sigma_b$	$\mu_b - \sigma_b$	$\mu_b + \sigma_b$
		Scenario I					
	0	0.3114	0.2034	−2.1839	−1.7473	−0.1681	−0.6751
Bubaexpected	1	0.4910	0.4924	0.4665	−0.4141	0.0139	−0.0468
	2	0.1976	0.3041	1.7174	2.1615	0.0513	0.2441
		Scenario II					
Bubaexpected	0	0.3498	0.2362	−2.2556	−1.8770	−0.1545	−0.6246
+	1	0.4831	0.5004	0.7308	−0.1123	0.0210	−0.0120
Reported = 1	2	0.1672	0.2635	1.5248	1.9892	0.0439	0.2123
		Scenario III					
Bubaexpected	0	0.2669	0.1698	−2.0024	−1.5403	−0.1798	−0.7129
+	1	0.5001	0.4843	0.1397	−0.7061	0.0044	−0.0848
Reported = 0	2	0.2329	0.3459	1.8627	2.2464	0.0536	0.2397

Note: The variables μ_b and σ_b denote the mean and the standard deviation of the series *bubaexpected*, respectively.

---

[84] For a discussion of the advantages of using elasticities in interpreting the results of qualitative response models and an application of this concept to evaluating problems in economics, see Krafft (1997).

market interventions of the Bundesbank tended to be more effective whenever it was not publicly known that the German central bank was participating in foreign exchange trading. Moreover, the marginal effects and the corresponding elasticities suggest that a small intervention raised the respective probabilities that $S_t = 2$ and $S_t = 1$ and lowered the probability that $S_t = 0$. The elasticities reveal that the probability that S_t^* settles in category 2 increased by more in response to a small intervention than the probability that the intervention is only partially effective. Furthermore, a large-scale intervention served to allocate probability mass from category 1 to category 2.

While these figures corroborate the impression that the intervention policy of the Bundesbank was a success, the relative magnitudes of the probabilities presented in Table 4.6 corroborate this impression far less. Comparing the magnitudes of the probabilities that S_t^* falls into partition j of its state space, it can be seen that the probability that $S_t = 1$ dominates in all cases. In other words, when conducting an intervention, the Bundesbank had a good chance that the intervention would either serve to narrow the wedge between the actual exchange rate and its implicit target level *or* contribute to decreasing the expected variability of the spot rate. For a small intervention, the relative magnitudes of the probabilities even indicate that the probability of a complete failure of the intervention exceeds the probability that the intervention is effective. The figures in the table further reveal that switching from a small to a large intervention increases the probability that $S_t = 2$ by about ten percentage points and serves to depress the probability that $S_t = 0$ by approximately the same amount. Thus, though the interventions are found to be statistically significant in the ordered probit models estimated above, the magnitude of the effect on the probability that S_t^* settles in category 2 is only moderate. This, in turn, casts doubts that the intervention policy conducted by the Bundesbank during the years following the Louvre Accord was successful in statistical rather than in economic terms.

4.3   Summary

In this chapter, it has been taken into account that since the breakdown of the Bretton Woods system central banks have often attempted to influence the dynamics of real-world exchange rates by intervening in foreign exchange markets. The theoretical section of Chapter 4 was utilized to offer a currency option pricing model featuring infrequent central bank interventions. In the second part of this chapter, the empirically testable predictions of the model were used to

evaluate the effectiveness of the intervention policy of the Bundesbank
conducted during the years following the Louvre Accord.

The exchange rate model developed by Lewis (1995) was employed to argue
that an effective intervention policy influences not only the level and the volatility of the exchange rate but also the premia of the corresponding foreign currency options. The impact of infrequent central bank interventions on the premia
of foreign currency options was analyzed within the context of an appropriately
modified GK model. It was argued that a variation in the intervention probability
might either increase or decrease the option premium. The ambiguity of the
effect of infrequent interventions on FX option prices arises due to the fact that
an increase in the probability of a central bank intervention not only dampens
exchange rate volatility but also affects the domestic and the foreign risk-free
rate of interest. Using the intervention and interest rate data collected for a three-
year period following the Louvre Summit to set up the theoretical model, it was
argued that for the sample period investigated in the empirical part of the chapter
an effective intervention policy served to depress volatilities implicit in US$/DM
foreign currency option prices.

In Chapter 4.2 I analyzed the effectiveness of the intervention policy of the
Bundesbank in terms of a success criterion which allows the impact of central
bank foreign exchange market interventions on the level and on the expected
volatility of the exchange rate to be modeled simultaneously. Following Bonser-
Neal and Tanner (1996) and Madura and Tucker (1991), I measured the exchange rate volatility in terms of volatility quotes implicit in FX option premia.
With this multifactor success criterion at hand, I studied the success of interventions of the Deutsche Bundesbank in the US$/DM spot market during a
sample period ranging from January 2, 1987, to March 12, 1990.

The main results of estimating ordered probit models can be summarized as
follows. *First*, the absolute amount of Bundesbank interventions increased the
probability of a decline in both the wedge between the actual exchange rate and
the implicit target level and the volatility of the spot rate implicit in foreign
currency option prices. *Second*, foreign exchange market interventions were less
effective when market participants were aware that the Bundesbank participated
in FX trading. *Third*, the magnitude of the effect of raising the absolute intervention amount on the probability of an effective FX market intervention was
only moderate. Though the intervention variable turned out to be significant in
the estimated ordered probit models, the overall impression derived from the
models is that the intervention policy of the Bundesbank was successful in
statistical rather than in economic terms. Thus, the results of the empirical work
contained in this chapter differ from the findings reported in a recent related

study by Humpage (1999). The reason for these conflicting results is that Humpage frames his paper in terms of an approach which allows only the impact of central banks foreign exchange market interventions on the level of the spot rates to be studied whereas the quantitative framework suggested above renders it possible to examine both the level and the volatility effects of interventions simultaneously in an unified framework.

Future research could extend the present analysis in three interesting and important directions. *Firstly*, it would be possible to adopt the research strategy used in Chapter 4 to simultaneously model the impact of the interventions of other major central banks like the US Federal Reserve or the Bank of Japan on the level and the volatility of exchange rates. Given that it is often found in the empirical literature that the sign and the significance of the effects of central banks' interventions depend upon the specific sample period under investigation, it would also be an important exercise to carry out the computations not only for the years following the Louvre Accord but also for the post-Plaza and the post-Louvre periods. *Secondly*, it would be interesting to adopt my success criterion and the ordered probit model to analyze the simultaneous impact of interventions on the level and the volatility of spot exchange rates using high-frequency data. The insights obtained by carrying out such an analysis could then be compared to the findings reported in the literature examining the effects of central bank interventions in "continuous" time (see, e.g., Peiers 1997, Goodhart and Hesse 1993, and Dominguez 1999). *Thirdly*, it would be interesting to use other options data to assess the effectiveness of central banks' foreign exchange market interventions. For example, one could extend the work of Galati and Melick (1999) and exploit the informational content embodied in the prices of risk reversals to analyze whether interventions cause market participants' exchange rate expectations under the equivalent martingale measure to become skewed in the direction suggested by the FX market intervention. The multifactor success criterion suggested in this chapter could then be employed to investigate the impact of central bank interventions on the level of the exchange rate and on the skewness of the respective implied equivalent martingale probability density within a unified framework.

5   Conclusion

Faced with the empirical shortcomings of the first-generation foreign exchange (FX) option pricing models, many fruitful attempts have been undertaken in the finance literature to develop alternative valuation models for the pricing of contingent claims whose payoff depends upon the level of the underlying exchange rate. In particular, models have been suggested capable of providing theoretical explanations of the biases resulting when the baseline Garman and Kohlhagen (GK) (1983) model is employed to price derivative contracts in real-world financial markets. The fundamental idea distinguishing many of the various extensions of the GK foreign currency option valuation model is to price derivative contracts by employing stochastic asset price processes reproducing the empirically observed leptokurtic shape of exchange rate returns distributions.

In the second chapter of this study, a set of important extensions of the GK model developed in this strand of research was reviewed and the implications of the various competing refinements of the pricing of foreign currency options were studied. The review demonstrated that the refinements of the GK model discussed in the literature help to explain the deviations of real-world foreign currency option premia from those predicted by the GK model. A drawback of the extended valuation approaches, however, is that the exchange rate dynamics utilized to replace the geometric Brownian motion employed in the first-generation models are specified in an ad hoc manner. Thus, while attractive from a technical point of view, a central flaw of the models surveyed is that they resort to arguments founded in mathematical rather than in economic theory to reconcile the predictions of option pricing theory with the way derivative contracts are priced in actual FX option markets. The exogeneity of the exchange rate process used in these models implies that convex and skewed volatility strike structures inferred from foreign currency options are exogenous phenomena.

This observation motivated the analyses contained in Chapter 3 of this study which contributed to the area of research concerned with the construction of an economic theory of the volatility strike structure. I used a modified and extended version of a heterogeneous agents monetary flex-price model of exchange rate determination introduced into the literature by Krugman and Miller (1993) to derive a continuous-time noise trader foreign currency option valuation model. In contrast to approaches by Grossman and Zhou (1996) and by Platen and Schweizer (1998), I analyzed the cross section of volatilities implicit in foreign currency option premia in the presence of technical spot traders following a state-dependent trend-extrapolative investment strategy. In my noise trader foreign currency option valuation model, important economic determinants of the volatility smile are the width of the interval of inaction of technical traders, the position of the prevailing spot rate relative to the trading triggers placed by noise traders, and the trading elasticity of technical traders. A Monte Carlo simulation was coded up to underscore that this model provides a rich and flexible framework which permits explicating smile and smirk effects observed in volatility strike structures in real-world FX options markets in economic rather than exclusively in technical terms.

I used real-world spot rate data for a broad set of major exchange rates to set up volatility-based empirical tests allowing assessment of whether the assumptions regarding the trading behavior of economic agents needed to derive a convex volatility strike structure in my theoretical framework are also valid from an empirical point of view. Based on the predictions of the theoretical model, I exploited the fact that the noise trading hypothesis of the volatility smile requires the conditional volatility of the exchange rate to rise (to fall) as the spot rate reaches a destabilizing (stabilizing) trading trigger stimulating technical investors to enter or to exit the market for domestic-currency-denominated assets.

In a first step, I used a traditional volatility-based quantitative approach to test the implications of the model. This setting allowed me to test for the presence of implicit trading-induced price barriers at potentially psychologically important exchange rate realizations ending in zero at the second and third digit after the decimal point. Results of GARCH-based empirical tests, however, were found to provide only very weak evidence supporting this interpretation of the barriers hypothesis of the volatility smile. Given these results, I performed an alternative volatility-based test for implicit trading regimes in FX markets. This alternative test mixes elements of technical filter and moving-average-based trading strategies and permits one to analyze whether exchange rate volatility is amplified whenever the absolute deviation of the prevailing spot rate from a medium-term target level exceeds certain critical threshold levels. The results of this alternative volatility-based test for noise-trading-induced implicit trading regimes in markets for foreign currency are encouraging. I documented that the conditional volatilities of the returns of the exchange rate under investigation computed upon estimating GARCH models contain a significant state-contingent component. Furthermore, for the overwhelming majority of currency pairs included in the empirical analysis these findings are supported by the results of a nonparametric test, of kernel density regressions, and of vector autoregressions. Against the background of these empirical findings, I concluded that noise trading and implicit trading regimes may be important factors determining the shape of the volatility strike structures implicit in FX options contracts on these exchange rates. Motivated by this finding, I supplemented the analysis by discussing the impact of chartism and fundamentalism on the pricing of contingent claims in a watered-down noise trading FX option valuation model with a closed-form solution for option premia.

The material contained in the third chapter of the study provided tools which allowed me to *explain* the observed mispricing of the first-generation option pricing frameworks. In Chapter 4, in contrast, I presented a model which showed how policymakers can use data on actual foreign currency option premia to *exploit* the pricing errors of the first-generation option pricing model. This application of option pricing theory was motivated by the fact that even since the abolition of the Bretton Woods system, major central banks often attempted to influence the dynamics of exchange rates by intervening in FX markets. Following, for example, Bonser-Neal and Tanner (1996), I used time-varying volatility quotes implicit in foreign currency options to assess the effectiveness of central banks' foreign exchange market interventions. To derive empirically testable hypotheses regarding the impact of effective infrequent central bank FX market interventions on options-implied volatilities, I used a model of exchange rate determination developed by Lewis (1995) to set up a foreign exchange option pricing model featuring infrequent central bank interventions. Using this model, I analyzed the impact of infrequent central bank FX interventions on the premia of FX options premia within the context of an appropriately modified GK model. I argued that the sign of the effect of a variation in the intervention probability on FX option premia depends upon the moneyness of the contract and upon the relative magnitude of the impact of the intervention probability on exchange rate volatility and on the international interest rate differential. I employed this feature of the model to argue that in empirical studies using option premia to disentangle effective from ineffective central bank FX market interventions, it is important to evaluate carefully the impact of central bank interventions on both international interest rates and exchange rate volatility.

Based on the predictions of the theoretical model, I analyzed the effectiveness of intervention policy of the German central bank during the Louvre period by using a multifactor success criterion. The distinguishing feature of this success criterion is that it allows one to model the impact of this type of FX market interventions on the level and on the expected volatility of the spot rate within a unified framework. The criterion was used as the dependent variable in an ordered qualitative response model. This model was estimated to test for a potentially significant relation between the spot market interventions carried out by the Bundesbank during a three-year period following the Louvre Summit, which took place in Paris in February 1987, and the following change in the level of, and in the implied volatility embedded in options on, the US$/DM exchange rate.

According to the multi-factor success criterion, an intervention was classified as effective if it helped to narrow the wedge between the prevailing exchange rate and an implicitly given target level and, at the same time, served to lower the volatility of the US$/DM spot price as anticipated by traders involved in the trading of the corresponding foreign currency options. If one of these conditions was not satisfied, the intervention was rated as partially effective. If both conditions did not hold, the intervention was rated as completely ineffective. Thus, rather than differentiating between completely effective and completely ineffective interventions only, my success criterion also allows for partially effective interventions and renders it thus possible to paint a picture of the effectiveness of central banks' FX market interventions, which is potentially more colorful than those painted in many related studies in this area of research.

Based on my success criterion, the findings of estimating ordered probit models indicate that the absolute amount of Bundesbank interventions increased the probability of a decrease in the absolute distance between the actual exchange rate and its implicit target level and the volatility of the spot rate embedded in FX options prices on the US$/DM spot rate. The quantitative importance of this effect, however, was found to be small. My empirical results further suggest that the foreign exchange market interventions of the Bundesbank were less effective when market participants were aware that the German central bank was participating in FX trading. All in all, the empirical evidence indicates that increasing the absolute intervention amount exerted only a rather moderate effect on the probability that a FX market intervention would turn out to be effective. I concluded that the FX market intervention policy of the Bundesbank during the Louvre period was effective in statistical rather than in economic terms. Thus, the results based on a multifactor success criterion provide evidence supporting the view that central banks should be somewhat reserved and cautious when the question arises whether interventions in foreign exchange markets are an appropriate policy instrument to support the domestic currency.

References

Abken, P.A., and S. Nandi (1996). Options and Volatility. *Federal Reserve Bank of Atlanta Economic Review* 81(3) (December): 21–35.

Ackert, L.F., J. Hao, and W.C. Hunter (1997). The Effect of Circuit Breakers on Expected Volatility: Tests Using Implied Volatilities. *Atlantic Economic Journal* 25(2): 117–127.

Aguilar, J., and Nydahl, S. (2000). Central Bank Intervention and Exchange Rates: The Case of Sweden. *Journal of International Financial Markets, Institutions and Money* 10(3/4): 303–322.

Aitchison, J., and S.D. Silvey (1957). The Generalization of the Probit Analysis to the Case of Multiple Responses. *Biometrika* 44(1/2): 131–140.

Ait-Sahalia, Y., and A.W. Lo (1998). Nonparametric Estimation of State-Price Densities Implicit in Financial Asset Prices. *Journal of Finance* 53(2): 499–547.

Alexander, V. (1998). Geldpolitik and Volatilitäten auf Finanzmärkten. In E. Baltensberger (ed.), *Spekulation, Preisbildung und Volatilität auf Finanz- und Devisenmärkten*. Berlin: Duncker and Humblot.

Allen, H., and M.P. Taylor (1990). Charts, Noise, and Fundamentals in the London Foreign Exchange Market. *Economic Journal* 100(400): 49–59.

Allen, H., and M.P. Taylor (1992). The Use of Technical Analysis in the Foreign Exchange Market. *Journal of International Money and Finance* 11(3): 304–314.

Almekinders, G.J. (1995). *Foreign Exchange Interventions: Theory and Evidence*. Aldershot: Edward Elgar Publishers.

Almekinders, G.J., and S.C.W. Eijffinger (1994). Daily Bundesbank and Federal Reserve Interventions: Are They a Reaction to Changes in the Level and Volatility of the DM/-rate? *Empirical Economics* 19(1): 111–130.

Almekinders, G.J., and S.C.W. Eijffinger (1996). A Friction Model of Daily Bundesbank and Federal Reserve Intervention. *Journal of Banking and Finance* 20(8): 1365–1380.

Amin, K.I., and R.A. Jarrow (1991). Pricing Foreign Currency Options Under Stochastic Interest Rates. *Journal of International Money and Finance* 10(3): 310–329.

Amin, K.I., and V.K. Ng (1997). Inferring Future Volatility from the Information in Implied Volatility in Eurodollar Options: A New Approach. *Review of Financial Studies* 10(2): 333–367.

Arrow, K.J. (1964). The Role of Securities in the Optimal Allocation of Risk-Bearing. *Review of Economic Studies* 31(85): 91–96.

Baillie, R.T., and T. Bollerslev (1989). The Message in Daily Exchange Rates: A Conditional Variance Tale. *Journal of Economics and Business Statistics* 7(3): 297–919.

Baillie, R.T., and W.P. Osterberg (1997a). Why Do Central Banks Intervene? *Journal of International Money and Finance* 16(6): 909–919.

Baillie, R.T., and W.P. Osterberg (1997b). Central Bank Interventions and Risk in the Forward Market. *Journal of International Economics* 43(3): 483–497.

Bakshi, G.S., and Z. Chen (1997). Equilibrium Valuation of Foreign Exchange Claims. *Journal of Finance* 52(2): 799–826.

Bakshi, G.S., and D. Madan (1999). Crash Discovery in Stock and Option Markets. Working Paper. Robert H. Smith School of Business. University of Maryland, College Park, Md.

Bakshi, G.S., C. Cao, and Z. Chen (1997). Empirical Performance of Alternative Option Pricing Models. *Journal of Finance* 52(5): 2003–2049.

Balduzzi, P., G. Bertola, and S. Foresi (1995). Asset Price Dynamics and Infrequent Feedback Trades. *Journal of Finance* 50(5): 1747–1766.

Balduzzi, P., S. Foresi, and D.J. Hait (1997). Price Barriers and the Dynamics of Asset Prices in Equilibrium. *Journal of Financial and Quantitative Analysis* 32(2): 137–159.

Ball, C.A., and A. Roma (1994). Stochastic Volatility Option Pricing. *Journal of Financial and Quantitative Analysis* 29(4): 589–607.

Bank for International Settlements (1996). *Central Bank Survey of Foreign Exchange and Derivatives Market Activity 1995*. Basle.

Bank of Japan (1995). Empirical Analyses of the Information Content of Implied Volatility. *Bank of Japan Quarterly Bulletin* 3(2): 64–88.

Bardhan, I. (1995). Exchange Rate Shocks, Currency Options and the Siegel Paradox. *Journal of International Money and Finance* 14(3): 441–458.

Barone-Adesi, G., and R.E. Whaley (1987). Efficient Analytic Approximation of American Option Values. *Journal of Finance* 42(2): 301–320.

Bates, D.S. (1996a). Testing Option Pricing Models. In G.S. Maddala and C.R. Rao (eds.), *Handbook of Statistics. Vol. 14: Statistical Methods in Finance*. Amsterdam: Elsevier Science.

Bates, D.S. (1996b). Jumps and Stochastic Volatility: Exchange Rate Processes Implicit in PHLX Deutsche Mark Options. *Review of Financial Studies* 9(1): 69–107.

Baxter, M., and A. Rennie (2000). *Financial Calculus — An Introduction to Derivative Pricing*. Cambridge: Cambridge University Press.

Bera, A.K., and C.M. Jarque (1982). Model Specification Tests: A Simultaneous Approach. *Journal of Econometrics* 20(1) Supplement: 59–82.

Bera, A.K., and M.L. Higgins (1993). ARCH Models: Properties, Estimation, and Testing. *Journal of Economic Surveys* 7(4): 305–366.

Berndt, E.K., B.H. Hall, R.E. Hall, and J. Hausman (1974). Estimation and Inference in Nonlinear Structural Models. *Annals of Economic and Social Measurement* 4(3): 653–665.

Bertola, G., and R.J. Caballero (1992). Target Zones and Realignments. *American Economic Review* 82(3): 520–536.

Bertola, G., and L.E.O. Svensson (1993). Stochastic Devaluation Risk and the Empirical Fit of Target-Zone Models. *Review of Economic Studies* 60(3): 689–712.

Bick, A. (1987). On the Consistency of the Black–Scholes Model with a General Equilibrium Framework. *Journal of Financial and Quantitative Analysis* 22(3): 259–275.

Biger, N., and J. Hull (1983). The Valuation of Foreign Currency Options. *Financial Management* 12(1): 24–28.

Björk, T. (1996). Interest Rate Theory. In W.J. Runggaldier (ed.), *Financial Mathematics*. Berlin: Springer-Verlag.

Black, F., and M. Scholes (1973). The Pricing of Options and Corporate Liabilities. *Journal of Political Economy* 81(3): 637–654.

Bodurtha, J.N., Jr., and G.R. Courtadon (1987a). Test of an American Option Pricing Model on the Foreign Currency Options Market. *Journal of Financial and Quantitative Analysis* 22(2):153–167.

Bodurtha, J.N., Jr., and G.R. Courtadon (1987b). The Pricing of Foreign Currency Options. Salomon Brothers Center for the Study of Financial Institutions at the Graduate School of Business Administration of New York University. Monograph Series in Finance and Economics 4/5. New York.

Bollerslev, T. (1986). A Generalized Autoregressive Conditional Heteroscedasticity. *Journal of Econometrics* 31(3): 307–327.

Bollerslev, T., and J.M. Wooldridge (1992). Quasi-Maximum Likelihood Estimation and Inference in Dynamic Models with Time-Varying Covariances. *Econometric Reviews* 11(2): 143–172.

Bollerslev, T., R.Y. Chou, and K.F. Kroner (1992). ARCH Modeling in Finance: A Review of the Theory and Empirical Evidence. *Journal of Econometrics* 52(1/2): 5–59.

Bonser-Neal, C., and G. Tanner (1996). Central Bank Intervention and the Volatility of Foreign Exchange Rates: Evidence from the Options Market. *Journal of International Money and Finance* 15(6): 853–878.

Borensztein, E.R., and M.P. Dooley (1987). Options on Foreign Exchange and Exchange Rate Expectations. *IMF Staff Papers* 34(4): 643–680.

Boughton, J.M. (1987). Tests of the Performance of Reduced-Form Exchange Rate Models. *Journal of International Economics* 23(1/2): 41–56.

Box, G.E.P. (1953). A Note on Regions for Tests of Kurtosis. *Biometrika* 40(June): 465–469.

Boyle, P.P. (1977). Options: A Monte Carlo Approach. *Journal of Financial Economics* 4(3): 323–338.

Boyle, P.P., M. Broadie, and P. Glasserman (1997). Monte Carlo Methods for Security Pricing. *Journal of Economic Dynamics and Control* 21(8): 1267–1321.

Breeden, D.T. (1979). An Intertemporal Asset Pricing Model with Stochastic Consumption and Investment Opportunities. *Journal of Financial Economics* 7(3): 265–296.

Breeden, D.T., and R.H. Litzenberger (1978). Prices of State-Contingent Claims Implicit in Option Prices. *Journal of Business* 51(4): 621–651.

Brennan, M.J., and E.S. Schwartz (1978). Finite-Difference Methods and Jump Processes Arising in the Pricing of Contingent Claims: A Synthesis. *Journal of Financial and Quantitative Analysis* 13(3): 462–474.

Brennan, M.J., and E.S. Schwartz (1989). Portfolio Insurance and Financial Market Equilibrium. *Journal of Business* 62(4): 455–476.

Breuer, P. (1999). Central Bank Participation in Currency Options Markets. IMF Working Paper WP 99/140. International Monetary Fund, Washington, D.C.

Breusch, T.S. (1978). Testing for Autocorrelation in Dynamic Linear Models. *Australian Economic Papers* 17(31): 334–355.

Buch, C.M., R.P. Heinrich, and C. Pierdzioch (1998). Taxing Short-Term Capital Flows — An Option for Transition Economies? Kiel Discussion Paper 321. Kiel Institute of World Economics, Kiel.

Butler, C., and N. Cooper (1997). Implied Exchange Rate Correlations and Market Perceptions of European Monetary Union. *Bank of England Quarterly Bulletin* 37(4): 413–423.

Campa, J.M., and P.H.K. Chang (1995). Testing the Expectations Hypothesis of the Term Structure of Volatilities Implicit in Option Prices. *Journal of Finance* 50(2): 529–547.

Campa, J.M., and P.H.K. Chang (1996). Arbitrage-Based Tests of Target-Zone Credibility: Evidence from ERM Cross-Rate Options. *American Economic Review* 86(4): 726–740.

Campa, J.M., and P.H.K. Chang (1998). ERM Realignment Risk and Its Economic Determinants as Reflected in Cross-Rate Options. *Economic Journal* 108(449): 1046–1066.

Campa, J.M., P.H.K. Chang, and R.L. Reider (1997). ERM Bandwidths for EMU and After: Evidence from Foreign Exchange Options. *Economic Policy* 24(April): 54–89.

Campbell, J.Y., A.W. Lo, and A.C. MacKinlay (1997). *The Econometrics of Financial Markets*. Princeton, N.J.: Princeton University Press.

Catte, P., G. Galli, and S. Rebecchini (1992). Exchange Markets Can Be Managed! *International Economic Insights* 3(5): 17–21.

Ceuster, M.J.K., G. Dhaene, and T. Schatteman (1998). On the Hypothesis of Psychological Barriers in Stock Markets and Benford's Law. *Journal of Empirical Finance* 5(3): 263–279.

Chang, P.H.K., and C.L. Osler (1999). Methodical Madness: Technical Analysis and the Irrationality of Exchange-Rate Forecasts. *Economic Journal* 109(459): 636–661.

Chen, R.-R., and L.O. Scott (1995). Interest Rate Options in Multifactor Cox–Ingersoll–Ross Models of the Term Structure. *Journal of Derivatives* 3(2): 53–73.

Cherian, J.A., and R.A. Jarrow (1998). Options Markets, Self-Fulfilling Prophecies, and Implied Volatilities. *Review of Derivatives Research* 2(1): 5–37.

Chesney, M., and L.O. Scott (1989). Pricing European Currency Options: A Comparison of the Modified Black–Scholes Model and a Random Variance Model. *Journal of Financial and Quantitative Analysis* 24(3): 267–284.

Christensen, P.O., D. Lando, and K.R. Miltersen (1998). State-Dependent Realignments in Target Zone Currency Regimes. *Review of Derivatives Research* 1(4): 295–323.

Christie, A. (1982). The Stochastic Behavior of Common Stock Variances. Value, Leverage and Interest Rate Effects. *Journal of Financial Economics* 10(4): 407–432.

Cox, J.C., and S.A. Ross (1976). The Valuation of Options for Alternative Stochastic Processes. *Journal of Financial Economics* 3(1/2): 145–166.

Cox, J.C., J.E. Ingersoll, Jr., and S.A. Ross (1985a). An Intertemporal General Equilibrium Model of Asset Prices. *Econometrica* 53(2): 363–384.

Cox, J.C., J.E. Ingersoll, Jr., and S.A. Ross (1985b). A Theory of the Term Structure of Interest Rates. *Econometrica* 53(2): 385–407.

Cox, J.C., S.A. Ross, and M. Rubinstein (1979). Option Pricing: A Simplified Approach. *Journal of Financial Economics* 7(3): 229–263.

Cyree, K.B., D.L. Domian, D.A. Louton, and E.J. Yobaccio (1999). Evidence of Psychological Barriers in the Conditional Moments of Major World Stock Indices. *Review of Financial Economics* 8(1): 73–91.

David, A., and P. Veronesi (1999). Option Prices with Uncertain Fundamentals: Theory and Evidence on the Dynamics of Implied Volatilities. Working Paper 47. Board of Governors of the Federal Reserve System, Washington, D.C.

Davutyan, N., and W.R. Parke (1995). The Operations of the Bank of England, 1890–1908: A Dynamic Probit Approach. *Journal of Money, Credit and Banking* 27(4): 1099–1112.

Debreu, G. (1959). *The Theory of Value. An Axiomatic Analysis of Economic Equilibrium.* New York: John Wiley & Sons.

De Grauwe, P., and D. Decupere (1992). Psychological Barriers in the Foreign Exchange Markets. *Journal of International and Comparative Economics* 1(2): 86–101.

De Grauwe, P., and H. Dewachter (1992). Chaos in the Dornbusch Model of the Exchange Rate. *Kredit und Kapital* 25(1): 26–54.

De Grauwe, P., H. Dewachter, and M. Embrechts (1993). *Exchange Rate Theory: Chaotic Models of Foreign Exchange Markets.* Oxford: Blackwell Publishers.

DeGroot, M.H. (1989). *Probability and Statistics.* Reading, Mass.: Addison-Wesley.

De Long, J.B., A. Shleifer, L.H. Summers, and R.J. Waldman (1990). Noise Trader Risk in Financial Markets. *Journal of Political Economy* 98(4): 703–738.

Diebold, F.X., and J.A. Lopez (1995). Modeling Volatility Dynamics. Research Paper 9522. Federal Reserve Bank of New York.

Diebold, F.X., and M. Nerlove (1989). The Dynamics of Exchange Rate Volatility: A Multivariate Latent Factor ARCH Model. *Journal of Applied Econometrics* 4(1): 1–21.

Dixit, A.K. (1993). The Art of Smooth Pasting. In J. Lesourne and H. Sonnenschein (eds.), *Fundamentals of Pure and Applied Economics*. Vol. 55. Chur: Harwood Academic Publishers.

Dixit, A.K., and R.S. Pindyck (1994). *Investment under Uncertainty*. Princeton, N.J.: Princeton University Press.

Dominguez, K.M. (1998). Central Bank Intervention and Exchange Rate Volatility. *Journal of International Money and Finance* 17(1): 161–190.

Dominguez, K.M. (1999). The Market Microstructure of Central Bank Interventions. Working Paper 7337. National Bureau of Economic Research, Cambridge, Mass.

Dominguez, K.M., and J.A. Frankel (1993a). Does Foreign-Exchange Intervention Matter? The Portfolio Effect. *American Economic Review* 83(5): 1356–1369.

Dominguez, K.M., and J.A. Frankel (1993b). *Does Foreign Exchange Intervention Work?* Institute for International Economics, Washington, D.C.

Donaldson, R.G. (1990). International Evidence on Psychological Barriers in Asset Prices and the Efficient Market Hypothesis. Financial Research Center Memorandum 116. Department of Economics, University of Princeton, Princeton, N.J.

Donaldson, R.G., and H.Y. Kim (1993). Price Barriers in the Dow Jones Industrial Average. *Journal of Financial and Quantitative Analysis* 28(3): 313–330.

Döpke, J., and C. Pierdzioch (1999). What Can the ECB Learn from Bundesbank Interventions? Evidence on the Link Between Exchange Rate Volatility and Interventions. Kiel Working Paper 955. Kiel Institute of World Economics, Kiel.

Dornbusch, R. (1976). Expectations and Exchange Rate Dynamics. *Journal of Political Economy* 84(6): 1167–1176.

Dothan, M.U. (1987). A Random Volatility Correction for the Black–Scholes Option Pricing Formula. *Advances in Futures and Options Research* 2: 97–115.

Drost, F.C., and T.E. Nijman (1993). Temporal Aggregation of GARCH Processes. *Econometrica* 61(4): 909–927.

Dufresne, P.C., W. Keirstead, and M.P. Ross (1996). Pricing Derivatives the Martingale Way. Mimeo. Haas School of Business, University of California at Berkeley.

Dumas, B. (1991). Super Contact and Related Optimality Conditions. *Journal of Economic Dynamics and Control* 15(4): 675–685.

Dumas, B., L.P. Jennergren, and B. Näslund (1993). Currency Option Pricing in Credible Target Zones. *Review of Futures Markets* 12(2): 323–340.

Dumas, B., L.P. Jennergren, and B. Näslund (1995a). Siegel's Paradox and the Pricing of Currency Options. *Journal of International Money and Finance* 14(2): 213–223.

Dumas, B., L.P. Jennergren, and B. Näslund (1995b). Realignment Risk and Currency Option Pricing in Target Zones. *European Economic Review* 39(8): 1523–1544.

Dumas, B., L.P. Jennergren, and B. Näslund (1995c). Comment on 'Exchange Rate Shocks, Currency Options and the Siegel Paradox' by Indrajit Bardhan. *Journal of International Money and Finance* 14: 459–460.

Dunis, C. (1989). Computerised Technical Systems and Exchange Rate Movements. In C. Dunis and M. Feeny (eds.), *Exchange Rate Forecasting*. London: Woodhead-Faulkner.

Edison, J.J. (1993). The Effectiveness of Central Bank Interventions: A Survey of the Post-1982 Literature. Special Papers in International Economics 18. International Finance Section, Department of Economics, Princeton University, Princeton, N.J.

Eichengreen, B., M.W. Watson, and R.S. Grossman (1985). Bank Rate Policy under the Interwar Gold Standard: A Dynamics Probit Model. *Economic Journal* 95(September): 725–745.

Eijffinger, S.C.W., and A.P.D. Gruijters (1991). On the Short-term Objectives of Daily Intervention by the Deutsche Bundesbank and the Federal Reserve System in the U.S.: Dollar/Deutsche Mark Exchange Market. *Kredit und Kapital* 24(1): 50–72.

Eijffinger, S.C.W., and A.P.D. Gruijters (1992). On the Effectiveness of Daily Intervention by the Deutsche Bundesbank and the Federal Reserve System in the U.S. Dollar–Deutsche Mark Exchange Market. In E. Baltensperger and H.W. Sinn (eds.), *Exchange-rate Regimes and Currency Unions*. London: MacMillan Press.

Ekvall, N., L.P. Jennergren, and B. Näslund (1993). Currency Options Pricing with Mean Reversion and Uncovered Interest Rate Parity: A Revision of the Garman–Kohlhagen Model. Working Paper 6524. Stockholm School of Economics, Stockholm.

Elliott, R.J., and P.E. Kopp (1998). *Mathematics of Financial Markets*. Berlin: Springer-Verlag.

Emanuel, D., and J. MacBeth (1982). Further Results on the Constant Elasticity of Variance Call Option Pricing Model. *Journal of Financial and Quantitative Analysis* 17(4): 533–554.

Enders, W. (1995). *Applied Econometric Time Series*. New York: John Wiley & Sons.

Engle, R.F. (1982). Autoregressive Conditional Heteroscedasticity with Estimates of the Variance of U.K. Inflation. *Econometrica* 50(4): 987–1007.

Europäische Zentralbank (2000). Der Informationsgehalt von Zinssätzen und ihren Derivaten für die Geldpolitik. *Monatsbericht*. Mai. Frankfurt am Main.

Fama, E.F. (1965). The Behavior of Stock Market Prices. *Journal of Business* 38(1): 34–105.

Fastrich, H., and S. Hepp (1991). *Währungsmanagement international tätiger Unternehmen*. Stuttgart: Poeschel Verlag.

Fatum, R. (2000). On the Effectiveness of Sterilized Foreign Exchange Intervention. Working Paper 10. European Central Bank. Frankfurt am Main.

Fatum, R., and M. Hutchison (1999). Is Intervention a Signal of Future Monetary Policy? Evidence from the Federal Funds Futures Market. *Journal of Money, Credit and Banking* 31(1): 54–69.

Feeny, M. (1989). Charting the Foreign Exchange Market. In C. Dunis and M. Feeny (eds.), *Exchange Rate Forecasting*. London: Woodhead–Faulkner.

Finucane, T.J. (1989). Black–Scholes Approximations of Call Option Prices with Stochastic Volatilities: A Note. *Journal of Financial and Quantitative Analysis* 24(4): 527–532.

Flood, R.P., and A.K. Rose (1995). Fixing Exchange Rates: A Virtual Quest for Fundamentals. *Journal of Monetary Economics* 36(1): 3–37.

Föllmer, H., and M. Schweizer (1993). A Microeconomic Approach to Diffusion Models for Stock Prices. *Mathematical Finance* 3(1): 1–23.

Frankel, J.A. (1996). How Well Do Foreign Exchange Markets Work: Might a Tobin Tax Help? In M. ul Haq, I. Kaul and I. Grunberg (eds.), *The Tobin Tax: Coping with Financial Volatility*. New York: Oxford University Press.

Frankel, J.A., and K.A. Froot (1988). Chartists, Fundamentalists, and the Demand for Dollars. *Greek Economic Review* 10(1): 49–102.

Frankel, J.A., and K.A. Froot (1990). Chartists, Fundamentalists, and the Demand for Dollars. In A.S. Courakis and M.P. Taylor (eds.), *Private Behaviour and Government Policy in Interdependent Economies*. Oxford: Clarendon Press.

Frenkel, M. (1997). Exchange Rate Dynamics with Chartists, Fundamentalists, and Rational Speculators in the Foreign Exchange Market. *International Journal of Business* 2(1): 1–24.

Frey, R., and A. Stremme (1997). Market Volatility and Feedback Effects from Dynamic Hedging. *Mathematical Finance* 7(4): 351–274.

Funabashi, Y. (1988). *Managing the Dollar: From the Plaza to the Louvre*. Washington, D.C.: Institute for International Economics.

Galati, G., and W. Melick (1999). Perceived Central Bank Intervention and Market Expectations: An Empirical Study of the Yen/Dollar Exchange Rate, 1993–96. Working Paper 77. Bank for International Settlements, Basle.

Garber, P.M., and G. Spencer (1996). Dynamic Hedging and the Interest Rate Defense. In J.A. Frankel, G. Galli, and A. Giovannini (eds.), *The Microstructure of Foreign Exchange Markets*. Chicago: Chicago University Press.

Garman, M.B., and S.W. Kohlhagen (1983). Foreign Currency Option Values. *Journal of International Money and Finance* 2(3): 231–237.

Geiger, U. (1996). *Heterogene Erwartungen am Devisenmarkt: Das Portfoliomodell der Wechselkursbestimmung unter dem Einfluß autoregressiver Erwartungen*. Tübingen: Francke Verlag.

Gennotte, G., and H.E. Leland (1990). Market Liquidity, Hedging, and Crashes. *American Economic Review* 80(5): 999–1021.

Geske, R.L. (1979a). A Note on an Analytical Valuation Formula for Unprotected American Call Options on Stocks with Known Dividends. *Journal of Financial Economics* 7(4): 375–380.

Geske, R.L. (1979b). The Valuation of Compound Options. *Journal of Financial Economics* 7(1): 63–81.

Geske, R.L., and H.E. Johnson (1984). The American Put Option Valued Analytically. *Journal of Finance* 39(5): 1511–1524.

Gesser, V., and P. Poncet (1997). Volatility Patterns: Theory and Some Evidence from the Dollar–Mark Option Market. *The Journal of Derivatives* 5(2):46–61.

Ghosh, A.R. (1992). Is It Signalling? Exchange Intervention and the dollar-Deutsche mark rate. *Journal of International Economics* 32(3): 201–220.

Giddy, I.H. (1983). Foreign Exchange Options. *Journal of Futures Markets* 3(2): 143–166.

Glosten, L.R., R. Jagannathan, and D.E. Runkle (1993). On the Relation between the Expected Value and the Volatility of the Nominal Excess Return on Stocks. *Journal of Finance* 48(5): 1779–1801.

Godfrey, L.G. (1978). Testing for Higher Order Serial Correlation in Regression Equations When the Regressors Include Lagged Dependent Variables. *Econometrica* 16: 1303–1310.

Goodhart, C.A.E., and T. Hesse (1993). Central Bank Forex Interventions Assessed in Continuous Time. *Journal of International Money and Finance* 12(4): 368–389.

Goodman, L.S., S. Ross, and F. Schmidt (1985). Are Foreign Currency Options Overvalued? The Early Experience of the Philadelphia Stock Exchange. *Journal of Futures Markets* 5(3): 349–359.

Grabbe, J.O. (1983). The Pricing of Call and Put Options on Foreign Exchange. *Journal of International Money and Finance* 2(3): 239–253.

Greene, W.H. (1997). Econometric Analysis. Upper Saddle River, N.J.: Prentice Hall.

Grossman, S.J. (1988). An Analysis of the Implications for Stock and Futures Price Volatility of Program Trading and Dynamic Hedging Strategies. *Journal of Business* 61(3): 275–298.

Grossman, S.J., and Z. Zhou (1996). Equilibrium Analysis of Portfolio Insurance. *Journal of Finance* 51(4): 1379–1403.

Hafner, C.M. (1998). *Nonlinear Time Series Analysis with Applications to Foreign Exchange Rate Volatility*. Heidelberg: Physica-Verlag.

Hamilton, J.D. (1994). *Time Series Analysis*. Princeton, N.J.: Princeton University Press.

Hammersley, J.M., and D.C. Handscomb (1964). *Monte Carlo Methods*. London: Chapman and Hall.

Hansen, G. (1993). *Quantitative Wirtschaftsforschung*. München: Verlag Franz Vahlen.

Härdle, W. (1990). *Applied Nonparametric Regression*. New York: Cambridge University Press.

Harrison, J.M., and D.M. Kreps (1979). Martingales and Arbitrage in Multiperiod Securities Markets. *Journal of Economic Theory* 20(3): 381–408.

Hausman, J.A., A.W.-C. Lo, and A.C. MacKinley (1992). An Ordered Probit Analysis of Transaction Stock Prices. *Journal of Financial Economics* 31(3): 319–379.

Heckman, J.J. (1979). Sample Selection Bias as a Specification Error. *Econometrica* 47(1): 153–161.

Heston, S. (1993). A Closed-Form Solution for Options with Stochastic Volatility with Applications to Bond and Currency Options. *Review of Financial Studies* 6(2): 327–343.

Hogan, K.C. Jr., K.F. Kroner, and J. Sultan (1997). Program Trading, Nonprogram Trading, and Market Volatility. *Journal of Futures Markets* 17(7): 733–456.

Hsieh, D.A. (1988). The Statistical Properties of Daily Foreign Exchange Rates: 1974–1983. *Journal of International Economics* 24(1/2): 129–145.

Hsieh, D.A. (1989). Testing for Nonlinear Dependence in Daily Foreign Exchange Rate Changes. *Journal of Business* 62(3): 339–368.

Hull, J. (1993). *Options, Futures, and Other Derivative Securities*. Englewood Cliffs, N.J.: Prentice-Hall.

Hull, J., and A. White (1987a). The Pricing of Options on Assets with Stochastic Volatilities. *Journal of Finance* 42(2): 281–300.

Hull, J., and A. White (1987b). Hedging the Risks from Writing Foreign Currency Options. *Journal of International Money and Finance* 6(2): 131–152.

Hull, J., and A. White (1988). An Analysis of the Bias in Option Pricing Caused by a Stochastic Volatility. *Advances in Futures and Options Research* 3: 29–61.

Humi, M., and W.B. Miller (1992). *Boundary Value Problems and Partial Differential Equations*. Boston: PWS-Kent Publishing Company.

Humpage, O.F. (1999). U.S. Intervention: Assessing the Probability of Success. *Journal of Money, Credit and Banking* 31(4): 731–747.

Hung, J.H. (1997). Intervention Strategies and Exchange Rate Volatility: A Noise Trading Perspective. *Journal of International Money and Finance* 16(5): 779–793.

Ingersoll, J.E. (1987). *Theory of Financial Decision Making*. Totowa, N.J.: Rowman & Littlefield.

Ingersoll, J.E. (1997). Valuing Foreign Exchange Rate Derivatives with a Bounded Exchange Rate Process. *Review of Derivatives Research* 1(2): 159–181.

Jackwerth, J.C., and M. Rubinstein (1996). Recovering Probability Distributions from Option Prices. *Journal of Finance* 51(5): 1611–1631.

Jeanne, O., and A.K. Rose (1999). Noise Trading and Exchange Rate Regimes. Working Paper 7104. National Bureau of Economic Research, Cambridge, Mass.

Johnson, H.E. (1983). An Analytical Approximation for the American Put Price. *Journal of Financial and Quantitative Analysis* 18(1): 141–148.

Johnson, H.E., and D. Shanno (1987). Option Pricing When the Variance Is Changing. *Journal of Financial and Quantitative Analysis* 22(2): 143–151.

Jorion, P. (1988). On Jump Processes in the Foreign Exchange and Stock Markets. *Review of Financial Studies* 1(4): 427–445.

Judge, G.G., R.C. Hill, W.E. Griffiths, H. Lütkepohl, and T.C. Lee (1988). *Introduction to the Theory and Practice of Econometrics*. New York: John Wiley & Sons.

Kaminsky, G.L., and K.K. Lewis (1996). Does Foreign Exchange Intervention Signal Future Monetary Policy? *Journal of Monetary Economics* 37(2): 285–312.

Kempa, B., and M. Nelles (1994). Target Zones and Heterogeneous Expectations. Discussion Paper 84. Department of Economics, University of Essen, Germany.

Kempa, B., M. Nelles, and C. Pierdzioch (1998). Valuing Currency Options with Reflected Mean Reversion and Stochastic Realignment Risk. Mimeo. University of Essen, Germany.

Kho, B.C. (1996). Time-varying Risk Premia, Volatility, and Technical Trading Rule Profits: Evidence from Foreign Currency Futures Markets. *Journal of Financial Economics* 41(2): 249–290.

Kim, I.J. (1990). The Analytic Valuation of American Options. *Review of Financial Studies* 3(4): 547–572.

Koch, H.J. (1992). *The Pricing of Foreign Currency Options*. Ph.D. Thesis. Yale University.

Koedjik, K.G., and P.A. Stork (1994). Should We Care? Psychological Barriers in Stock Markets. *Economics Letters* 44(4): 427–432.

Kolb, R.W. (1997). *Options*. Malden, Mass.: Blackwell Publishers.

Krafft, M. (1997). Der Ansatz der logistischen Regression und seine Interpretation. *Zeitschrift für Betriebswirtschaft* 67(5): 625–642.

Krugman, P.R. (1987). Trigger Strategies and Price Dynamics in Equity and Foreign Exchange Markets. Working Paper 2459. National Bureau of Economic Research, Cambridge, Mass.

Krugman, P.R. (1991). Target Zones and Exchange Rate Dynamics. *Quarterly Journal of Economics* 106(3): 669–682.

Krugman, P.R., and M. Miller (1993). Why Have A Target Zone? *Carnegie–Rochester Series on Public Policy* 38(June): 279–314.

Lastrapes, W.D. (1989). Exchange Rate Volatility and U.S. Monetary Policy: An ARCH Application. *Journal of Money, Credit and Banking* 21(1): 66–77.

Leahy, M.P., and C.P. Thomas (1996). The Sovereignty Option: The Quebec Referendum and Market Views on the Canadian Dollar. International Finance Discussion Paper 555. Board of Governors of the Federal Reserve System.

LeBaron, B.D. (1999). Technical Trading Rule Profitability and Foreign Exchange Market Interventions. *Journal of International Economics* 49(1): 125–143.

Lehment, H. (1980). Devisenmarktinterventionen bei flexiblen Wechselkursen — die Politik des Managed Floating. Kieler Studien 162. Tübingen: Mohr Siebeck.

Levich, R.M., and L.R. Thomas (1993). The Significance of Technical Trading-Rule Profits in the Foreign Exchange Market: A Bootstrap Approach. *Journal of International Money and Finance* 12(5): 451–474.

Levin, J.H. (1997). Chartists, Fundamentalists, and Exchange Rate Dynamics. *International Journal of Finance and Economics* 2(4): 281–290.

Lewis, K.K. (1995). Occasional Interventions to Target Rates. *American Economic Review* 85(4): 691–715.

Ley, E., and H. Varian (1994). Are There Psychological Barriers in the Dow Jones Index? *Applied Financial Economics* 4(3): 217–224.

Lindberg, H., and P. Söderlind (1994). Intervention Policy and Mean Reversion in Exchange Rate Target Zones: The Swedish Case. *Scandinavian Journal of Economics* 96(4): 691–715.

Lintner, J. (1965). The Valuation of Risky Assets and the Selection of Risky Investments in Stock Portfolios and Capital Budgets. *Review of Economics and Statistics* 47(1): 13–37.

Ljung, G., and G. Box (1978). On a Measure of Lack of Fit in Time Series Models. *Biometrica* 65: 297–303.

Lo, A.W., and J. Whang (1995). Implementing Option Pricing Models When Asset Returns Are Predictable. *Journal of Finance* 50(1): 87–129.

Lui, S., and B.W. Brorsen (1995). Maximum Likelihood Estimation of a GARCH-Stable Model. *Journal of Applied Econometrics* 10(3): 273–285.

Lux, T. (1997). Time Variation of Second Moments from a Noise Trader Infection Model. *Journal of Economic Dynamics and Control* 22(1): 1–38.

Lux, T., and M. Marchesi (2000). Volatility Clustering in Financial Markets: A Microsimulation of Interacting Agents. *International Journal of Theoretical and Applied Finance* 4(4): 675–702.

MacBeth, J., and J.L. Merville (1980). Tests of the Black–Scholes and Cox Call Options Valuation Models. *Journal of Finance* 35(2): 285–301.

MacMillan, L.W. (1986). Analytic Approximation for the American Put Option. In F.J. Fabozzi (ed.), *Advances in Futures and Options Research* 1 (Part A). Greenwich, Conn.: Jai Press Inc.

Madura, A.L., and J. Tucker (1991). Impact of the Louvre Accord on Actual and Anticipated Exchange Rate Volatilities. *Journal of International Financial Markets, Institutions, and Money* 1(2): 43–59.

Malz, A.M. (1996). Using Option Prices to Estimate Realignment Probabilities in the European Monetary System: The Case of Sterling–Mark. *Journal of International Money and Finance* 15(5): 717–748.

Malz, A.M. (1997). Estimating the Probability Distribution of the Future Exchange Rate from Option Prices. *Journal of Derivatives* 5(2): 18–36.

Mandelbrot, B. (1963). The Variation of Certain Speculative Prices. *Journal of Business* 36(4): 394–419.

McDonald, J.B., and W.K. Newey (1988). Partially Adaptive Estimation of Regression Models via the Generalized T Distribution. *Econometric Theory* 4(4): 428–457.

Meese, R.A., and K. Rogoff (1983). Empirical Exchange Rate Models of the Seventies. *Journal of International Economics* 14(1/2): 3–24.

Melick, W.R., and C.P. Thomas (1997). Recovering an Asset's Implied PDF from Option Prices: An Application to Crude Oil Prices During the Gulf Crisis. *Journal of Financial and Quantitative Analysis* 32(1): 91–115.

Melino, A., and S.M. Turnbull (1990). Pricing Foreign Currency Options with Stochastic Volatility. *Journal of Econometrics* 45(1): 239–265.

Melino, A., and S.M. Turnbull (1991). The Pricing of Foreign Currency Options. *Canadian Journal of Economics* 24(2): 251–281.

Menkhoff, L. (1997). Examining the Use of Technical Currency Analysis. *International Journal of Finance and Economics* 2(4): 307–318.

Merrill Lynch (2000). FX Strategies. Bi-Weekly Themes and Forecasts. February 2000. Fixed Income Strategy. Global Securities Research and Economics Group.

Merton, R.C. (1973). The Theory of Rational Option Pricing. *Bell Journal of Economics and Management Science* 4(1): 141–183.

Merton, R.C. (1976). Option Pricing When Underlying Stock Returns Are Discontinuous. *Journal of Financial Economics* 3(1/2): 125–144.

Mittnik, S., and S.T. Rachev (1993). Modeling Asset Returns with Alternative Stable Distributions. *Econometric Reviews* 12(3): 261–330.

Mizrach, B. (1996). Did Option Prices Predict the ERM Crises? Working Paper 96–10. Department of Economics, Rutgers University, New Brunswick, N.J.

Mossin, J. (1966). Equilibrium in a Capital Asset Market. *Econometrica* 34(4): 768–783.

Naik, V. (1993). Option Valuation and Hedging Strategies with Jumps in the Volatility of Asset Returns. *Journal of Finance* 48(5): 1969–1984.

Neely, C.J., P.A. Weller, and R. Dittmar (1997). Is Technical Analysis in the Foreign Exchange Market Profitable? A Genetic Programming Approach. *Journal of Financial and Quantitative Analysis* 32(4): 405–426.

Neftci, S.N. (1996). *An Introduction to the Mathematics of Financial Derivatives.* San Diego, Calif.: Academic Press.

Nelson, D.B. (1991). Conditional Heteroskedasticity in Asset Returns: A New Approach. *Econometrica* 59(2): 347–370.

Nelson, D.B., and C.Q. Cao (1992). Inequality Constraints in the Univariate GARCH Model. *Journal of Business and Economic Statistics* 10(2): 229–235.

Neuhaus, H. (1995). Der Informationsgehalt von Derivaten für die Geldpolitik: Implizite Volatilitäten und Wahrscheinlichkeiten. Diskussionspapier 3/95. Volkswirtschaftliche Forschungsgruppe der Deutschen Bundesbank, Frankfurt am Main.

Nielson, L., and J. Saá-Requejo (1993). Exchange Rate and Term Structure Dynamics and the Pricing of Derivative Securities. Working Paper 92/72/Fin. INSEAD, Fontainebleau.

Obstfeld, M., and A.M. Taylor (1998). The Great Depression as a Watershed: International Capital Mobility over the Long Run. In M.D. Bordo, D.C. Goldin, and E.N. White (eds.), *The Defining Moment: The Great Depression and the American Economy in the Twentieth Century*. Chicago: Chicago University Press.

Pagan A.R., and G.W. Schwert (1990). Alternative Models of Conditional Stock Volatility. *Journal of Econometrics* 45(1): 267–290.

Paolella, M. (1999). *Tail Estimation and Conditional Modeling of Heteroscedastic Time-Series*. Berlin: Pro Business.

Peiers, B. (1997). Informed Traders, Intervention, and Price Leadership: A Deeper View of the Microstructure of the Foreign Exchange Market. *Journal of Finance* 52(4): 1589–1614.

Peterson, D.R., E. Scott, and A.L. Tucker (1988). Tests of the Black–Scholes and Constant Elasticity of Variance Currency Call Option Valuation Models. *Journal of Financial Research* 111(3): 201–212.

Pierdzioch, C. (2000). The Effectiveness of the FX Market Interventions of the Bundesbank During the Louvre Period: An Options-Based Analysis. Kiel Working Paper 971. Kiel Institute of World Economics, Kiel.

Pierdzioch, C., and G. Stadtmann (2000). Komplexe Aktien- und Wechselkursdynamik in einem makroökonomischen Modell mit heterogener Erwartungsbildung. *Kredit und Kapital* 33(3): 377–409.

Platen, E., and M. Schweizer (1998). On Feedback Effects from Hedging Derivatives. *Mathematical Finance* 8(1): 67–84.

Pring, M.J. (1990). *Handbuch Technische Kursanalyse*. Darmstadt: Verlag Hoppenstedt & Co.

Rabenmananjara, R., and J.M. Zakoian (1993). Threshold ARCH Models and Asymmetries in Volatility. *Journal of Applied Econometrics* 8(1): 31–49.

Roll, R. (1977). An Analytical Valuation Formula for Unprotected American Call Options on Stocks with Known Dividends. *Journal of Financial Economics* 5(2): 251–258.

Rose, A.K. (1994). Are Exchange Rates Macroeconomic Phenomena? *Federal Reserve Bank of San Francisco Economic Review* 1: 19–30.

Rosenberg, M.R. (1996). *Currency Forecasting: A Guide to Fundamental and Technical Models of Exchange Rate Determination*. Chicago: Irwin Publishing Company.

Rubinstein, M. (1994). Implied Binomial Trees. *Journal of Finance* 49(3): 771–818.

Schäfer, K. (1993). *Optionsbewertung mit Monte-Carlo-Methoden*. Bergisch-Gladbach: Verlag Josef Eul.

Scheide, J. (1986). Mehr Stabilität durch Wechselkurszielzonen? *Die Weltwirtschaft* (1): 38–46.

Schlittgen, R. (1998). *Einführung in die Statistik: Analyse und Modellierung von Daten.* München: Oldenbourg Verlag.

Schöbel, R., and J. Zhu (1999). Stochastic Volatility with an Ornstein–Uhlenbeck Process. *European Finance Review* 3(1): 213–46.

Schroder, M. (1989). Computing the Constant Elasticity of Variance Option Pricing Formula. *Journal of Finance* 44(1): 211–219.

Schwartz, E.S. (1977). The Valuation of Warrants: Implementing a New Approach. *Journal of Financial Economics* 4(1): 79–93.

Schwert, G.W. (1989). Why Does Stock Market Volatility Change over Time? *Journal of Finance* 44(5): 1115–1153.

Scott, E., and A.L. Tucker (1989). Predicting Currency Return Volatility. *Journal of Banking and Finance* 13(6): 839–851.

Scott, L.O. (1987). Option Pricing When the Variance Changes Randomly: Theory, Estimation, and an Application. *Journal of Financial and Quantitative Analysis* 22(4): 419–438.

Scott, L.O. (1997). Pricing Stock Options in a Jump-Diffusion Model with Stochastic Volatility and Interest Rates. *Mathematical Finance* 7(4): 413–426.

Sharpe, W. (1964). Capital Asset Prices: A Theory of Market Equilibrium Under Conditions of Risk. *Journal of Finance* 19(3): 425–442.

Shastri, K., and K. Tandon (1986). Valuation of Foreign Currency Options: Some Empirical Tests. *Journal of Financial and Quantitative Analysis* 21(2): 145–160.

Shastri, K., and K. Wethyavivorn (1987). The Valuation of Currency Options for Alternative Stochastic Processes. *Journal of Financial Research* 10(4): 283–293.

Siebert, H. (1994). *Außenwirtschaft.* 6. Auflage. UTB für Wissenschaft. Stuttgart: Fischer Verlag.

Siebert, H. (2000a). *Außenwirtschaft.* 7. Auflage. UTB für Wissenschaft. Stuttgart: Fischer Verlag.

Siebert, H. (2000b). The Japanese Bubble: Some Lessons for International Macroeconomic Policy Coordination. *Aussenwirtschaft* 55(2): 233–250.

Siegel, J.J. (1972). Risk, Interest Rates, and the Forward Exchange. *Quarterly Journal of Economics* 86(2): 303–309.

Silverman, B.W. (1986). *Density Estimation for Statistics and Data Analysis.* London: Chapman and Hall.

Sims, C. (1980). Macroeconomics and Reality. *Econometrica* 48(1): 1–48.

Sircar, K.R., and G. Papanicolaou (1998). General Black–Scholes Models Accounting for Increased Market Volatility from Hedging Strategies. *Applied Mathematical Finance* 5(1): 45–82.

Söderlind, P. (1998). Extracting Expectations about 1992 UK Monetary Policy from Option Prices. Discussion Paper 1823. Centre for Economic Policy Research, London.

Söderlind, P., and L.E.O. Svensson (1997). New Techniques to Extract Market Expectations from Financial Instruments. *Journal of Monetary Economics* 40(2): 383–429.

Sorensen, C. (1997). An Equilibrium Approach to Pricing Foreign Currency Options. *European Financial Management* 3(1): 145–160.

Stein, E.M., and J.C. Stein (1991). Stock Price Distributions with Stochastic Volatility: An Analytical Approach. *Review of Financial Studies* 4(4): 727–752.

Svensson, L.E.O. (1992). An Interpretation of Recent Research on Exchange Rate Target Zones. *Journal of Economic Perspectives* 4(4): 119–144.

Szakmary, A.C., and I. Mathur (1997). Central Bank Intervention and Trading Rule Profits in Foreign Exchange Markets. *Journal of International Money and Finance* 16(4): 513–535.

Tobin, J. (1958). Estimation of Relationships for Limited Dependent Variables. *Econometrica* 26(1): 24–36.

Vasicek, O.A. (1977). An Equilibrium Characterization of the Term Structure. *Journal of Financial Economics* 5(2): 177–188.

deVries, C.G. (1994). Stylized Facts of Nominal Exchange Rate Returns. In F. van der Ploeg (ed.), *The Handbook of International Macroeconomics*. Oxford: Blackwell Publishers.

Weber, A. (1996). Is Central Bank Intervention Effective in Stabilizing Exchange Rates? In F. Bruni (ed.), *Risk Management in Volatile Financial Markets*. Financial and Monetary Policy Studies 32. Dordrecht: Kluwer Academic Publishers.

Whaley, R.E. (1981). On the Valuation of American Call Options on Dividend-Paying Stocks with Known Dividends. *Journal of Financial Economics* 9(2): 207–211.

Whitelaw, R.F. (1994). Time Variations and Covariations in the Expectations and Volatility of Stock Market Returns. *Journal of Finance* 49(2): 515–541.

Wiggins, J.B. (1987). Option Valuation Under Stochastic Volatility: Theory and Empirical Estimates. *Journal of Financial Economics* 19(2): 351–372.

Wilmott, P., J. Dewynne, and S. Howison (1995). *Option Pricing: Mathematical Models and Computation*. Oxford: Oxford Financial Press.

Xu, X., and S.J. Taylor (1994). The Term Structure of Volatility Implied by Foreign Exchange Options. *Journal of Financial and Quantitative Analysis* 29(1): 57–74.

Youssefmir, M., and B.A. Huberman (1997). Clustered Volatility in Multiagent Dynamics. *Journal of Economic Behavior and Organization* 32(1): 101–118.

Zhang, P.G. (1996). *Exotic Options: A Guide to Second Generation Options*. Singapore: World Scientific Publishing.

Zimmermann, H. (1998). *State-Preference Theorie und Asset Pricing: eine Einführung*. Heidelberg: Physica-Verlag.

Index

Absolute diffusion model *25–26*

Autoregressive conditional heteroskedasticity
Diagnostic statistics *95–97, 112–113, 175*
GARCH model *85–88, 165–167, 174–175*
GED function *88*
Likelihood function *88*
Schwert's method *114–115*
TARCH model *175*

Boundary conditions
for American options *14–16*
for European options *10, 15, 20–21, 31, 68, 151*
High contact *16*
in the noise trader model *61–63*
Smooth-transition *63*
Transversality condition *61*
Value matching *15, 62*

Bretton Woods system *1, 145*

Central bank interventions
and FX option pricing *145–159*
and the Louvre Summit *145–146*
Constructing an instrument for interventions *175–177*
Effectiveness *178–183*
Literature on effectiveness *161–167*
Literature on interventions and implied volatilities *164–167*
Occasional interventions and exchange rates *149–152*
Target value during Louvre period *168*

Central bank reaction function *176*

CEV model *24–27*

Chapman–Kolmogorov equation *20*

Characteristic function *34, 36, 132*

Data
Bundesbank intervention data *171–172*
Exchange rate data *89–91, 171–172*
Implied volatility data *28, 170–172*

Differential equations
Ordinary differential equation *36, 60, 150*
Partial differential equation *9–10, 25, 29, 31, 35–36, 40, 68, 151*
Stochastic differential equation *8, 24, 29, 35, 38, 58, 67, 69, 126–128, 149–150*

Early exercise premium *14–15, 18*

Economic fundamentals *46, 52, 57–58, 61–67, 149–151*

Equivalent martingale measure (*see* martingale)

Exchange rate expectations *59, 130–131*

Fat tails *23–24, 38*

Free boundary problem *16*

Garman and Kohlhagen model *8–11*

Girsanov's theorem *21*

Hedging *1, 2, 5, 11–12, 29–30, 39, 53–56*

International interest rate differential
Decomposition formula *151*
Uncovered interest rate parity *58, 149*

Jensen's inequality *32, 62, 74*

Jump models
    Jump-diffusion model *38–42*
    Jumps-in-volatility model *42*

Leverage effect *27*

Martingale *10, 16, 19, 21, 39, 69–70*
Monetary model *52, 56–67, 149–151*
Monte Carlo simulation
    (*see* numerical simulation)

Noise trader
    and volatility smiles *72–80*
    in exchange rate models *47, 57–66, 125–132*
    in the FX option pricing model *50, 67–80*
    in the Heston-style model *132–136*
Numerical simulation
    American options *16–17*
    Monte Carlo simulation *22, 47, 69–72, 105*
    of the CEV model *25–26*
    of the Heston-style model *134–135*
    of the Hull and White model *32–33*
    of the jump diffusion model *41, 42*
    of the model featuring interventions *152–159*

Option sensitivities *11–13*
    delta *12–13*
    rho *13*
    theta *13*
    vega *13, 33*
Options
    American style *14–18*
    European style *8–11, 19–20*
Ordered probit model *167–170*
    Elasticities *170*
    Likelihood function *170*
    Marginal effects *182*
    Multifactor success criterion *169–170*
    Regressors *173–175*

Price barriers
    Empirical evidence on price barriers (*see* volatility-based empirical tests)
    Literature on price barriers *52, 81–83*
    Neighborhood of barriers *84, 103*
Put-call-parity *11–12*
Put option *10, 12, 14, 23*

Radon–Nikodym derivative *69*
Risk-neutral probability density function *22–23, 70*
Risk-neutral valuation *10, 11, 19–23, 70*
Risk premium
    for bearing exchange rate risk *8, 11, 20, 21, 68*
    for bearing volatility risk *30–31, 35*

Stochastic volatility model
    Heston model *24, 31, 34–37, 72*
    Hull and White model *24, 28–34, 72*
Stock market volatility *174–175*

Term structure of interest rate *131–132*
Tobit model *177*

Volatility smile
    (*see* volatility strike structure)
Volatility-based empirical tests
    Alternative test *98–114*
    Traditional test *85–87, 91–97*
    Kernel density estimation *117–120*
    Wilcoxon test *115–117*
Volatility strike structure
    Definition of *2*
    in the Heston-style noise trader model *134–135*
    in the noise trader FX option pricing model *72–80*

Symposia and Conference Proceedings

Horst Siebert, Editor

Elemente einer rationalen Umweltpolitik
Expertisen zur umweltpolitischen Neuorientierung
Tübingen 1996. 378 pp. Hardcover.

Monetary Policy in an Integrated World Economy
Tübingen 1996. 280 pp. Hardcover.

Towards a New Global Framework for High-Technology Competition
Tübingen 1997. 223 pp. Hardcover.

Quo Vadis Europe?
Tübingen 1997. 343 pp. Hardcover.

Structural Change and Labor Market Flexibility
Experience in Selected OECD Economies
Tübingen 1997. 292 pp. Hardcover.

Redesigning Social Security
Tübingen 1998. 387 pp. Hardcover.

Globalization and Labor
Tübingen 1999. 320 pp. Hardcover.

The Economics of International Environmental Problems
Tübingen 2000. 274 pp. Hardcover.

The World's New Financial Landscape: Challenges for Economic Policy
Berlin · Heidelberg 2001. 324 pp. Hardcover.

Tübingen: Mohr Siebeck (http://www.mohr.de)
Berlin · Heidelberg: Springer-Verlag (http://www.springer.de)

KIELER STUDIEN · KIEL STUDIES

Kiel Institute of World Economics

Editor: *Horst Siebert* · Managing Editor: *Harmen Lehment*

304. **Environmental Tax Reforms and the Double Dividend. A Theoretical and Empirical Analysis for Germany,** *Christian M. Scholz*
Tübingen 2000. XIX, 323 pp. Hardcover.

305. **Wettbewerbsorientierte Reformen der Stromwirtschaft,** *Lars Kumkar*
Tübingen 2000. XIII, 500 pp. Hardcover.

306. **Leistungsbilanzentwicklung ausgewählter Schwellenländer Asiens und Lateinamerikas. Ursachen und wirtschaftspolitische Konsequenzen,** *Rainer Schweickert*
Tübingen 2000. IX, 122 pp. Hardcover.

307. **Structural Change of the Production Process and Unemployment in Germany,** *Axel Schimmelpfennig*
Tübingen 2000. XX, 232 pp. Hardcover.

308. **Globalisierung, Strukturwandel und Beschäftigung,** *Jörn Kleinert, Axel Schimmelpfennig, Klaus Schrader, Jürgen Stehn*
Tübingen 2000. XIII, 247 pp. Hardcover.

309. **Wirtschaftliche Auswirkungen einer EU-Erweiterung auf die Mitgliedstaaten,** *Hugo Dicke, Federico Foders*
Tübingen 2000. XIV, 224 pp. Hardcover.

310. **The Integration Process between Eastern and Western Europe,** *Daniel Piazolo*
Berlin · Heidelberg 2001. XVII, 178 pp. Hardcover.

311. **Bildungspolitik für den Standort D,** *Federico Foders*
Berlin · Heidelberg 2001. XII, 125 pp. Hardcover.

312. **Der Euro als Ankerwährung. Die mittel- und osteuropäischen Beitrittsländer zwischen Transformation und Integration,** *Rainer Schweickert*
Berlin · Heidelberg 2001. (In Vorbereitung).

313. **Noise Trading, Central Bank Interventions, and the Informational Content of Foreign Currency Options,** *Christian Pierdzioch*
Berlin · Heidelberg 2001. XVII, 207 pp. Hardcover.

More information on publications by the Kiel Institute at http://www. uni-kiel.de/ifw/pub/ pub.htm, more information on the Kiel Institute at http://www.uni-kiel.de/ifw

Tübingen: Mohr Siebeck (http://www.mohr.de)
Berlin · Heidelberg: Springer-Verlag (http://www.springer.de)